The Basic Book
of Antiques

Other Books by George Michael

Antiquing with George Michael

The Treasury of New England Antiques

Treasury of Federal Antiques

The Basic Book of
ANTIQUES

by George Michael

ARCO PUBLISHING COMPANY, INC.
219 Park Avenue South, New York, N.Y. 10003

Line drawings by Sue Bard

Second Printing, 1975

Published by Arco Publishing Company, Inc.
219 Park Avenue South, New York, N.Y. 10003

Library of Congress Catalog Card Number 74-77072
ISBN 0-668-03433-5

Printed in the United States of America

Contents

Introduction

There has long been a need for a basic book on antiques. Teachers and students have struggled with the subject, with no text that could provide a sensible working guide to the structure of classes and topic matter.

This volume covers ten years of instructing experience when I benefited from the questions and responses of many students. As antiques are a very visual subject, colored 35 mm slides were used to implement the course. I took many of these myself, but some were purchased at museums and historical societies which maintain libraries of such slides. Students brought in items related to the course and chapter of study for each session, and these made for lively discussion and analysis.

I wish to thank my many teachers over the years—some were scholars and some were scoundrels—but I learned the appreciation of art in its many forms from them all. My students are told that if they can just become aware of what they are looking at the course will have been a success. Meeting them at auctions and shows over the years, it has been a pleasure to know that instruction in antiques and antiquing is a very viable and practical endeavor. May those of you who are embarking on your antiquing adventures gain something of value from this book, and let us hope it makes it easier on your teacher, no matter who he or she may be.

My thanks are also extended to all the students who have challenged their teacher—it keeps one sharp and discourages laziness in the learning experience.

Additional thanks go to the many scholars, museums, historical societies, private collectors, auctioneers, show promoters, and others who have cooperated in providing the information and pictures which helped make this book possible. Consider this a primer of instruction—the people mentioned above will help you continue your education if you will pursue it in your contact with them as a student and/or buyer. Until you start buying and selling, you will never know what anything is really worth. Until you start visiting museums to sharpen your eye as to the best and most interesting items to seek for your own, you cannot hope to learn to evaluate quality antiques properly. Antiquing is a learning process—I hope this book will encourage you to continue yours.

George Michael
Merrimack, New Hampshire

The Basic Book
of Antiques

Chapter 1

How to Collect and Enjoy Antiques

If you purchased this book with the intention of learning something about antiques and how to collect and enjoy them, you have just embarked on one of the most interesting adventures in your life. There is no mystery to antiquing. Newcomers to the field are fascinated by the actions and know-how of the old timers in the game, not realizing that once they too were taking the plunge which would involve them in a business which combines a form of gambling, suspense, intrigue, and adventure which is really quite harmless in its nature, yet very rewarding to those who have the fortitude to stick it out and learn the rules.

Before getting involved, you must judge just how deeply you want to get into the nitty gritty of antiquing, and then try to hold the line in conformance with your plans. Some have likened the antique business to a disease which gradually possesses you, drawing you deeper until there is no retreat or escape, but do not let this deter you. Along the way you will have lots of fun, meet many interesting people, win a little, lose a little, and above all, come away with at least one very important advantage—you will be more aware of the beauty in our art and antique objects. If this awareness is the only profit you receive, you will be well-rewarded.

This quality of "awareness" is the most important asset you can have in the antiques field. Some people are born with it—they have an affinity for the arts and can translate and relate their feelings to them quite easily. Others have to acquire this affinity through study and hard work. Still others acquire it by buying and selling. I have always told those who have asked, "The more rapidly I lost money on antiques, the more rapidly I learned about them. You never forget your lessons."

1

Everyone experiences a certain amount of this type of learning. No matter how long people remain in the antique business, they find they make occasional mistakes. In many cases buying and selling is based on personal judgment alone, since one of a kind items keep turning up, and you must gamble on your feelings toward the piece. My old traveling partner, Frank Rowe, once told me after such a losing experience, "When you find you have made a mistake, sell out, and get out." My father once told me, "You make your money when you buy, not when you sell; goods well bought are half sold." I keep this in mind at all times, but there are many occasions when factors such as a possible eventual buyer, personal emotion for the piece, or just the gambling spirit make me plunge into items which later prove to be duds. A dealer once remarked about one of his mistakes, "I showed it to the world, and nobody wants it." This is why it is so important that you judge the type of collector-dealer you want to be before you get involved in serious buying and selling. There is no separation between collecting and dealing. Even though you may not have a shop with a shingle hanging out front stating that you are in the antique business, you will find that before long you will be buying and selling to upgrade your collection. Items bought when money was tight will eventually give way to better items acquired through good buys or during a period of more affluency. This swapping off can make you money as well as providing an outlet for any gambling instincts you have, and will give you the satisfaction of creating a collection of which you can be proud.

Everyone has an instinct to collect something, and this urge can be directed in several ways. First, there are those who collect to impress their friends with something of interest or beauty which can also be used as decoration. There are those who collect only functional items, such as chairs, tables, chests of drawers, and beds, and those who collect decorative pieces like oils, glass, and fine porcelain. Others combine their desire to enjoy the items they buy with the idea of treating them as an investment, with liquidation for a profit in the future. Then there is the final category of people who are outright dealers, those who buy and sell for profit alone, along with the pleasure of having quality items pass through their hands. The person who stuffs cupboards full of creamers or salt and pepper shakers is a delight to auctioneers and dealers who otherwise would not know what to do with many of the items available for sale. Collections of this type are mostly dust collectors, and unless they are of really high quality can represent only the satisfaction of a squirrel-like need to stuff something away.

People who collect to impress their friends are usually affluent people who have little thought of buying or selling or upgrading their pieces. They collect art for art's sake and enjoy it on that level, which is a very good one if you can afford it.

Those who collect functional items probably make up the greatest proportion of buyers today. People have learned that if you are going to buy a table, chairs, chests, etc., it is much more sensible to buy old than new. New furniture is worth about half its price when it is delivered to your home, and it continues to depreciate rapidly. Good antique furniture will almost always rise in value, and you can usually sell it at a good profit if necessary. In the meantime, you can enjoy the pieces, whether they are furniture or decorative, since all of them have a much warmer and more comfortable look because of the patina which comes with age.

Those who treat antiques as an investment are wise in their choice. We are continually made aware of fantastic increases in value as auction sale prices are reported. Quality antiques have always risen in value faster than stocks, and provide a much greater return than bank interest. If you buy quality, you need have little fear of a decline in value. It is much more pleasurable to enjoy a fine oil painting on the wall than it is to read figures in a bank book, especially with the realization that the painting is increasing in value much more rapidly than your bank account. Quality items can always be liquidated rapidly for cash, so they represent a very fluid form of capital investment.

People who buy and sell as dealers are the ones who do most of the work of acquiring good antiques for those who want them. They are the ones who scrounge about in attics, barns, and cellars and spend long hours at auctions, shows, and flea markets, searching out the means to their living. It is a rather thankless job in many respects, but the rewards are more than financial, and this helps keep most dealers in the business. You must be curious and have a great deal of imagination to remain in the business and you must be willing to spend long hours at it. Many dealers have to empty attics which are roasting hot from the summer sun and no ventilation. Others have to paw through mountains of rusty junk in garages and barns, often risking their lives by lowering pieces down from haylofts. The best buys at flea markets are made when the dealers are setting up, sometimes as early as 6:00 a.m. and this means rising very early to be there for the first crack at the new merchandise when it is being unwrapped. Dealers will often spend long hours manning booths at shows and flea markets as well as running a shop at home. You have to be quite dedicated to the field to be a dealer—you will earn everything you work for, but the work will be fun.

Perhaps the greatest introduction to antiques is professional instruction in the field in which you are interested. This is very important in developing the most important attribute in the business—being "aware" of what you see. If you want to specialize in collecting ceramics, it would be advisable to take an eight week course at whichever local school, university, arts and science center, or historical society sponsors one. Although you may never become a fancy or recognized potter, at least you will learn the makeup of ceramics, recognize the problems faced in making and decorating such pieces, and acquire a feeling for quality. And when you begin collecting it will not be difficult for you to separate the good from the bad. This advice also applies to those who are interested in furniture, oil painting, pewter, brass, silver, copper, iron, jewelry, sewing, and rugmaking, or any other craft. Your courses of instruction will give you a better appreciation of the problems faced by an artist, and this will result in your being better able to judge quality work.

Above all, read the many good books available and become a frequent visitor to museums and restorations in order to see, first hand, the items in which you are interested. An excellent place to begin your education is at an auction—you can sit and listen to the auctioneer describe the pieces sold, you can note the interest and activity in bidding, and you can learn the price at which representative pieces sell. Go to good shows and shops and talk

"I have not yet begun to fight," is part of the new "America Remembers" limited edition collection in pewter from Wallace silversmiths. It captures the moment of John Paul Jones' stirring reply to the British demand for surrender during a naval engagement of the Revolutionary War. Such limited edition works are among the collectibles of today. In time, limited editions of this type will rise in value, as long as the work is of good quality.

with the dealers. You will find them friendly, interesting, and full of information. They are business people who want to cultivate you as a buyer and friend. The old clichés which deal with the reliability of dealers and auctioneers are as dead as dodo birds. There are scoundrels in every business—the antiques business should not be singled out as a particular area in which many of them are active. I find that dealers and auctioneers are much more reliable to do business with than people in private homes who often could care less if they never saw you again. The dealers and auctioneers want you to come back and they will treat you as a valued customer if you are responsible in your business dealings with them.

1850   1903

IN MEMORIAM
ALBERT TEELE DUNN

"I have fought a good fight,
I have finished my course,
I have kept the faith."

Gravestone rubbings are popular, as are the sayings that appear on them. Once in a while an authentic stone comes up for sale. The message on this one epitomizes the Puritan ethic.

Even ice boxes are coming back into favor. Not long ago, this one (now priced at $35) would have been relegated to the town dump.

There is new interest in the work of American artists in marble. This child putting on her sock makes an appealing subject. Late nineteenth century American, unsigned.

One of the most confusing aspects of the antique business is determining just what constitutes an antique. There are many descriptions, but perhaps the following will clear up your misconceptions. An antique is primarily an object which is wholly or partially handmade. We buy the work of an artisan's hands, and appreciate the feeling, depth, and dimension he has put into his work. This applies to all fields of art—furniture, glass, paintings, ceramics, silver, pewter, and the rest. The creative ability of an artist turns out a piece which speaks to us in terms of quality. Quality is made up of good taste, good design, and good construction or workmanship. Hand workmanship and quality are the first requirements of an antique.

An item made in good taste is one which has good proportions; if it is carved, the work must be pleasant and not too over-embellished or ostentatious; if it is colored, the colors must harmonize and be pleasing to the eye. Good design insures that the piece has the look of the period in which it was made. Items which contain design features of two or more periods are considered transitional and will have no place in the collections of purists. A design can also be pleasing or offensive—your eye and the appeal of the object to you will determine this. Do not expect everyone to share your appreciation for a piece, but as long as you like it, you can judge whether or not you should own it. A craftsman may have good ideas but if he cannot use good workmanship in their realization and creation, his work cannot be considered as quality. Your awareness of these requirements will grow as you see more and more pieces and suddenly they will speak to you rapidly—a glance will do, whereas now you may have to study them.

If a piece meets the requirements of being handmade and of good quality, generally the older it is the more valuable it is. This is where age enters the picture, and not before. Age alone does not make an antique. If an item was a monstrosity two hundred years ago it will be a monstrosity today, and age will not have improved it one bit. However, many fairly new works of art are prized more than much older ones, so you must be careful in using age as a criteria. You can see pieces of Roman glass two thousand years old dug from ruins and selling at nominal prices. These pieces of glass meet the standards of an antique in that they are handmade and of good quality. When these Roman pieces are placed beside pieces made by eighteenth-century artisans like Casper Wistar, Frederick Amelung, and Baron Stiegel, they will bring but a fraction of what the latter pieces will command. The price and the collecting fever are raised by desirability. When the supply does not meet the demand, prices go up—age and the other criteria have little to do with price if there is no desire for the item.

A great fireplace with all the necessities of home life in the eighteenth century. (Museum Village, Smith's Clove, Monroe, New York)

The interior of seventeenth century Plympton House, the oldest American house in Greenfield Village, Dearborn, Michigan, which was moved there from South Sudbury, Massachusetts. It is a one-room home with a free-standing fireplace built to provide heat on all sides. The covered well located inside the house is an unusual feature. (Henry Ford Museum, Dearborn, Michigan)

All items made by machine fall into the category of "collectibles," since they may be reproduced at any time, and do not reflect the individual work of a craftsman's hands. Machine-printed pictures cannot compare with those painted by hand with oils, brush, and palette. A printed picture is a lifeless rendition, but in an original painting, the artist projects his feelings with depth and dimension and he communicates with us on an artistic level. The same rule applies to all forms of antiquity: furniture, silver, pewter, glass, ceramics, etc. Machine-made furniture is rather harsh and stiff when compared to the early handmade pieces. Spinning a silver dish on a lathe does not require the painstaking work expended in hammering it out by hand and finishing it with crude tools. Some early machine-made work such as pressed glass will be discussed later, and you will learn that these pieces have value in the context of rarity and design. There are some items like mechanical banks which have risen to great values, but only because they are rare, and because they perform an interesting function. On the whole, you will find that the handmade item is much more desired than its machine-made counterpart.

You cannot set any particular date as to when items acquire the aura of age which helps in their desirability and value. We do know that the year 1830 is used as the approximate turning point when America turned from hand to machine work. This was the time of the industrial revolution, when the steam engine became practical as a source of energy, factories of all kinds were set up, and machinery took the long hours and drudgery out of manufacturing. Unfortunately, along with the industrial change-over, there was also a changeover in the amount of attention given to style and good craftsmanship. Products turned out after 1830 must be examined in the light of their quality and method of manufacture.

Manufacturers found that machines could turn out more products more rapidly and were willing to sacrifice quality for speed and quantity to satisfy the growing demand. However, in rural regions away from the seaports and large cities, we know that many workers relied on hand craftsmanship as late as the Civil War period, as most of them could not afford the new machinery, and perhaps they did not want to use it either. Hand craftsmanship has never died. It has always been with us and is still here today, although you must accept the fact that it has declined since 1830, and after the Civil War was only a small factor in production.

You may have heard the saying that "anything a hundred years old or older is an antique." This misconception arose during the 1920's, when dealers revolted against paying duty on the antiques they imported. They argued that an old object offered no competition to the modern industrial worker and that duties had been set up as a protection against such competition. The Government went along with this, and in 1930 a bill was passed stating that anything made before 1830 would be admitted duty free as an antique. This rule remained in effect until 1966 when President Johnson signed a new bill which used one hundred years of age as the determining factor, rather than the inflexible 1830 rule. The new bill was implemented because antiques of the Empire and Victorian periods which came after 1830 had become fashionable due to the growing scarcity of pre-1830 artifacts. So the hundred year rule is still in effect, but only as a determination as to whether duty shall be collected when a piece is imported. The Government did not attempt to aesthetically describe an antique.

This should help clear up some of the confusion which will arise when you see a glass paperweight made by Domenic Labino a year ago in his home in Ohio sell for ten times more than one made a hundred years ago at famed Bacarrat Factory in France. Many of the pieces turned out in the art noveau style by the factory of Louis Comfort Tiffany as late as the early 1930's sell for considerably more than their counterparts of many years ago. When the Dedham, Massachusetts Pottery closed in 1948, you could have bought hand-decorated, handmade dinner plates there for three dollars—today it would be difficult to find one you could buy for less than fifty. The famed Mount Washington-Pairpoint Factory of New Bedford, Massachusetts, which closed in 1958, left behind a heritage of handmade merchandise which is eagerly sought by collectors, although it is not very old. These are but a few examples which show that age alone has little effect on the desirability and price of antiques.

We are fortunate in one area—our parents and grandparents collected the items, purely by chance, which we enjoy as antiques today. These were the objects they used in their homes, and some were undoubtedly handed down as family pieces. The owners had no idea that these items would be prized today as art objects, finding places in museums and selling for enormous prices. They used these pieces as everyday artifacts and if they survived the trips to the dump and the trashman who cleaned out barns and attics, we were lucky.

You can collect the antiques of the future by choice, and these require a relatively small investment as opposed to the antiques of today. By applying the requirements listed earlier, you can examine contemporary work and judge whether the work fills them. This is a little like betting on a horse race by studying the past performance of the participants. You should check on the awards and recognition won by the artist, and check each particular work in the light of good taste, good design, and good construction. You can then visualize if it meets what you feel will be the desires of collectors in the future, since they will be little changed from what they are today as far as art appreciation is concerned. You can then begin buying the works of those whom you feel meet the test with the hope the artist will some day "arrive" and be recognized, thus making his works more desirable. In the meantime, most such investment is small when compared to investing in antiques, and the items may be enjoyed just as much in your home. Whether the artist "arrives" really isn't of great importance as long as you enjoy his work. You can only hope for the other.

When collecting either antiques or contemporary work, insist on all the documentation of the piece which is available. The past history of ownership of an old item can help in tracing its maker someday. Insist that present-day artists sign their work in some manner, and preserve this documentation. We must begin creating birth certificates for our antiques and collectibles so research on them in the future will be made easier. It also helps to raise the value when works can be traced to important craftsmen as well as important owners. Borrowing an etching pencil from your local police department to inscribe your social security number on your valued possessions is becoming popular today. This should not hurt the value of it if the number is put in an inconspicuous place, and it will aid in identification and help curb the increasing wave of fine arts thefts. The name of the maker can be put on with the same etching pencil if need be.

Collecting antiques should be fun and owning them should be even more pleasurable. Yet there are very few people who really know how to enjoy antiques. Many people worry about them because of their value and the thought of possible fire and theft is always in their minds. If you cannot enjoy an antique, you should sell it to someone who can. If you find that any items are a source of concern when you are away from your home, or when there are children about, it is high time you sold them. Some people are so concerned that they hire "antiques sitters" as a protection when they leave their homes. This defeats the idea of enjoyment and if you are going to get this involved with material possessions, think twice before embarking on a collection. You should have your items appraised, use the appraisal to insure them under a less expensive fine arts policy, and then let your insurance man worry about them when you are away. This is what you are paying him for.

At the back of this book there is a bibliography of the latest available books which will be of great help to you in pursuing further information and instruction in your chosen phase of antiquing. This book is intended as an introduction to the identification, collection, and enjoyment of antiques. I hope it lays a good groundwork for you to use in the future. Above all, if I have been able to make you more "aware" of what you are looking at and have shown how to judge the piece in the light of its contemporaries, I will feel I will have accomplished this goal. Personal tastes in antiques and appreciation of them differs sharply. Just as you would not attempt to buy such a personal thing as clothing for another, neither can you presume you know his artistic tastes, since these may vary greatly from yours. Learn, look, and examine. Do not be casual in your appraisal, as many good pieces are passed over because of this.

The possible fields for antique and memorabilia collecting are limitless. Let your eye be your guide to quality, and let your experience at shows, auctions, and flea markets be your guide to values. You must be immersed in the business to buy and sell wisely—a part time, on-again, off-again collector will not keep himself advised sufficiently enough to do well at it. Talk to dealers and collectors in the field in which you are interested. Go to museums to see the objects on display and study their characteristics. Above all, read good books on the subject. You will find that there is a wealth of material that will help you, if you will only seek it out.

Design Periods In America

1620-1670 Pilgrim
1670-1694 Jacobean
1694-1710 William and Mary
1710-1750 Queen Anne
1750-1775 Chippendale
1775-1800 Hepplewhite ⎫
1800-1830 Sheraton ⎭ Federal
1810-1840 Empire ⎫ American
1840-1890 Victorian ⎭ Home
1890-1910 Mission
1895-1920 Art Noveau
1920-1940 Art Deco

Chapter 2

Furniture

On page 14 I have listed the approximate dates of period designations for the designs which were most prominent in both our country and England. In seventeenth century America we managed to keep abreast of the motherland in design, since commerce brought with it manufactured items which could be copied. Design books became plentiful in the middle of the eighteenth century and we were faithful in following these so that the settlers here could live in the manner of their forebears.

We have read that John Alden was our first cabinet-maker—whether this is true is academic. What is most apparent is that if the Mayflower had been loaded with all the furniture and artifacts attributed to it, it could never have left the dock. The Pilgrims came with the barest of necessities, and it is unlikely there was any furniture aboard. Actually, not much of our seventeenth century furniture has survived. Most would have been made from the easily worked pine and some from the plentiful oak, birch, and maple. I would refer to the early part of the century as the Pilgrim period, for want of a better designation. Furniture would have been quite crude, yet functional. More time was needed for tilling the soil and hunting than for decoration of household artifacts. Much early furniture has probably been lost through attrition and over the years just thrown out as old and out of style. Most of what has survived has been snatched up by museums and restorations.

Toward the latter part of the century (at the time of the restoration in the 1660's) we were influenced by the prevailing Jacobean styles of heavily turned oak furniture, and its counterpart was made here. The rest of the periods came under the influence of cabinetmakers who worked independently, though some were fortunate enough to have their names attached to styles in which they worked and which influenced cabinetry on both sides of the ocean.

15

Carved oak chest of the Pilgrim period, seventeenth century. This is pleasing work done with crude tools at a time when Indians and starvation were greater concerns than the beautification of furniture.

Throughout furniture identification we see the importance of leg design in each period. This is perhaps the most important feature to recognize for rapid identification. I have explained these leg stylings with accompanying pictures and further explaining of design techniques. We must be careful in using the word "style" as there is evidence that cabinetmakers, especially in the country, refused to let go of some designs and continued to work in them long after new styles came into popular use. It is best to refer to a piece as being of "Queen Anne Style" since we know that such pieces were made almost until the nineteenth century, though the most popular years for it were during the first half of the eighteenth century. Some changes in methods of workmanship might give an indication as to whether the piece is early or late, but sometimes this type of attribution can be hazardous.

Leg designs graduated from the heavily turned ball-type construction to the more graceful yet ruggedly designed William and Mary legs, whose turnings were influenced by Dutch design. Early in the eighteenth century, at the time of Queen Anne, the graceful cabriole leg and varied type pad feet were conceived as a breakaway to light and airy furniture more in keeping with the delicate monarch herself. There are many leg variations in this period more fully explained in the pictures.

The noted cabinetmaker, Thomas Chippendale, was influenced by his contemporaries and freely copied their ideas. He published his first *Cabinetmaker's Guide* in 1754, and it influenced work on both sides of the Atlantic for many years. In fact, today his designs are the most copied in reproductions. Names like William Jones, Ince and Mauhew, Robert Manwaring, Matthias Lock, Batty Langley, and Sir William Chambers are less known to collectors, yet all pioneered some forms adapted by Chippendale, though he got credit for them. The Adams Brothers in England were architects who designed homes and were then called upon to sketch the furniture for them. Chippendale is known to have made many pieces for the Adams', hence his willingness to borrow from them. He continued the use of the cabriole leg but gave it a new look with the ball and claw or the ball and talon foot. He featured no decoration with veneering or inlay and beautified his pieces with carving instead. Another leg form to be remembered is the squared, fluted leg on chairs and tables. Some have designated these as "country" Chippendale in style, using the term "city" to denote those with the more fancy leg and foot. The bases of his chests of drawers might feature a very short leg, sometimes called a "bandy-leg," which is a version of the cabriole leg with a ball and claw foot. They sometimes feature what is called the "bracket base," made up of boards, front and sides, with cutouts to form legs and to beautify the piece.

The Hepplewhite period is characterized by the simple squared, tapered leg, which many feel is the finest in pure design. George Hepplewhite's *Cabinetmaker and Upholsterer's Guide* was published shortly after his death by his wife, Alice, who kept his shop going. Though he used carving as a decoration in his early work, he popularized a growing interest in veneers and inlays. American multicolored woods made such veneering quite pretty, but nowhere did this style reach greater heights of expression than in the northeastern section of the country where such woods were plentiful. Fine figured maple was found as far south as Pennsylvania and as far west as Ohio, and we see very good examples of work from these states as well as from the New York-New England area. The ultimate work seems to have been done in this period in the Boston to Portsmouth (New Hampshire) region, where great classic pieces were made to satisfy the retiring captains, shipowners, and wealthy merchants along the seacoast.

Thomas Sheraton was a contemporary of Hepplewhite and he utilized the tapered leg in his early construction. However, he turned to the reeded or simple turned leg as a change from the austere square design, and it found immediate favor. Some legs were carved in a bulbous design as well, which gave them added strength as well as a graceful look. There is some confusion in telling Hepplewhite chairs from early pieces by Sheraton, which feature the tapered leg. There is one fairly simple rule to follow. If the back is designed with rounded forms, such as the familiar shield back, the style is Hepplewhite. If the back of the chair is designed in geometric and squared forms, it should be considered Sheraton. Both might feature tapered legs with what is known as a spade foot—an enlargement on the taper, right at the foot.

The incoming Empire period brought with it a great deal of carving and attention to the French style, and this became prevalent after the turn of the century, especially in our seaport cities. Leaf and fruit carving became popular, and outswept leg pedestal-based tables in the Duncan Phyfe style became the rule. Brass pawed animal feet, some with a hairy appearance, were regarded as the latest in high fashion. The curved or scimitar leg and the Roman shaped curule leg were in favor. Rope and twist carved legs were stylish as well. Though there were some very graceful pieces made in the empire period, the earlier designs gave way to some rather horrible ideas which brought forth such monstrosities as the elephant trunk style. This style plagued the upper sections and bases of furniture which was otherwise quite well-made and in good design. It was during this period that the machine age set in and as less and less hand work was required for difficult pieces, good taste and design seems to have gone out the window. During this and the later Victorian period there was much carving featured, but most of it was done by machine. In the same manner as in cutting a new key, it became possible to trace over an original design, actuating several other machines which would reproduce the carving faithfully. It is not safe to assume that much furniture was hand-carved after the machines arrived. We know that some must have been done, but in purchasing most of this period it would be safer to assume that it was machine-carved. Artisans like John Belter in New York City continued to make quality pieces, though quite heavy, and it is believed that hand-carving was still in vogue with him. He was quite progressive, as the wood he shaped for chair backs was almost always made up in laminations, as in our present-day plywood. This was easily bent, was quite strong, and lent itself to carving. The cut out designs must have been done by hand, hence the importance and interest in his furniture today.

The Victorian period was aptly named after the British monarch. There was a return to dark stained woods and designs which closely resembled those of Chippendale a hundred years before. The cabriole leg and ball and claw foot returned along with carving (machine or otherwise) used as decoration rather than veneering and inlay.

The following periods, which include the Eastlake stylings in oak, the mission period of oak, and work during the art noveau and art deco periods will be discussed at length, later in this chapter. Let us examine the work of each period since the seventeenth century.

Jacobean

The Jacobean furniture of the early seventeenth century was rectangular and low in proportion, reflecting the low ceilings popular at that time. Most legs were straight, with some turnings, and a melon shape was popular. Legs were braced with stretchers, and were most often close to the floor. The later Jacobean period (which came after the restoration of Charles II to the throne in 1660) brought with it much carving and even caning of chairs. Charles married a Portuguese princess, Catherine of Braganza, and her dowry included furniture from the continent.

Some refer to this as the Carolean period, which was characterized by the introduction of S and C scrolls with mixed Dutch,
Portuguese, Flemish, Spanish, and French-Italian influences.
Spiral turned legs appeared and geometric moldings were
favored. The Dutch had perfected the turning lathe, which made
the spiral moldings possible, at a time when the English and
other artisans were still carving them totally by hand. At this time,
padded backs appeared on chairs and bun or ball feet were the
rule. Needlepoint, velvet, leather, and brocades were used for
upholstering. The great wood carver Grinling Gibbons left his
mark with work which has perhaps never been duplicated. Motifs
included acanthus leaves, roses, crowns, and scrolls.

During this time, there were produced crude stools; benches;
trestle tables, which were long dining tables; low box type chests;
bible boxes; and simple bed frames with rope supports for a
feather or cornhusk filled mattress. There was little attempt at
beautification, but we do find good examples of carving in
specific areas. In the western Connecticut–western Massachusetts
sections, a school of carvers is recorded near Hadley which left us
a fine heritage of their work. Some pieces are called "sunflower"
chests because of their floral decoration, and others are simply
called Hadley chests as a means of identifying the school of work
they represented. Oak was a popular wood for this work, and
because of this many pieces have survived. English counterparts
of these chests are also collected, and you must determine their
provenance by the decorative motifs. Study of the decoration
which existed at the time both here and overseas is a great help, as
this can help in attribution. To do it solely by workmanship at
this early period is hazardous.

Historians tell us that the term Jacobean might be applied to
several periods in the seventeenth century. The name is loosely
adapted from *Jacobus,* the Latin name for King James I who
reigned early in the century. James I was succeeded by Charles I,
who was later beheaded by Cromwell and his associates. Some
refer to the years 1649–1660 as Cromwellian, as they feel there
was a definite change in design to reflect the absence of the
monarchy, which until then had supported and inspired
craftsmen. Furniture from this period is characterized by stiff

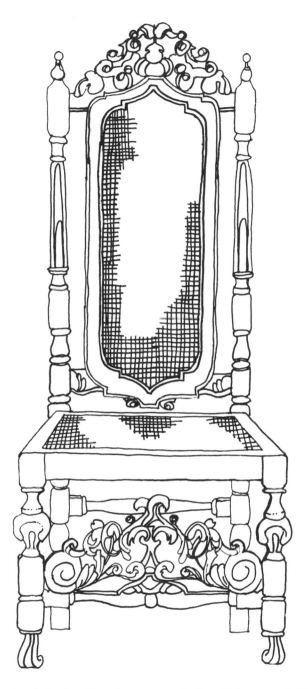

Chair of the late Jacobean period, English, around 1670, when caning was popular. The carving was influenced by work done in the Mediterranean area at the time.

lines, with little embellishment, but this should be of little concern to the American collector as there is little available either here or in England.

Until recently, styles of this period were not much in favor here in America, since the cased pieces are bulky and the chairs and settees are quite uncomfortable. Also, one would find it almost impossible to acquire a complete set of chairs, or other multiple items, as time has taken its toll of many of them. Our practice of wanting complete sets held down interest in such seventeeth century furniture. The English reproduced much of it in the nineteenth century, and you must be careful in your purchases if you want the early work. Perhaps the best clue is to look for pegs in the framework. The English were using pegs to join furniture right into the Queen Anne period early in the eighteenth century, but at that time such work began to disappear. However, almost all seventeenth century work should show pegs. Also, you should check the underframe of any furniture to look for new screws or angle cut braces. In the early days, craftsmen glued crude blocks of wood at joining points, whereas later work shows machine-cut braces held in by screws. You should look for early marks left by saws, planes, and chisels. Later work done by machine will be perfectly smooth, with very tight joints.

William and Mary

James II, the son of Charles II, seemed to have little better luck in ruling than Charles I, and he fled the country, leaving his daughter, Mary, to rule with her husband, William, who was Dutch. Though they only ruled from 1688 to 1702, William and Mary managed to have an influence on furniture and other art styles. Many Huguenot craftsmen were coming into England at this time to escape religious persecution caused by the revocation of the Edict of Nantes. The Dutch and French influence was immediately felt, and for the first time furniture took on graceful lines and proportions. It featured a combination of curved and straight lines, and chair backs were heightened. The seats were most often square, with backs slanted for comfort. Turned legs

Tall chest in the William and Mary style. A classic example of the period, it is veneered in burl walnut and bears the brass tear-drop pulls of the late seventeenth and early eighteenth centuries. The bold trumpet turnings are very good.

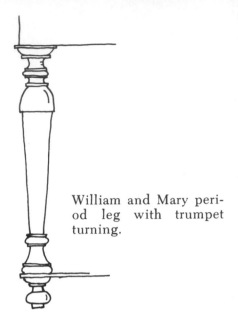

William and Mary period leg with trumpet turning.

Early eighteenth century ball foot chest from New Hampshire, in William and Mary style. Made in pine, which is much rarer than maple. The glass knobs are replacements; it most likely originally came with brass tear-drop pulls.

with vase and ring, trumpet, and inverted cup designs became the rule. Ball and bun feet were still used on low chests for strength, but longer legs with stretchers framing them became the rule for the taller cased pieces. The chests and highboys were soon decorated with marquetry inlay, painted decorations, and well-grained veneers. Some royal furniture was gilded, and some appeared with marble tops. The cockleshell was popular in carving, and some chair legs had feet with toe and even ball and claw carvings. China cabinets were popular, as antique collecting became a pastime for the wealthy. Tall clocks appeared, and the game tables introduced at the time of Charles I became the rage as cards and other games of chance swept the nation. The long, rigid refectory tables of the preceeding years gave way to graceful gateleg and other drop leaf designs. One of the most important designers of the period was a Huguenot, Daniel Marot, and as a result his work shows the influence of the Louis XIV styles then prevalent in France. This was a period of high style, and represented the transition from the rigid and functional to the graceful and beautiful in furniture.

Queen Anne

The advent of Queen Anne to the throne in 1702 brought with it a further refinement in style, with the pieces becoming perhaps more delicate and beautiful than those of any other period. The heavy underbracing of the preceding periods gradually disappeared, and graceful cabriole legs, designed from the architectural cyma curve, became the rule. Anne ascended the throne after the death of William of Orange, who had given Parliament the power of absolute rule in England, reducing the monarchy to a titular role as far as governing was concerned. With the monarchy no longer dictating style, cabinetmakers exercised their own imagination, yet most came up with a refinement of the continental styles which were still most appreciated. The Dutch influence was strongly felt during Anne's reign, and we are fortunate that it was, since it left us with a heritage of fine furniture. In America, cabinetmakers in Boston, Portsmouth,

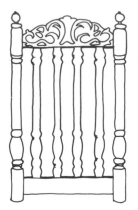

Detail showing the split spindle bannister back of a Queen Anne period armchair, early eighteenth century. The spindles were made by clamping two pieces of wood together before shaping them as a round spindle. When separated, they were used on the chair back with the flat surface forward and the rounded surface to the rear.

A beautiful oval-topped Queen Anne style table. A deeper skirt with cutouts would have improved it, but its size and proportions place it high on the desirability list.

This grouping features a delicate Queen Anne style table with cabriole leg and toed foot. Chairs are in the bannister back style of the same period. (Roger Bacon, New Hampshire)

Cabriole leg of the Queen Anne period fitted with the pad foot (often called duck or Dutch). Some feel that this is the most graceful leg ever put on furniture.

A good spoon back Queen Anne chair with cabriole leg and pad feet. This chair would have been improved if the rear legs had matched the front.

Bonnet-topped highboy in Queen Anne style, American, early eighteenth century. The pieces bear this name due to the hooded bonnet which extends from the broken arch back to the wall. The legs are graceful, and the proportions are very good.

Newport, New York, and Philadelphia brought the style to perfection in design.

Walnut and mahogany were favored woods in England at the time, but in this country the artisans skillfully used the lighter colored and highly figured maples, mahoganies, cherry, and birch in their work. American craftsmen used little or no veneer or inlay, preferring to paint or japan (lacquer and gild) the cased pieces to beautify them. Carving was relegated to fans or shells on drawers, and perhaps some cutout work on the tops of highboys and fancy finials. Late in the period, the Philadelphia craftsmen carried this even further, with carvings on the knees of the legs. Chairs became quite comfortable and the upholstered wingback with overstuffed cushions became the rule. The short cabriole leg was referred to as a "bandy-leg," and was often used on the frames of tall and short chests and on chests on chest. Backs of side chairs were shaped in "spoon" fashion for greater comfort. Others featured a split spindle or bannister back, which is nothing more than a combination of upright supports spaced in proportion. Drop leaf tables were very popular because they conserved space. The cabriole leg was the rule in fancy furniture, and it is felt that the Dutch had imported the idea from the Orient. Even before Chippendale's time, some legs were designed with ball and claw feet. This style had deep significance to the Chinese, as it represented the foot of a dragon holding a pearl. It was left to Chippendale to really popularize it, in his period which followed.

In examining the construction details of Queen Anne's time, note again that the English gradually did away with pegging the joints during this period, whereas American craftsmen pegged furniture right into the beginning of the nineteenth century. Dovetail joints in the cases and in the drawers were widely spaced, as opposed to those of later years. Pine was most often the secondary wood used in America, whereas deal or other soft wood not native to our shores would appear in the English pieces. Little walnut was used in England at the time, as blight had hit the trees in France, where most of it came from. Perhaps the most telling feature is the width of the boards used in drawer bottoms and on the backs of pieces, and the direction in which they run. England had long before run out of wide boards, as their trees had suffered indiscriminate cutting for centuries. As a result, the English used two or three boards to make up a drawer bottom, with the grain running from front to rear in the drawer. The Americans still had huge pine boards available and usually used one single piece with the grain running from end to end in the drawer. The English also ran their back boards vertically, while the Americans ran them horizontally. Actually, if you were able to study pieces side by side, you would see that American furniture is basically lighter and more graceful than its English counterparts of any period.

Chippendale

Until the middle of the eighteenth century, the names of furniture styles and periods had been taken from those of monarchs. It was at about this time that the name of Thomas Chippendale became quite prominent in cabinetry circles in England. The son of a cabinetmaker and wood carver from Worcester, he took to his father's trade and built a reputation unmatched by any other craftsman in his field. In 1754, he published a book of furniture designs which showed that he was not hesitant about borrowing ideas from others, both in England

Chippendale period cherry chest with serpentine front and ball and talon feet; New England. This piece of furniture has class. Note that the rear legs were made to match the front.

and elsewhere. He was inspired by Gothic and Oriental motifs, and carried them to perfection in a blending of functional use as well as beauty. Chippendale might be called the first true English style which evolved from many others, and which was carried to perfection by other cabinetmakers as well. Here in America, the craftsmen seized on this departure from the reserved Queen Anne style, and turned out classic pieces using our beautiful woods. This was the era of the famous Goddard and Townsend families in Newport, and their creations in the Chippendale style are considered to be the epitome of cabinetmaking in this country.

Chippendale favored mahogany, and used curves freely. He continued the use of the cabriole leg, and placed the ball and claw and the ball and talon foot firmly in leg design. He favored carving over veneering for beauty. The back rails of chairs were most often serpentine or of curved shape, and many are characterized by pronounced ears at the juncture of the side posts and crest rail. Chair arms were curved and often flared at the ends, and the supports were angled forward at the side rails of the seat. The ladderback design was carried to its greatest height, and many featured intricate piercing and carving on the rails. Chippendale's carvings featured acanthus leaf (which was brought to its fullest fruition early in the nineteenth century), scrolls, French rococo, fruit and flowers, and even lion heads. The breakfront made a dramatic appearance in Chippendale's time, and he furthered the making of sideboards, which are generally credited to Thomas Shearer, another English designer.

Other designers of note were also in great favor during this time. Perhaps Chippendale was most influenced by Thomas Johnson, a well-known designer and carver in London. Johnson was a master of the French styles which we label as Louis XV. Sir William Chambers went to the Orient, and on his return pioneered the use of oriental influences in furniture, and this caught Chippendale's fancy. The "Chinese Chippendale" design was created as a result. Chambers published his *Designs For Chinese Buildings, Furniture, Dresses, Etc.* in 1757, and Chippendale was quick to use it. Robert Manwaring published the *Chairmaker's Guide* in 1766 and this, along with a furniture style book done by Matthias Darly, had great influence on

Chippendale. Robert and James Adams were primarily architects, but wealthy patrons had them design furniture to match their house designs. The shops of Chippendale and another up-and-coming cabinetmaker, George Hepplewhite, were used for its manufacture. Needless to say, both were influenced by the Adams styles, about which little is known in this country as so little of it was made or sent here. The Adams brothers returned to the use of fluting in legs after excavations in Greece had uncovered such designs, and they are also credited with stressing the use of veneers and inlays to beautify furniture.

Fancy carved ball and talon foot of the Chippendale period. If the foot has animal claws, it is called ball and claw; if it has bird claws, it must be called ball and talon.

A cabriole leg design used during the Chippendale period, with a ball and talon foot. This design was revived during the Victorian period, so you must determine the age of the piece by the other means of construction used.

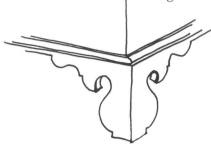

Leg of the Chippendale period, mid-eighteenth century. The shape and cutouts suggest that it is of Connecticut origin.

Six drawer tiger maple Chippendale style chest. The wide top molding, fan carving, and "C" scroll cutouts at the base give it a lot of character. It is typical of New Hampshire work of the third quarter of the eighteenth century.

You should be suspect of this Chippendale style rocking chair. Side chairs like this one were not made in rocking chair fashion, so this must be a conversion, which destroys its value.

Block front four drawer chest of the Chippendale period, made in mahogany with ball and talon feet. Although this has the appearance of being a product of the Townsend and Goddard families of Newport, Rhode Island, I would judge that it isn't, since they were known to undercut the talons so that there would be a space between them and the ball. This is not evident in this chest.

Bow-front Chippendale style mahogany chest with ball and talon feet, bandy leg; American, third quarter of the eighteenth century. On a good piece of furniture all four legs will be the same. Cabinetmakers often economized on their time by making the back legs in simple fashion since they were not as obvious. The fan inlay at the corners of the drawers is a nice touch of beauty.

Transitional chair with a Queen Anne base and Chippendale back. This would be labeled a Chippendale chair, although it is not pure in design.

Chippendale style chair in pure design, made of tiger maple with a rush seat, about 1750–1770. "Ears" at the top of the leg posts were quite common in this design. The square legs of this piece set it apart from the more highly styled "city" type of furniture.

Impressive chest-on-chest, with the top a perfect 36″ width, mid-eighteenth century. The case construction is typically Chippendale, but the bandy legs with pad feet are in the Queen Anne style. The wing brasses are Chippendale.

Interesting side chair with Chippendale style back and cabriole legs which feature carved Flemish feet. This is a transitional piece in that it combines features from two periods of design.

American arm chair, Chippendale style, about 1770–1785. It is from the Boston area, and the initials SF are stamped on the inside of the backseat rail. The knuckles carved at the ends of the arms are interesting. The well cut and carved back makes this a fine piece. (Museum of Fine Arts, Boston)

Hepplewhite

George Hepplewhite, another noted London cabinetmaker, was responsible for a radical departure in furniture style, doing away with the curved legs and fancy carvings of Chippendale's time. Though contemporary with Chippendale in his early years, Hepplewhite took his inspiration from the then recent excavations at Pompeii, which prompted a revival in interest in the classic lightness, grace, and elegance of pieces unearthed. He did away with bizarre decoration and trusted to purity and simplicity of line to create a whole new idea. Louis XV had died, and across the channel the French designers noted the change in tastes and paralleled Hepplewhite with their version of the Louis XVI style. Both featured the slender tapered leg, often with a spade foot. Bowfront chests made their appearance, and the convex fronts were often terminated at concave corners, another Hepplewhite form. A favorite of the Prince of Wales, Hepplewhite utilized a feather carving on many pieces, inspired by the feathers on the Prince's hats. He adapted the Crusader shield as a shape for the backs of chairs and also for mirrors. Short, curved arms were used on chairs, as was a rail above the seat to reinforce the back. Chairs were usually upholstered with the material extending over the frame and covering it entirely. If you should find a Hepplewhite designed chair with slip or removable seat, be cautious, as this is not the norm. Some say Hepplewhite's styles reflected the austerity of the period after the Revolutionary War. Be that as it may, there are students today who consider his styles perhaps the most classic of all. Such beauty was created with simplicity, using the coloring of well-grained woods, either veneered or solid, along with restraint in any carving. New appreciation is growing for work done in this style in America, since from Boston north to Portsmouth, New Hampshire, it was brought to full development in beauty and fine cabinetry.

Chests of this period most likely would feature the "French leg," or out-turned tapered leg, often reinforced with a pronounced toe. The cutouts on the skirts of such pieces are important, as this work determines much of the value, based on the ingenuity of the maker. Though we generally record that the

A rather plain shield-back chair in Hepplewhite design, late eighteenth century. The maker did not exert himself to beautify it with carvings or inlay. (New Hampshire Historical Society, Concord, N.H.)

Hepplewhite style was going out of favor in America at about 1800, we have found documented pieces made in this fashion as late as the 1830's, despite the advent of two period changes at the time. This was still an era of hand construction, and one would go to a cabinetmaker and order the piece made up as he saw fit. It would not be unusual to have pieces made to match earlier ones handed down in a family. Because of this, it is much safer to refer to a piece by style, such as "Hepplewhite style," as you cannot be sure whether a piece was made during his lifetime or during the time his designs were most popular. This would apply to all periods. The Dunlap family (a group of cabinetmakers in New Hampshire from 1740 to 1830) is known to have worked in the Queen Anne style as late as the 1790's, as this is what their customers wanted.

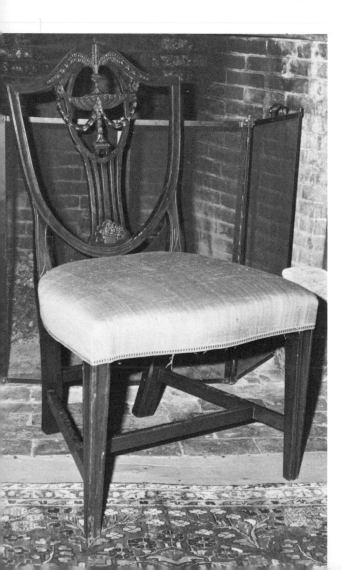

Beautifully styled Hepplewhite shield-back chair. The carving is reminiscent of that of Samuel McIntire, the noted craftsman who worked in the late eighteenth and early nineteenth centuries in Salem, Massachusetts.

Pure Hepplewhite style armchair with tapered leg and spade feet. It features the Prince of Wales feather carving on the back. Hepplewhite was a friend of the Prince and used this design in tribute to him, since the Prince wore feathers in his hat.

Late eighteenth century work-table with tapered Hepplewhite legs. The top and legs are of birch, the secondary wood is pine, and the drawer is veneered in tiger maple. Although this is a pure country piece, the cabinetmaker beautified it with the drawer veneer. The pull is hickory, held on the inside by a wooden peg.

While the preceding periods had produced tall chests and highboys, they went out of favor during Hepplewhite's time, and none has appeared in his style. Some of the four drawer chests made in the north-shore Massachusetts and Portsmouth, New Hampshire, areas are fast approaching (and in some cases have exceeded) the values of chests of previous periods. These are outrageously beautiful pieces most often made in mahogany, or mahogany-stained birch, and veneered with striking figured birch or maple woods. Those featuring a drop-panel, which is nothing more than a decorative rectangular or oval veneered decoration beneath the bottom drawer, are highly sought because this distinctive feature is rare.

Tilt-top game table, attributed to the Dunlap Circle of cabinetmakers, New Hampshire. The cut corners, diamond inlay, and stringing of marquetry around the top are typical of their work. Late eighteenth or early nineteenth century.

Tilt top game tables reached their height in beauty and style at this time. Many are made with a single board top and swing leaf, and when veneered are done with our highly figured light colored woods which offer a great contrast to the popular mahogany or cherry legs and frame. The small tilt top candle stands, which were so popular during the Chippendale era, were restyled by Hepplewhite with squared legs and tops with cut out corners, as well as veneering in the panels and on the legs. Sideboards were developed to perfection, with the delicate legs and high veneering setting them apart from those which came before. The design is one which fits well with just about any contemporary home, so is it is quite acceptable and highly sought after for decoration.

A very pure Sheraton style table leg, which shows fine turnings at the top and bulbous reeding descending to a well-turned ankle and toe. This style was used extensively during the 1800–1830 period.

The simple turned leg of a worktable such as this marks it as Sheraton in style, about 1800–1830. If the table is made of hardwood, the top should be within 16″ × 19″ in size and should be no thicker than ⅝″. A top thickness of up to ¾″ is acceptable in pine. These tables are rated on the quality of the wood and its graining, as well as on proportions and workmanship.

Sheraton

The turn of the century brought with it a change to the style of Thomas Sheraton, another London cabinetmaker who published a book which found ready favor with other artisans. Working at the same time as Hepplewhite, he was influenced by the tapered leg, and used this in his early creations. Sheraton seized on Chamber's revival of the fluted classic leg, and refined this by turning out what is called a reeded leg. The former is hollowed out in convex fashion, where the latter is shaped in concave fashion. Coupled with graceful turnings, such legs were used on

Chest of drawers with dressing glass, Sheraton style, attributed to Salem, Massachusetts, about 1800–1810, and from the family of Elizabeth Derby West. The chest is mahogany with figured birch veneer on the drawers. The leg posts are in a well-reeded design, terminating in cookie corners. (Museum of Fine Arts, Boston)

Sheraton fancy armchair of a style which was popular in the early nineteenth century. Bamboo turnings were popular then; hence its Oriental look.

Five drawer chest of the late Sheraton–early Empire period, around 1830, in a mahogany-stained birch with tiger maple drawer veneer. The overhanging upper drawers and bold front posts are typically Empire in design. Furniture of this type could have been made as late as the Civil War in the upper sections of New England.

all types of furniture and in America they may be attributed to Sheraton style. Sheraton carried on Hepplewhite's attention to the classic Greek proportion of 5 x 7 with relation to height and width. However, in four drawer Sheraton chests made in northern New England there is one dimension which must be observed. They should measure just about the same in height and width. If a chest from this region is shorter than its width, you must examine it to determine if the legs have been cut.

Sheraton also carried on the making of small work tables which made their first appearance under his predecessors. Work table is a better name for what many call a night or bedside table. Most feature at least one and sometimes up to three drawers, and some are made with drop leaves. They might be made in any combination of woods. If one is found in hard wood and its top measures less than 16" or more than 19" in either direction, or is thicker than 5/8", it should be examined carefully for replacement. These are the proper maximum and minimum measurements. If the table is pine, the top thickness can be 3/4", as this is the dimension of a 1" planed board.

The Sheraton style held up well and was made by country cabinetmakers as late as the Civil War. Despite the inroads of other styles and the machines which made more ornate work possible, many country artisans simply filled orders as they were placed, and quite often did not buy the more sophisticated machinery since they could not afford it.

Fine Sheraton style tilt-top game table with reeded legs. The veneer is figured birch, and the legs and top are mahogany. It is typical of the fine tables made in the Boston-Portsmouth area early in the nineteenth century. (Owned by Robinson Wright, Connecticut)

A real country storekeeper's or stationmaster's desk in pine with birch legs. The molding at the top is quite Empire in design, and this, along with the turned legs, would classify it as a late Sheraton–early Empire piece, about 1830–1840. Although this is a rough looking piece, it could be refinished into a fine one; the doors have a beautiful crotch mahogany veneer.

Ogee foot, popular in the third quarter of the eighteenth century and used extensively on chests. This differs from the French leg popular at this time because it is curved in cyma style.

Graceful sidechair in the Empire (or French Directoire) style, about 1820–1830. It features the front sabre leg which was widely used in this period.

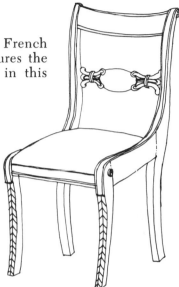

Empire secretary veneered in mahogany. The front turned posts place it in this period. Its size, proportions, and workmanship are good, which helps increase its value.

Empire

After the French Revolution, there was great sympathy here for the people of the country who had assisted us in our own revolution. Until this time, America had been dominated by the tastes and styles of our mother country, England, and it was not until after our separation that we began to develop our own tastes. After 1800, American tastes leaned strongly toward the French. France and America entered into trade, to the discomfort of the English, and soon our seaports were deluged with the latest fashions from France. New York became a leader in the furniture revolution, and soon the best of the French Empire or Directoire styles were being copied here. Decorations in carving featured the acanthus leaf, pineapples, animal and bird feet, flowers, lyres, cornucopia, and scrolls. Heavy cornices and moldings were prominent. This is a rather enigmatic period since some good furniture was created, as well as some that was outright monstrous. In the early part of the period, which extended from about 1810 to 1830, furniture with tasteful proportions and decoration was made by such artisans as Duncan Phyfe and Henri Lannuier in New York and Anthony Quervelle and Henry Connelly in Philadelphia. When machines came into general use, about 1830, the art of hand craftsmanship began to die out, and with it the true lines of beauty in furniture. The Empire styles which came after began to show the effects of poor design and construction, and by the time the Victorian designs achieved a foothold, the look of fine furniture had all but disappeared.

During the Empire period, mahogany was most favored as a wood. When it was not available, country workmen would often veneer simple pine with mahogany to create a more expensive look. Four posted beds were quite popular. Some were made with a simple tester frame on which a skirt would be hung, while some were made with the full canopy. The poorer people settled for high legged beds made with posts as much as four or five feet from the floor, and those which featured pineapple or cannonball carvings at the tops were popular. The tall posts were often reeded in Sheraton style, and acanthus leaf carving was used to beautify them. You may see canopy topped beds with reeded posts at the foot and tapered posts at the head—this is perfectly all right, as reeded posts were difficult to make, and the artisans possibly felt the head posts were pretty much out of sight anyway. Sleigh beds made their appearance, and set the stage for the look of future beds. Until the appearance of the Hollywood style bed in this century, most beds were very conventional, with a headboard, footboard, and spring and mattress of some kind. Rope springing beneath the mattresses gave way to coil springs and flat springs at about the time of the Civil War. A man by the name of Samuel Pratt is credited with inventing coil springs for furniture in the 1820's, but they did not seem to make their appearance as bed springs until the aforementioned time. At least we know that furniture upholstered with springs did not come before the 1820's. Attribution as to the age of chairs and sofas can often be based on this, unless there is evidence that springs were added later.

Horsehair as an upholstery material came into full use, though it is known that Thomas Shearer featured it in the third quarter of the eighteenth century. The fetish for putting animal paws and bird feet on chairs, sofas, and cased pieces has never been explained. Some approximated the grotesque and in later years—in fact right up until the 1950's—many pieces were thrown into dumps and otherwise disposed of. Renowned cabinetmakers like John and Thomas Seymour, who worked in Boston during the Federal Period (1770–1830), left some elegant works of construction for us to marvel at today, but some of these have animal feet which distract from the aesthetics of the whole piece.

DUNCAN PHYFE

Duncan Phyfe came from Scotland and settled in Albany, New York, in 1783. He later moved to New York City where he became the darling of the social set, and received many commissions to make fine furniture. In attempting to adapt the French Empire style to American tastes, he managed to create some really fine pieces, which were graceful, delicate, and beautiful. However, when the heavier Victorian ideas began to permeate toward the end of this period, his styling suffered and the result was a decline in the quality of his work. Phyfe's early furniture was practically all curves, as he was a master in harmonizing them. Tables were made with pedestal bases and outstretched legs, and his name has forever been attached to them. He featured the lyre

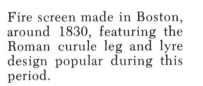

A table base and leg style attributed to Duncan Phyfe, the noted nineteenth century New York cabinetmaker. Although he adapted from other forms rather than pioneering new ones, Phyfe created a harmony of flowing lines and grace which marks his work.

Fire screen made in Boston, around 1830, featuring the Roman curule leg and lyre design popular during this period.

for decoration, along with carvings of cornucopias, acorns, swags, drapery, bow knots, medallions, palms, oak and laurel leaves, wheat, eagle wings, and even lion's feet. Some feel Phyfe originated a style that was native to America, based on the Empire designs, but if you study, you will discover that he was merely emulating the work of many designers who had come before— varying the shapes slightly and using the woods which were native.

Victorian

Queen Victoria was a buxom woman, and some feel that her ascent to the throne prompted the massive furniture that appeared at about the same time, 1840. Some designers reverted to the styles of Chippendale, and the cabriole leg with ball and claw foot made a dramatic return. Others were plainer in concept, but carving, mostly done by machine, became the favored decoration. Decorative veneering and inlay all but disappeared. The machines made mass production possible and reduced the output for fine handcrafted furniture to a few scattered shops throughout the country. However, away from the cities, good furniture of this period was still made by the country cabinetmakers who could not afford machinery, or would not bother to use it. Such pieces may show evidence of good hand work, and may be prized accordingly.

There was much delicate Victorian furniture, and much that was heavy and cumbersome. You must judge it on the merit of quality as outlined in the Introduction. However, a problem exists so far as age is concerned. As this styling extended for such a long period and has been reproduced so much in this century, you cannot always be sure in judging age. This merely underscores the problem of collecting machine-made items which may be reproduced at will. Several large furniture companies in the 1920's and 1930's did nothing but make fine reproductions of Empire and Victorian styles, and many of these pieces are now touted as 125-year-old originals based solely on the fact that someone's grandmother owned them.

This was a period popular for its marble-topped pieces and you should insist on pure white American marble as opposed to the often used colored marbles from overseas. Mahogany and walnut were the most popular woods, but some rosewood has appeared on American pieces. Secondary woods were pine, ash, poplar, chestnut, and elm. More elm wood was used than is generally realized, as it was an inferior wood for burning, and could not be relied on for surface construction of any furniture. However, once dried properly, it was strong and fairly stable. If elm is used on a surface, and exposed to the elements of heat and cold, it is prone to split. Leg styles reverted back to the late seventeenth and mid-eighteenth centuries, reviving the heavy ball and the cabriole leg with various feet. The graceful sweep of the Louis XV leg of the mid-eighteenth century is very evident. Rounded forms were used on chair backs and carvings of grapes, flowers, swags, and even rococo motifs were used for adornment.

The increased affluence of the populace in the growing industrial complex resulted in the need for more closet space in which to hang clothing. Since such space was at a premium in older houses, the wardrobe experienced a great revival. The Dutch and Germans had been making their *kas* and *schrank* since coming to this country and settling in Pennsylvania and New York, but New England and the South had few counterparts of these until the Victorian period. The well chest became popular, with raised smaller drawers offsetting the larger ones, and mirrors became a part of almost every bureau. Dark stains which hid the beautiful wood graining were the rule, as some people felt it would make the massive pieces look smaller.

American Home

While fine furniture was being made for the well-to-do, there was a lower class being turned out for the masses. Little has been written about the work then being done for the factory worker who could not afford expensive furniture. Little attention has been given to placing such work in a category by itself for easier identification. Just to lump it together with Victorian style antiques is not wholly accurate. There has been some talk about reclassifying the entire Empire and Victorian periods into an American theme, as we really had no direct connections to either designation. The Hepplewhite and Sheraton periods have been lumped together as the Federal period to give a more accurate designation to the work turned out in this country, and perhaps it is time to give such attention to the second and third quarters of the nineteenth century. An old work I saw many years ago, gave reference to the American Home period, using this as a proper designation. Perhaps we should adjust to this as easily as we did to Federal.

Small candle or tea table in birch, New England, early nineteenth century. The early tables of this style featured legs which were mortised into the post. Later ones, such as this, had legs applied to the post by dowelling or pegs.

Nineteenth century chair-table in pine, with a top 6′ in diameter. This is one of the largest you can find. The chair section would often have a lift cover with storage underneath, but this one is unusual in that it has drawers.

Lift-top commode which was originally part of a bedroom set made of pine. The solid plank sides are good, but a better commode would have rounded corners. This one has a single drawer on the left, with a dummy knob on the right to give it balance. The base cutout and painted decoration help to make it valuable.

The reasons are many. It is not easy to classify this pine furniture—bedroom sets, drop leaf tables, kitchen chairs, and benches—as Victorian. Can we honestly identify sleigh beds and rockers, Morris chairs, and platform rockers with the basic Victorian furniture? There were many oddities created, such as beds which dropped out of phony chests of drawers, and even a set of shelves on an iron frame which could be swung parallel to each other to form a table top. There were shapes in chairs and settees not found in Europe: such as arrowbacks and Hitchocks and the Shaker style, created by the well-known religious sect. Painting and stencilling of furniture was quite popular, and quite often one will see a bedroom set decorated with the scenes at a farm, where an itinerant painter might take lodging in return for his work. Is this a technique which can be ascribed to whose who did honor to Queen Victoria? The last of the monarchs to lend a royal name to a period style cannot be credited with (or blamed for) all that was done then.

In short, I feel that the era from 1830–1890 should be designated the American Home Period, leaving the more classic designations to those who enjoy them overseas.

SHAKER AND ZOAR

To broaden our knowledge of the Shakers, whose industry helped create many artifacts that are high on the collectable list today, we must recall the movement started here late in the eighteenth century when Ann Lee left England with a band of followers and founded the first colony at Mt. Lebanon, New York. A celibate sect, it grew, nevertheless, and locations for colonies extended all through New England and as far away as Kentucky. The Shakers supported themselves as food and herb growers, and also by the manufacture of furniture and other household items. Their furniture is light and delicate, yet very strong. The lines are simple with no ornament, and in this simplicity project great beauty. They worked with the woods at hand, and created pieces like chairs, cupboards, desks for the Eldresses, tables of all kinds, and just about everything which was made of wood. Their buildings, which still stand today in several colonies, were

Impressive Shaker store desk made in nineteenth century New England. Five feet long, it is one of the many functional, clean-lined pieces made by this religious sect. (Bud Foster Antiques, Wexford, Pennsylvania)

Shaker twelve drawer, long tailor's work counter with a Shaker lidded box, drying rack or "swift," and pierced tin and painted pine footwarmer on top. (Sotheby-Parke Bernet, New York)

designed with strength and durability in mind. One may see them in their original state at Canterbury, New Hampshire; Sabbathday Lake, Maine; Hancock, Massachusetts; and Pleasant Hill, Kentucky; as well as at other lesser known locations. Most of the groups sold off their material possessions as their numbers dwindled, and during the depression many of the homes and buildings were emptied in order for the Sisters and Brothers to make ends meet. Shaker furniture is high on the desired list today, not only with private collectors, but with those who are busy restoring Shaker buildings to their original look. The Canterbury colony has recently been incorporated in order that it may be preserved in its original appearance and condition for posterity.

In 1817, a group of separatists from the Lutheran Church in Germany came to America and eventually created a village in Ohio, named Zoar. The group was active until 1898, and during this time practiced great industry, as did their other religious counterparts in this country. Zoar furniture is quite rigid and stiff in appearance, and is rugged. Unlike the Shakers, who developed their own designs, the Zoars (along with other religious sects) generally made furniture in the style of the day but did not bother to beautify it with carvings or veneer. The community is being restored today, and more is being learned about what they made. There is a limited amount of furniture that can now be documented, so you may never know if you possess a Zoar piece unless you do your homework.

Eastlake

Almost no oak was used during the golden age of furniture, which extended from the time of Queen Anne through the Federal period. It was sparsely used during the years thereafter until Charles Eastlake, an English designer, published his *Hints on Household Taste* in 1868. He set forth a style departing from the heavier Victorian motifs and stressed that oak and walnut should be the preferred woods. The curved line was out, the straight line was in, and his ornamentation of the wood expressed

A custom made oak dining set which would bring a lot of money today, but
had little value as recently as the 1960's. Custom pieces in oak are uncommon,
and you can see that this one is not of common design or construction.

Custom made desk and chair in oak, late
nineteenth century. Regarded as untouchable
only a few years ago, quality oak furniture is
now commanding a respectable price.

Marble-topped walnut table in the style of
Charles Eastlake, late nineteenth century.
His designs were quite architectural, and a
new wave of furniture started after his
book was published in England in 1868.

his training as an architect. His designs were very structured, but they represented a departure from the old concepts, and the public, looking for a change after the Civil War, readily accepted them. American architects Frank Furness and Henry Hobson Richardson seized on the design change and helped popularize it in this country. Naturally, the huge furniture factories in Michigan and in the South began making the poor man's Eastlake, and until recently Eastlake has been regarded as the bottom in design and construction of all our periods.

Actually, there were many well-styled functional pieces and these command good prices now. Round tables should have claw feet—those with the elephant trunk foot are not as good. Oak hall trees used to land in dumps and were cut up for firewood, but some have now risen into the three-figure price range. The best ones should have brass hangers, a mirror, iron wells for umbrellas, and storage space for footwear. Oak ice boxes were thrown away for years, and now they are being turned into liquor and record cabinets. Kitchen chairs had designs pressed into them to give them the feeling of carving. Small commodes once available at anytime for a quarter, and the desks and bookcases given away by the Larkin Company as premiums for its soap wrappers have achieved new importance. Roll top desks were once the scourge of dealers, as they were heavy and cumbersome, but now they are a hot item. It seems obvious that the rise in interest in furniture of this period came about because of the increased cost of the better early furniture. Young people want inexpensive pieces, yet ones with age.

Mission

Another style crept in during the heyday of oak—that which has been identified as "mission." A takeoff from the furniture which was popular in the West, the style has its roots in the old Spanish missions which abound there. Made on square lines, the pieces are rugged indeed. Many town halls and other public buildings are still outfitted with Mission chairs, desks, and tables, since they are functional and nearly indestructible. The style

Heavy oak rocking chair of the type much in demand now. These chairs are virtually indestructible. The design on the back crest rail was stamped in under tremendous pressure when the wood was wet, and it is referred to as a "pressed back."

Late Victorian period couch in Eastlake style. The wood is walnut and the carving was done by machine. This couch would have been improved if wood had been used on the tops of the arms instead of upholstery.

would win no beauty award, but its clean lines are reminiscent of the comfortable Hepplewhite which has an enduring quality. Mission furniture has been exhibited in museums, so it has arrived so far as collectors are concerned.

Twentieth Century

Not much can be said for the styling of furniture during the twentieth century. America's burgeoning population gave growth to mass production which inundated us with very mediocre pieces, and supply seemed much more important than quality. The walnut waterfall, blonde oak, and gray oak became the hallmark for those who wished to be modern. The era spawned a host of factories which brought back "colonial" designs in maple and birch, but the reproductions left a lot to be desired as the workmanship was not good and the wood colorings ranged from red to very light blonde. Quality furniture has always been made, but buyers have always been limited because of cost. Concerns like Paine in Boston and Mayfair in Albany continued to turn out impeccable pieces and their work is gathering a lot of attention today from those who regard this work as classic in the same manner as you would assess a classic car, boat, or airplane. Private cabinetmakers have always been at work, and from time to time these individual pieces turn up to please their new owners. Those which are labeled are a prize, and if you should locate some of these, attempt to document their history if at all possible, while information might still be available. These pieces may be classics in museums someday, and such documentation will be very important.

It is not likely that there will be a return to the golden age of anything, as quick sale and profit seem to be the motivating force in our economy. Handcrafted furniture will always be with us and there is great interest in it today, but we can never hope to enjoy it on the scale it reached before 1830. You must live with your nostalgia if nothing more.

A New England cabinetmaker's demonstration box, which desplays his ability to make good mortised and dovetailed joints. The joinings are different at front and rear, as he needed to show all the different designs he could make.

Dressing table carrying the label of a chair factory operated by Thomas Brown on the banks of the Oyster River in New Hampshire, which runs through the university town of Durham. Most dressing tables of this type are made in pine, but this one is hardwood, most likely birch or maple.

Pier glass with gilded wood frame, about 1815–1820, presumably owned by the family of Nathaniel West of Peabody, Massachusetts. The carvings of the eagle and doves and the ribbons and balls which decorate the outer frame are outstanding. (Museum of Fine Arts, Boston—gift of Richard Edwards)

Centennial

During the third quarter of the last century, there was a revival of interest in the styles which were prevalent during the Revolutionary period almost a hundred years before. Fine reproductions were made of period styles popular then, using the same woods and same type of veneers and inlays. Another revival took place during the 1920's and 1930's, and the work was so good that anyone but an expert can be easily fooled. Old handmade drawers were often taken from undesirable Empire style chests, and were incorporated into good period frames made from old wood. Appraisers long ago labeled such work as "Centennial," and the name is in general use today. Many a poor chest or desk was altered with a new base, frame, legs, or feet, and was completely restyled to make it more desirable. Unscrupulous dealers have passed these on without saying too much about them—in one estate appraisal in Boston, eleven of the twelve cased pieces of furniture were Centennial, yet they were bought as antique. There must be some dealers who genuinely do not know that they are handling a reproduction, so they cannot be accused of misdealing. Actually, in many cases the furniture is just as finely made as its predecessors, and should be regarded as fine work. It should not command the same value, but you should not ignore it as it represents that which was classic in form and work. There are Centennial collectors who want nothing else, and they must confine their buying to the Boston and Philadelphia areas since this is where most of this work was done. What our Bi-Centennial will produce to match it is anybody's conjecture. The rule in buying is to look for as much handwork as possible, and to buy only quality in taste, design, and construction.

Veneering

Not long ago, the public was indoctrinated with the idea that the only good furniture was that made of solid wood. The horrible veneering of walnut and oak on our twentieth century furniture gave rise to this idea. However, with regard to the older

Perhaps the most outstanding slant top desk of all time is this eighteenth century carved ivory and bone rendition which is kept in the Summer palace at Pushkin, near Leningrad. It is a superb example of French artistry done at the time of Catherine the Great.

Hooded pine cradle, most likely from the eighteenth century, since the corners are dovetailed. These were made in sizes large enough to hold adults, who would sleep in them by the fireplace when ill.

antique pieces, you will find that veneered pieces will usually command a higher price than solid wood. In the Queen Anne and Chippendale periods, when veneering was at a minimum, there is naturally little comparison to be made. The Federal period brought with it a revival of this work, and in this era comparative pieces are valued according to the beauty and workmanship in them—not on whether or not they are veneered. The striking figured maple and birch which was most often used created works of art, not just functional pieces of furniture. In this respect, I feel that Federal period furniture is still highly underrated today, and will in many instances surpass the value of comparative pieces from the preceding periods before long. Age alone does not make a desired antique. Artistic beauty as a result of fine handcraftmanship will become more and more of a deciding factor in value. We are at the threshold of this renaissance now, so Federal furniture represents a much better buy for investment than the furniture which preceded it.

American Regional Styles

Once you have learned your periods, you may accept the new challenge of studying the regional characteristics of furniture. The different cultures abounding in America resulted in the variety of tastes evident in many types of artifacts. New England furniture is characterized by its delicate style, slender legs, and good proportions. When it is veneered, it is done in good taste with very highly figured woods. Dimensions are very important to this aesthetic, and this detail was unsurpassed elsewhere. In the case of a sideboard, New England pieces feature more leg and less body, whereas those from Philadelphia south are heavier bodied with shorter legs. Much carving was done, but not in the heavier rococo style which was the mark of Philadelphia work. Southern craftsmen relied heavily on dark stains in the manner of English work, but northern craftsmen were more content to use natural finishes and allow the wood grains to show in their own color. Northern five-legged game tables are a rarity, whereas they were the rule in the South. Charleston furniture is styled much

Dish-top, snake foot table, New Hampshire, eighteenth century. It is of light cherry, which is not common for this region. The legs are well-mortised into the main post as they should be for the period.

A rather classy eighteenth century high chair with a wide splay on the legs to prevent a child from tipping it. The legs are of tiger maple.

The painted decoration on this low pine Pennsylvania chest is enough to heighten its value considerably, although the work is not the best of this type to be found. Early nineteenth century.

like Boston, since many cabinetmakers from New England sought the more temperate climate and carried their influence with them. New York cabinetry was influenced for years by its Dutch heritage and culture, and the designs approximated much of what was being made overseas. In an era of cabriole legs, country furniture was rarely made with them, and much of the cased work was quite heavy in its look. Woods are a good clue, and you will find New England furniture in maple, pine, birch, cherry, and mahogany. Mahogany, walnut, and cherry were most popular in New York and Pennsylvania. Going south, you will find extensive use of walnut, mahogany, beech, and poplar, as well as the well-grained hard pine. Northern pine had little or no grain.

Some early furniture has snob appeal, and as a result great buys on New England furniture may be made in Philadelphia where there is little regard for New England work. Those who are enamored of the Newport work of the Townsends and Goddards feel there is nothing else to own or discuss. The clean lines of Dunlap work from New Hampshire will have little appeal to those whose tastes run to the fancy, no matter where they live. Some regard the highly veneered work of the Boston-North Shore Massachusetts-Portsmouth craftsmen as gaudy—merely a veneer over poor lumber beneath.

One may accept this as a clue to buy furniture where it is least appreciated, and this rule applies to all antiques. Victorian and Empire furniture is shipped by the truckload from New England, where it is not much in demand, and finds its way south to Texas where there are ready buyers who want the massive pieces for their high-ceilinged antebellum homes. A Victorian couch may begin its trip by selling for $25 or $50 in Maine, and after passing through the hands of several dealers sell for twenty times that in the South. Oak furniture is bought in New England, primarily to be shipped to the West coast where high prices are paid for it. Naturally, it must start its long journey by selling at a low price.

Much of our fine furniture has found its way overseas. Benjamin Frothingham worked in Charlestown, Massachusetts, and labeled his pieces as Charlestown, N.E. Not long ago a fine labeled highboy shipped from his shop overseas turned up in

Cophenhagen, Denmark. Another great highboy in an American museum was found in South Africa, and in 1952 a fine slant top desk bearing his label showed up in England and was brought back to be sold at an auction in New Hampshire.

Dimensions are important, as good proportion makes for a good looking piece. Dimensions also affect value. Perhaps the most desired width for a slant top desk, five or six drawer chest, or highboy top of the eighteenth century would be an even 36". Those which are wider command less money, and any which are smaller will usually command more. You must be very careful in any "just like" attributions, as the width of the piece is very important in relation to value. Short, squat legs, which lower the body of a chest to the floor do not give the graceful proportion of a tall, well-defined leg. Perhaps the greatest expression of this is in the cased pieces made in New Hampshire, which, for some reason, feature high legs which enhance the dignity of the pieces to which they are attached. Another New Hampshire characteristic is the wide moldings which are apparent at the tops of highboys and chests-on-chests. Traveling a few miles over the border in any direction will reveal narrower moldings made by nearby contemporaries. Maine furniture is styled very much like that of Massachusetts, as Maine was part of Massachusetts Commonwealth until 1818 and must have been influenced by this.

The furniture styles of the Boston-Salem-Portsmouth area have many characteristics which are similar, but there are differences. Chests, desks, and secretaries with a drop panel decoration were made from Salem north to Portsmouth and its area, but none has appeared with definite Boston attribution. They are known to have been made by Joseph Clark of Greenland (which is near Portsmouth), by the firm of Judkins and Senter of Portsmouth, and also by Nathaniel Appleton of Salem. Boston and Salem both featured a raised or top panel decoration on the tall cased pieces, but none has appeared on Portsmouth furniture. Salem and its area seems to be the only place where both raised and drop panels would be noted on the same piece, as Portsmouth featured only the drop panel. This small attention to detail is helpful, and illustrates what study will uncover in any field of antiquity and

Unusual oval-topped table with mid-eighteenth century styling, featuring splayed legs which are turned as they drop from the frame. The style is suggestive of Hepplewhite, but the concept of the table is early eighteenth century.

American Queen Anne highboy, early eighteenth century. This is a rather plain design, but it is built with very good proportions. The tops of such highboys should be 36″ wide—wider ones command less money as a rule, and narrower ones, which are more interesting and valuable, are scarce. The cabriole legs are very graceful.

American great chair of the Carver type, attributed to the Saybrook-Guilford area of Connecticut, late seventeenth, early eighteenth centuries. (Museum of Fine Arts, Boston)

Six drawer chest, commonly called a "Texas highboy." A product of the late nineteenth century, it features a locking corner post which swings out so that the drawers can be opened. These pieces derive their name from the fact that so many were shipped to Texas to meet a huge demand.

A rare pine slave's bed from the South, which doubled as a sleeping bench and storage chest. This one is of single board construction, in that each surface is made up of one wide board. This type is more desirable than those using two or more boards.

Early nineteenth century table with stretcher base and oval top whose feet are well worn. Typical of many tables of this type, except for the deep skirt it features, which is very desirable. A better one would have the skirt cut out in decoration, while lesser ones have narrow skirts. Condition is important, and single board tops enhance value.

how reasonable attribution may be made in the light of known facts. On some pieces of furniture the work is so similar that you would be hard put to specify the area of craftsmanship as this region was so full of fine cabinetmakers.

To attempt to explain the various details which must be studied in furniture of all areas would require space far beyond the bounds of this book. Its purpose is to make you "aware" of what you see. You must study history, for even the simple revelation of dates will prove instantly when the first work could have been done. The original thirteen colonies were the center of production until about 1820. The colonization beyond into Ohio, Indiana, Illinois, and into the Louisiana Purchase (which became our property in 1803) meant that craftsmen of all kinds helped in creating new settlements. It is highly unlikely that highly styled furniture would have been made until affluency was there to support it. You must content yourself with the study of the country pieces made during this time, gauging when the first real prosperity hit a community and created wealthy patrons who would demand the latest and best. The machine age began at about this time, and with the exception of those who still worked with hand tools away from most modern civilization, you may run into the mass production pieces which saturated the country—especially after the railroads came in and made mass distribution possible.

Unusual Regional Styles

An unusual situation occasionally comes about because of an event in history. At the time of the Revolution, Connecticut owned a strip of land which extended from its western border all the way to what is now Ohio. Congress later granted parts of this land to New York and Pennsylvania as it intersected their borders, and then granted new land at no charge to the Connecticut residents who wanted to pack up and move West. This land in the northern Ohio area is now known as the Western Reserve. Much fine Connecticut and other New England furniture may be found in this part of Ohio, since it was taken

This impressive chest-on-chest made by John Cogswell of Boston in 1782 was acquired by the Museum of Fine Arts in Boston in 1973. It has the bombe, or kettle-shaped base, a broken arch top, and is made of mahogany. This is highly styled furniture, rich in carvings, and on a par with any made in America. (William Francis Warren Fund)

there early in the nineteenth century. Some claim the first Hitchcock style chair was made in Ohio, but research shows it more likely that it was made up of parts furnished by Lambert Hitchcock from his factory in Connecticut. He is known to have made chair parts and shipped them disassembled from about 1815 to 1825, when he decided to make the complete chairs himself at his factory in Riverton. Much early Ohio furniture has the look of New England, as it was made by the Connecticut craftsmen who moved there.

Pennsylvania was dominated by a fine school of workmen who worked in strict adherence to English design. This work reached its greatest heights during the Chippendale era, and some feel the finest work in this country was done there and then. Baltimore housed many fine craftsmen who gave birth to ideas in style and veneering which were soon copied all over the colonies. One has but to see the elegant inlay work, the dainty Pembroke tables, and the magnificent banquet tables to realize how important Baltimore was as a center of fine furniture. Charleston and Annapolis had the wealthy clients a community needs to inspire great cabinetry, and the amount of it left in those areas can speak for itself. A trip to the area's museums and historic homes is highly recommended for further study of this work.

The growing ports of Mobile and New Orleans were definitely influenced by the French and Spanish furniture and artifacts which were easily imported over the sea—a much easier method than overland transport in those days. It inspired local cabinetry in the same style, and much study is now in progress to document such work.

Points of Identification

In conclusion, here are a few points of identification for furniture made during the "handmade" era prior to 1830.

You should always get beneath any piece of furniture to examine the leg and base structure, since this is the first place which will receive damage in moving or handling. You must examine the age (or patina) of the wood, to make sure that it is the same in all sections and that there are no replacements. Wood reinforcing blocks are glued at important joints to strengthen them. If corner blocks are held in with screws, you must determine if this is later construction or merely bracing which was added later to reinforce a weak spot. If screws are used, they must be of the hand cut variety, usually with the point tips cut off. In the old days, holes were drilled before the screws were put in, removing the necessity of a point. The slits in the screw heads will usually be off center as they were made quickly by hand. Machine screws are cut dead-center; this gives them away.

The drawer bottoms should preferably be single board and the grain should run from side to side in the chest. If the bottom has several boards running from front to rear, be suspicious, as you are most likely looking at an English piece. The drawer bottoms should be chamfered, or narrowed down at the edges, and should fit into slots at the drawer sides. The drawer sides should be dovetailed to the front and rear boards—generally, the wider and cruder the dovetail, the older it is. By the Federal period, dovetails were highly refined. The front dovetail will often be hidden with a molding or cockbeading which surrounds the drawer front. This is referred to as a "hidden dovetail," and it does not detract from the piece. The drawer bottom boards should show signs of hand planing or rough saw marks. Saw marks which are straight up and down and parallel to each other are evidence the board was cut on an up and down jacksaw. This was a two-man saw manipulated by a man standing atop the log and a man beneath in a pit, with the saw stroke moving up and down. The circular saw was not invented by the Shakers until the 1820's, so boards which show the marks of a circular saw must have been cut during that time or later.

Some experts can feel the leg of a piece and determine if the piece is old. New wood will still be quite round, while wood which has aged over the years will dry, with wood cut against the grain drying more slowly than wood cut with it. As a result, there is a slight oval shape to a turned leg if it is old, but you must sharpen your senses to work with this clue.

In American work, back boards on cased pieces should run horizontally, and usually are of pine, hewn, and chamfered. They

Gate-leg table in maple, late seventeenth or early eighteenth century. The turnings are quite good, and it is in excellent condition for a piece of this period.

American desk on a frame, late seventeenth or early eighteenth century, made of oak. It is typical of the period.

The chair at the right bears the label of Benjamin Randolph, a Philadelphia cabinetmaker of the eighteenth century, but is a phony. The chair at the left is authentic. The former could be a good reproduction from the Centennial period of the 1870's, but close examination reveals its duplicity. Do not trust all labels, since they can be duplicated.

A walnut desk waiting its turn at a country auction in Wolfboro, New Hampshire. Its small size, well-grained wood, and good workmanship stimulated a good price, well into the three figures.

Oriental lacquered sewing table brought to this country in the nineteenth century American-China trade. It holds sewing artifacts carved from ivory and bone. These tables are quite desirable and none too plentiful.

Queen Anne style lowboy in maple and birch, early eighteenth century, has a New Hampshire history. The brasses are replacements from a later period. True lowboys are too small to be mistaken as bases for highboys. Many highboy bases have had boards added to create a "lowboy" look, but their proportions are not correct, and you should sense this immediately.

are generally held in by rough hand cut nails. However, such nails are now being duplicated, so do not use this as an absolute means of attribution. In Centennial furniture, the back boards are often a dead giveaway to the age of the piece. Many pieces were made with thin machine-cut wood, and they most likely came this way. You may suspect that fakers later replaced these with old hewn pine to mislead unwary buyers.

If you are buying a chest-on-chest or highboy, you should check to make sure it is not a married piece. Due to family disagreement on who should get the furniture, it would sometimes be divided, with separate halves going to different owners. A new frame would then be built to hold the upper half, creating a phony chest, and a top would be put on the lower section. In the case of a highboy, this lower unit is often miscalled a lowboy. Over the years, dealers and buyers have been re-uniting sections, even though they are not original to each other. You should pull out a drawer from each section and examine the dovetailing to make sure it matches perfectly. Moldings and beading on the upper and lower cases should be checked. Back boards must be identical and must show the same age. The base should show no signs of tampering. Holes for the brasses or pulls should be cut or drilled identically. Above all, the proportions must be right—be sure the molding supporting the top section on the base is not too wide, and that the height and width of the top is proportioned well in relation to the bottom. Of course, the wood must be the same, but diligent refinishing can make them match. Study the wood in both sections, and make sure they originated in the same cabinet shop. It has been suggested that more than one man may have worked on such big pieces, so there may be variances. It is most evident that this was very likely, but the work would have been divided with each man doing his specialty—one to cut, one to dovetail, one to carve, etc.—so all similar work on the two pieces should check out as the same.

It is quite difficult to determine the age of a chair by looking at it from the outside. You must examine the frame construction, since this is where the truth lies. This often means ripping out a dust cover. If you are not permitted to examine the interior framework, stay away from the chair, unless you are paying a reproduction price. Reinforcing blocks to strengthen the legs against the frame were glued on early pieces, and later construction used corner blocks with screws. The age of the wood is important. Look for many tack marks where the upholstery was changed over the years. Look for hewn marks on the inside wood, as most were left a little rough and are not as smoothly cut as a machine driven saw would have left them. To judge by the leg backs alone is hazardous unless you know your woods and patina, and have a feel for the correctness of the piece. Even collectors this knowledgeable turn the pieces over.

The type, age, and condition of brasses is important. From the tear drop pulls of the late seventeenth century the turn of the century style advanced to bale handles with brass plates behind. The pre-1830 brasses or knob pulls featured a threaded post. This was inserted from the front of the drawer to the inside, where it was held on with a hand cut nut, often round. Later brasses would be held by a bolt which would be inserted from the inside of the drawer and fastened to the bale handle or knob at the front. After you have seen really old brasses, you will have little difficulty in telling them from the new. However, new brasses do not fault a piece too much, as most collectors will accept them as long as they are in the proper period style. Many museums have new brasses and knobs on their furniture—perhaps because they came that way, and perhaps because of the problem of theft.

Wooden and brass knobs were used extensively in the eighteenth century, especially during the last quarter. They were very popular all through the Federal period, and a great deal of Empire furniture appears with them. Glass pulls were introduced in 1825 by Bakewell of Pittsburgh when he developed a pressing machine to make them. The Boston and Sandwich Glass Company of Cape Cod is known for its fiery opalescent drawer pulls. These became quite popular and appear on much late Sheraton and Empire furniture. After this time all sorts of metal, wood, and glass pulls and handles with back plates were used. There is such a variety that I would be lost in attempting to discuss them. Since most were not handmade, they have little importance in the collecting scheme.

A very nice tavern table of the early eighteenth century. Its bold turnings are very desirable, but it would have been improved if it had been made with a single board top, rather than a two board one.

Pennsylvania dower chest with a beautiful painted design. Chests with lower drawers such as this are not common to New England, so it is not too difficult to guess its origin both from this and from the floral decoration which is quite Pennsylvania German in feeling.

You should check the inside of the drawers to determine if the pulls are original. Pull knobs were quite often replaced with bale handles and an additional hole would have been drilled. Early artisans hollowed out the holes on the drawer interiors so that the bolts and nuts would not tear clothing. If you find a drawer with one hole hollowed and one just drilled to accommodate the bolt, it is obvious that the brass is a replacement. Sometimes two new holes have been drilled to accommodate a bale handle, and the single hole which once held the pull knob will be quite obvious from the interior, though it will be covered by the back plate at the front of the drawer.

Leg heights are important in all pieces of furniture. Many were damaged in careless handling; others may have been left on dirt floors in cellars, and some were too tall for their new surroundings, so out would come a saw to take them down to size or even them off. This hurts a piece of furniture as the change is quite visible to the eye which is interested in good proportion. There are no set rules for the height and width of most furniture, so you must judge the piece with your eye—either the proportion is pleasing, or it isn't. You may find evidence of new wood where the saw has been at work. The cutting may be very evident unless the legs are cut properly at the termination of a turning. No one can help you on this, so use your own judgment and it will not be long before your eye will make you suspect tampering.

There are sometimes very good buys in furniture when the piece needs some work. Repair and restoration are acceptable, as long as they are not evident or objectionably visible. A drawer front that is obviously new will hurt a piece. A new frame or legs beneath a chest, well cut, done in good proportion, and refinished so they cannot be told from the upper section will be quite acceptable, though a top price should not be paid. Interior bracing work (new drawer slides and the like) will not harm value too much as long as it is out of sight. However, your leniency over the liberties taken with a piece may not be shared by the next buyer when you wish to dispose of it. You must be careful in your judgment, especially if you feel that you may sell the piece someday.

If you are prone to refinishing or decorating pieces of furniture, remember that there is as much effort expended on a poor piece as on a good one. If extra work is needed, it is best to seek quality as it will be more rewarding as far as ownership and eventual resale is concerned. Always buy a piece with the thought that you may have to sell it someday, and you will be more cautious and better satisfied with your venture into this area of antiques.

Mahogany chest-on-chest in Chippendale style, attributed to Jonathan Gostelow, Philadelphia, around 1775. This example is decorated with more restraint than most of the high-styled Philadelphia chests of the period. The intricate carving at the top is magnificent, and it has ogee feet. (Philadelphia Museum of Art)

Furniture Glossary

Acanthus—A plant native to southern Europe used as a motif in carving throughout civilized history. Very popular in French Empire style furniture.

Acorn—A turning based on the shape of the acorn.

Apron—A board which joins the understructure of cased furniture, tables, and chairs—often cut out for beautification.

Armoire—A cupboard for the storage of clothing.

Ball foot—A simple ball turning which was joined to the bottom of chests by a turned dowel.

Baluster—A turning, often done with bulbous swellings. Very popular in the late seventeenth and early eighteenth centuries.

Banding—A contrasting narrow stripping of veneer used for beautification. Popular during the Federal period, especially on drawer fronts.

Baroque—The Italian equivalent of French rococo, defining quite busy carvings and decoration.

Bombe—A chest or secretary base with a rounded bulging front and sides. Believed to have originated on American furniture in Boston.

Bun foot—A flattened ball with slender ankle above.

Cabriole—A shaped leg based on the cyma curve, with wide knees and narrow ankles terminating in various feet. Used extensively in the Queen Anne, Chippendale, and Victorian periods.

Caryatid—A carved human figure used as support for an upper pediment or shelf in furniture.

Court cupboard—Late seventeenth or early eighteenth century cased piece used for linens and dining areas.

Cyma curve—An S-shaped double curve.

Dentil molding—A series of carved rectangular blocks with spaces between. Often called hound's tooth molding if shaped to points.

Dutch foot—Often called a duck foot. A simple pad used on cabriole legs during the Queen Anne period.

Escritoire—A simple writing desk, with drawers, pigeonholes, secret drawers, and the like. The secretary was derived from this.

Escutcheon—A brass plate used for decoration or to surround openings such as a keyhole.

Fiddleback—A violin-shaped splat found as early as the time of Queen Anne, but revived during the Empire period.

Finial—A turned decorative device usually found atop cornices of high chests, or even as drops at the front lower section of highboys and lowboys.

Fluting—A channeled carving which is done in straight lines parallel to each other.

Fretwork—Ornamental work created by cutting and perforation.

Highboy—A tall chest of drawers, originally called a tallboy in England; usually standing on high legs and made in two sections.

Ladderback—A chair back with the cross splats arranged in ladder fashion.

Lunette—An ornamental design in half moon shapes. Often used in veneering in the Federal period.

Lyre—Design patterned after the instrument of that name. Popularized during the Empire period.

Marquetry—Decorations formed by inlaying various woods, shell, bone, or metals into a wood surface. This is often done in a thin wood veneer, which then is glued to the surface of the piece to be decorated. The rarer "intarsia" is veneering directly to the main surface.

Ogee—A shape made from two cyma curves with their convex sides meeting.

Patina—An aged surface.

Reeding—Convex grooves, carved parallel to each other.

Ribband—A reference to a carved or cutout "ribbon" chair back.

Rococo—From the French *rocaille,* literally meaning a pile of rocks. Carved ornamentation full of curves and other fancy carving motifs.

Serpentine—A serpentine curve used on the fronts of furniture.

Spindle—A turned round such as that used on chair backs and frames.

Splat—The central figure in a chair back.

Stretcher—An underbracing beneath case pieces, chairs, and tables, with reinforcement joined leg to leg.

Swag—A carving of leaves, draperies, or flowers.

Tester—The frame of a high four post bed, to which a decorative skirt is attached at the top.

Veneer—A thin ornamental wood with desirable graining which is glued to a surface of lesser wood.

Handmade Persian saddle flask in olive green. These where shipped to America in great quantities about 1968–1969. Although all of the flasks look old, it is suspected that some are still being made and aged rapidly in the desert.

Chapter 3

Glass

Glass reputedly originated on the shores of the Mediterranean when a group of Phoenecian sailors built a fire to cook their evening meal. In the morning they found that the hot coals and flames had melted the sand beneath and this had hardened into a crude form of glass. There must have been a quantity of soda mixed with the sand, since soda is necessary as a flux to form the melted silica. Since that time various minerals and elements have been mixed with silica to produce different types of glass, each with its own peculiar qualities. Lime, ashes, lead, and even gold has been used to produce glass ranging from the inexpensive to the exotic. Little is recorded about early glassmaking until the time of the Romans.

Roman civilization developed every known method of making glass objects until refinements in the making of plate glass were discovered in France in the eighteenth century, and the pressing of glass was developed in America early in the nineteenth century. At first, vessels were made by molding forms of sand or clay, and hot threads of glass were spun around these in spiral fashion. These were then smoothed out as much as possible, joining the threads in the process. When the blowpipe was invented, artisans soon learned to form pieces, and even add decorations, handles, spouts, etc., using crude tools, most of which changed little until the early nineteenth century.

From a collecting standpoint, you should concentrate on those items made after the Revolutionary War since there is not much pre-Revolutionary American glass, as England supplied most of our finished glass, and very little of this has survived. New Englanders like to take pride in the fact that theirs was the earliest settled part of the country and that the region preceded the others in manufacture of all kinds. However, it was quite late in producing one glassmaking concern that remained in business for an appreciable length of time. We do know that glassmaking in this country was introduced in Jamestown, Maryland, as early as 1608, and that there were window glass and bottle-making houses in New England and other settled parts of the country after that time, but it was not until Caspar Wistar, a Dutch inhabitant of Pennsylvania, went to Salem County in New Jersey and opened a glassworks there in 1739 that America had a company whose product became well known by name and survived for some years. Wistar made glass in what is now termed the "South Jersey tradition," and under his direction and that of his son's, it survived until 1780, when the fires of the Revolution put them out of business. Not one whole documented piece has survived intact from this output. Designs like the lilypad, cross ribbing, and swirled ribbons originated here and spread throughout the colonies.

Next to Wistar in influence was a very colorful character named Henry William Stiegel. He came to this country from Germany and managed to marry the daughter of the ironmaster of the Elizabeth Furnace in Lancaster County, Pennsylvania. He opened his glasshouse in 1763, and began turning out pieces in the German tradition of glassmaking, which makes it difficult today to tell his work from the imported glass made at that time. Stiegel became wealthy, and the title of "Baron" was bestowed on him as a measure of respect by his fellow townspeople. His high spending habits resulted in his being thrown into debtor's prison, which brought a halt to a very colorful career and the very interesting quality glass for which he was responsible. After the demise of his plant, about 1773, Pennsylvania remained prominent as a location of glassmaking due to the availability of coal and silica. The Philadelphia Glass Works was organized at that time with many of Stiegel's former workmen, and this company prospered under varying ownerships well into the nineteenth century.

Another early glassmaker was John Frederick Amelung, who set up his New Bremen Works at Fredericktown, Maryland, in 1787. Lured here by promises of opportunities in the new world, he encouraged other workers to follow him into the venture, which survived only until 1795. America had not instituted tariffs

Aquamarine lilypad pitcher, possibly from New York State. This design originated in New Jersey early in the nineteenth century and was used extensively in New York, Vermont, and New Hampshire. (Currier Gallery of Art, Manchester, New Hampshire)

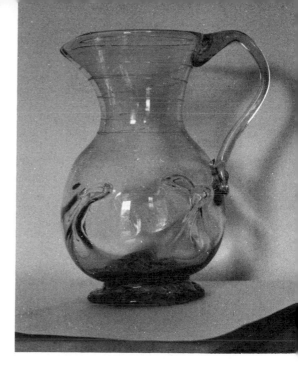

You must be careful when you buy items in pairs. Here is a "pair" of vases in ruby and clear glass made by the Pairpoint Company of New Bedford, Massachusetts. Because they are handmade, there are differences in dimensions which are quite evident in the handles. If you are a perfectionist, always hold pairs of anything close together for comparison.

Fifteen diamond nursing bottle made at the Mantua, Ohio, glass works, about 1821–1829. Working such a design into a blown flask required the skills of a master craftsman. (Jabe Tartar)

Glass held on a pointil rod being reheated in the glory hole of a furnace at Pikes Peak Glass Company, Colorado Springs, Colorado.

against imports which would have given local manufacturers protection from overseas competition. However, Amelung's glass won great favor, and there are good etched and signed pieces from his factory which have survived.

After the Revolutionary War, many glassworks were set up. None lived long enough to produce glass which has survived to be documented as from that period. It was really not until the beginning of the nineteenth century that any really large successful concerns were started, and examples of their work still survive. At the end of this chapter, I have listed the names of the prominent manufacturers whose work might be collected and indentified.

Glass is a combination of sand, flint, and spar or some other silicous substance with an alkali or some other material added as a flux. Of the alkalies, soda and potash were the first used successfully. Lead, borax, arsenic, nitre, and lime were used later. Sometimes pearl ashes, sea salt, and wood ashes were used. When red lead was used it gave the glass a yellow cast which could be corrected with nitre. If arsenic was used in excess the glass would turn milky. Pearl ashes were first used to make perfectly transparent glass. Borax was just as good, but it was more expensive and its use was mostly confined to making looking glasses.

The materials used for making glass were first reduced to a powder, either by pounding or by grinding in a horse mill. Then the powder was mixed with flux and calcined under intense heat for five or six hours. The resulting product was called "frit" and could be easily melted in the glass pots, with workmen skimming the scum from its surface. A typical mixture for a fine grade flint glass would be 120 pounds of white sand, 50 pounds of red lead, 40 pounds of pearl ashes, 20 pounds of nitre, and 5 ounces of magnesia. With the addition of a pound or two of arsenic, the material would fuse much more quickly and at a lower temperature. A cheaper mixture could be made by substituting sea salt for the arsenic. Crown glass (a popular product in the eighteenth century) was made from the following ingredients: 60 pounds of white sand, 30 pounds of pearl ashes, 15 pounds of nitre, one pound of borax, and a half pound of arsenic.

There were many "green glass" factories set up as early as the eighteenth century. A common mixture was as follows: 120 pounds of white sand, 30 pounds of unpurified pearl ashes, wood ashes well burned and sifted, 60 pounds of common salt, and 5 pounds of arsenic. In the rural glassmaking plants, a good green glass might be made by mixing 200 pounds of wood ashes with one hundred pounds of sand.

Colored glass has been with us for centuries, and the formulas have undoubtedly changed over the years. The following formulas come from recipes in use at the turn of the eighteenth into the nineteenth centuries, and in general use for many years after that.

To a glass mixture (such as the one outlined for flint glass above) add 9 pounds of copper precipitated from aqua fortis and two drachmas of precipitated iron for green. To ten pounds of glass add 6 drachmas of zaffre and one drachma of gold precipitated by tin for bright purple. Varying these formulas, you will find that for amethyst, magnesia was used; for black, magnesia and calcined iron; for white opaque, calcined horn, ivory, or bone; for ruby, gold precipitated by tin; for blue, calcined bones, horn or ivory, magnesia, and zaffre; for yellow, calcined iron or crude tartar and antimony.

After glass is formed, either by blowing or pressing, it must be annealed in an oven in which it cools gradually in order to retain its temper and strength. Etching was originally done by dipping the glass body into ordinary melted wax. After the wax hardened, an artisan would etch the outline of a decoration or picture into the wax on the glass body. It would then be dipped into a lead lined box which contained a fluoric acid which would etch the glass wherever it was not protected by the wax. Initials and monograms could be put on glassware in this manner. After a rinse in neutralizing water to flush away the acid, the remaining protective wax would be removed by dipping the piece in hot water and melting it away. A varnish coating was sometimes applied.

Engraving on glass is generally done by a spinning cutting wheel, with the artisan holding the glass body against the wheel to produce the desired decoration. The term "copper wheel cut"

Historical flasks are high on any collector's list. At left, one of the many varied designs of the Masonic flask turned out by the Marlboro Street Works at Keene, New Hampshire, about 1817–1825. At right, the Keene sunburst flask. These are blown molded in dark amber glass. In the oval on the flask at left, Keene is spelled KCCNC, which was easier to carve. At the right it is KEEN since there was no room for the final E.

Sandwich pattern glass goblets. Top, left to right: Sandwich star; diamond thumbprint; comet; and morning glory. Bottom, left to right: Chilson; scarab; bullseye and wishbone; and bullseye and block. All are of flint and of early manufacture. (Bourne Gallery)

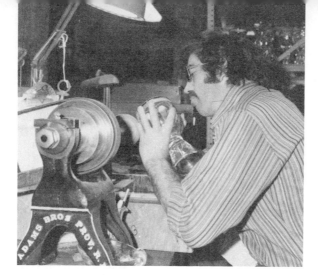

Bryant Sylvia at the glass cutting wheel, Pairpoint Glass Works, Sagamore, Massachusetts. Good contemporary work done by hand can well become a fine antique of the future.

Lamp made especially for Deming Jarves, founder of the Boston and Sandwich Glass Company. The shade and prisms are cut. His name is cut into the base, as this was a presentation piece. (Sandwich Glass Museum, Sandwich, Massachusetts)

Cut glass whiskey decanter flashed in ruby. The Boston and Sandwich Glass Company was known for its quality glass, and this piece is on display at the Sandwich Glass Museum on Cape Cod.

refers to such a method, with the wheel most likely sprinkled with diamond dust to speed the work. However, back in the early part of the nineteenth century, you could have purchased glass engraved in a more radical, simpler method. While the glass piece was hot, it would be dipped into a mixture of red lead, sand, and borax, heated and fused with what was called a menstrum—a mixture of pure cane sugar, water, and common writing ink, which would hold some oxide of manganese. The mixture might have also been painted on with a camel's hair brush or squirrel's foot. A simple etching or engraving tool would be used to cut away the desired decoration. The etching would appear in reverse, with the cut areas smooth and clear and the untouched areas appearing to have been roughened with a tool. Some artisans felt that clearer cuts could be made in this manner, with less possibility of unwanted glass powder being ground into the body at the edges of the cuts by the wheel.

Identifying the makers of early glass is quite difficult, as most melted the same metals according to the same or very similar formulas. Colors and pattern designs were copied freely, and neighboring concerns would often help each other when large orders came in, with each making up part of the order in similar molds. Workers in this industry were quite transient and always in demand, so they might take their own trade secrets with them from plant to plant, which would account for the similarities of workmanship.

Eighteenth Century Glass

We might categorize American glassmaking into different periods as an aid to identification. Eighteenth century glass must almost be lumped together so far as content and quality are concerned. Different blowing techniques and .types of decorations might aid in determining the origin of some pieces as far as regions are concerned, but due to continuous importation, it is quite difficult to tell American work from that which came from overseas. When mechanical pressing of glass was developed about 1825, glassmakers were able to run wild with mold designs,

Greentown glass made by the Indiana Tumbler and Goblet Company of Greentown, Indiana, about 1894–1903. Products like mustard and peanut butter were often packed in these to be sold in local grocery stores.

Rare lacy glass made at the Boston and Sandwich Glass Company, Sandwich, Massachusetts. Top, left to right: crossed strawberry and diamond bowl; lacy peacock eye bowl. Center: rare oval lacy deep bowl. Bottom, left to right: industry bowl; plate in acanthus and palmette pattern. All are flint glass and date early in the company's production. (Bourne Gallery)

and the industry diversified as it never could before. Suddenly, shapes, forms, designs, and pressing techniques could be identified, and glass from the Pittsburgh area took on a completely different look from that made in New England. New England benefited from the likelihood that immigrants would settle at their first port of call, where work might be available, rather than head into the less developed areas in the midwest. However, many workers got their start in New England and then went on to factories in the Pennsylvania, West Virginia, and Ohio areas, taking inland techniques and ideas learned on the coast. It is amazing how much we do know about the origin of much American glass, when so little of it was marked or otherwise documented.

In collecting glass, you will find it is best to concentrate your efforts in the regions where it was made. If you collect Hobbs and Brocunier, you should look for it in the Wheeling area. If you desire Sandwich glass, there is more of this on Cape Cod and in eastern Massachusetts than anywhere else. You will find the prices are generally lower in such areas since the law of supply and demand keeps them stable. You should look for Keene and Stoddard historical flasks in New Hampshire—looking for one made in Mantua, Ohio, might be rather futile. However, shipments of glass were made to different parts of the country, so you might examine the old records of companies preserved by historical societies and researchers, and you may locate what you are looking for elsewhere. The Boston and Sandwich Glass Company shipped glass to the west coast, so a lot of it can be found there. Some was even sent to Russia and other European nations. However, I have looked for specimens all over Europe (even in Russia) to no avail.

PRESSED GLASS

In 1825, a patent for pressing glass by machine was issued to Benjamin Bakewell at his plant in Pittsburgh. This was first used for pressing solid objects such as drawer pulls. In 1827, a further patent on pressing was issued to Deming Jarves at Sandwich for an improvement whereby hollowares might be made. The new technology was adopted around the world, and the resulting mass

Early glass from the Boston and Sandwich Glass Company. Top, left to right: a rare translucent blue acanthus pattern whale oil lamp; blue and clam water dolphin candlestick from the earliest mold; and a rare whale oil lamp with translucent blue base and opaque white font. Bottom, left to right: a purple-blue Three Printie vase; a light translucent blue candlestick cast in one mold; and a dark blue blown and molded decanter with shell and ribbed pattern. (Bourne Gallery)

production created so much glass made in so similar a manner and look that the smartest historians qualify their opinions on origin unless they are absolutely sure.

There are some who feel glass should be judged by its quality and not by the name of its maker. Unfortunately, most dealers and collectors do not agree with this premise. Documentation of glass is most important, as most is collected by maker's name. Early colored pressed glass is desirable, but patterns were often copied and this makes identification difficult. It was not until Ruth Webb Lee published her *Handbook of Early American Pressed Glass Patterns* in 1931 that collectors had a common glossary to use so that items could be advertised in a manner that all collectors could understand. Other patterns have been discovered since this book was published, but it remains an excellent guide. To this day, pattern glass is still made by basically the same mechanical means. This has made faithful reproduction of many of the old designs possible, much to the consternation of collectors. Collecting an item which can be reproduced has its own built in set of hazards, so you must arm yourself with great knowledge before venturing far in this field.

Art Glass

After the Civil War, industrial plants had to turn from making military items to consumer production, and glass companies struggled for their own piece of this business. Victorian England had been making fancy colored glassware which found favor here, and it was not long before England was challenged by native production. America entered what is often called the "art glass" period, when artistic design and color were the subject of much experimentation. Just about all of the existing glass plants boosted their production of this product while continuing production of conventional inexpensive tablewares and functional items. In the 1860's, William Leighton left the employ of the New England Glass Company for a new job at Hobbs and Brocunier in Wheeling, where he discovered the use of inexpensive lime as a flux instead of the more expensive lead or flint which was then in general use. The New England companies did not wish to cheapen their product and pretty much ignored this new technique. They suffered greatly from the competition of the midwestern factories, and eventually the two giants in the

Pieces from the art glass period of the late nineteenth century. Top row: agata glass; bottom row: peachblow, made by the New England Glass Company, Cambridge, Massachusetts. (Bennington Museum, Bennington, Vermont).

Mount Washington art glass. Left to right: Crown Milano cracker jar; Crown Milano berry bowl and silver stand; Cameo bowl in silver stand. (The Lola Kincaid Ford Collection, Corning Museum of Glass)

industry, the Boston and Sandwich Glass Company and the New England Glass Company, closed their doors in 1888. William Libbey moved the New England Glass Company to Toledo, Ohio, where it remains to this day. Since the New Englanders did not wish to compromise on the quality of their product, many collectors feel that the superior art glass was made in this region. You must understand that while the midwestern companies did make inexpensive lime glass, they also made quality items for the carriage trade, and these are comparable in quality and style to items made anywhere. In the nineteenth century, there was little activity in glassmaking beyond Indiana. Most glassmaking was concentrated in the West Virginia, Ohio, and western Pennsylvania areas at the end of the century, although there was some activity in New York State and New Jersey.

Tiffany Glass (Art Nouveau)

The turn of the century brought with it a change in style as art nouveau motifs, made popular in France, gradually came to our shores. Some people feel that the period from 1895 to 1920 was gaudy, others say it was sterile, and some feel it was an era when the most grotesque styles were perpetrated on the public. Glass felt the design changes more than anything else. Louis Comfort Tiffany helped to popularize the iridescent colored glasses, and his name is attributed to many items which may or may not be the product of his factory. His stained glass windows for churches and breakfast rooms in fancy homes are overshadowed only by the magnificent Tiffany glass curtain at the Palace of Fine Arts in Mexico City. To see this creation, you must go there on a Sunday morning since this is the only time it is lowered. It is made up of over two million pieces of glass fused together to show the two volcanos, Popocatepetl and Ixtaccihuatl, at different seasons of the year and at different times of day as lights are changed behind it. It is one of the most artistic creations of all times—made by an American glassmaker. Tiffany's European counterparts were very busy making and sending their iridescent and cameo-carved wares to America, where they found great favor with the wealthy.

Marking used by the Imperial Glass Company of Bellaire, Ohio before 1950.

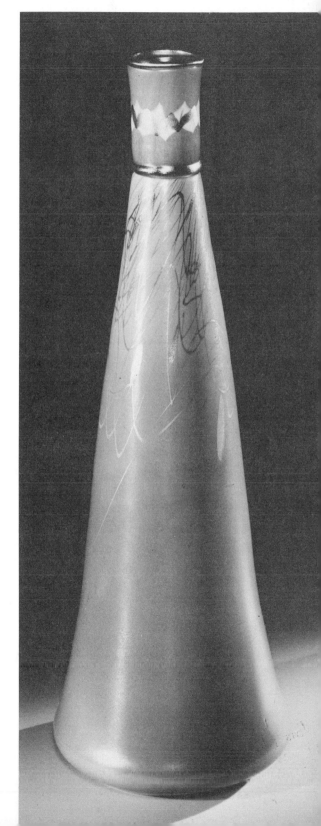

Vase of Tyrian glass designed by Frederick Carder and made by the Steuben Glass Works, about 1915–1917. This is a typical example of art nouveau iridescent glass. (Corning Museum of Glass)

Blown and cameo cut vase by Emile Galle, Nancy, France (1846–1904). Galle is the only maker who put his name on every piece he made or which was turned out in his factory. These pieces must be signed to be authentic.

Carnival glass made after 1910. The lamp with grape design is quite rare. Next to it are a corn holder in orange iridescent glass, an orange cruet, and a tumbler in blue helios. Most carnival glass was made in Pennsylvania, Ohio, and West Virginia.

Marking used by the Imperial Glass Company from 1950 to present is an I superimposed over a G.

Poor Man's Tiffany

During this periods commercial glassmakers were busy capitalizing on the new form and were turning out an inexpensive iridescent glass in fancy shapes and colors. Frank Fenton of Newark, Ohio, is credited with making the first efforts in this direction in 1907. He mixed iron oxide and iron chloride with the glass metal to give it its sheen. Other glass works picked up this development immediately, and soon such famous works as Imperial in Bellaire, Ohio; Millersburg and Westmoreland, both in Pennsylvania; and Fenton's former employer, Harry Northwood of Indiana, Pennsylvania, were turning out the poor man's Tiffany. No glass company in New England is credited with making the product. By this time, most New England glass works had closed or had moved to the midwestern area. The first new color in appearance was yellow, or marigold, but chemists soon explored the full range of colorings. Artists came up with designs ranging from the most popular grape through the tiger lily, fine cut heart, sunflower, sunken daisy, shell and jewel, fish scale and beads, open rose, scroll embossed, thistle, star, and singing birds, to name a few. Fruit bowls were popular, along with hatpin holders, powder jars, and pin trays. On the rarer side are ash trays, banks, jelly jars, paperweights, and electric lamps. Baskets and vases were popular, but most were for decorative rather than functional use. The pitcher and tumbler sets were favorite premium items and, in some cases, complete dinner sets were made.

In later years this was called "carnival glass," as it was often given away as a prize at carnivals and fairs and was also used as a premium by cereal and tea companies. It received this name during the depression years when companies found their warehouses full, with no ready market for distribution. Loads were dumped into the market and carnival operators seized on it as an inexpensive prize for their games of chance. Long regarded as an inferior product, carnival glass was an item which had to be sold by the boxful at auctions until a few years ago. Then collectors became interested in it as there were pieces which showed definite quality, reflected by the handwork incorporated in the making. Most people think the glass was all machine made, but research has proven that up to seven or eight men spent four or five minutes making each well-moulded piece. The inexpensive pieces look inexpensive, and those of value look it, so you do not have to be too bright to evaluate most of this glass. Depth of molding, design, color, iridescence, and proportions must be judged in determining quality.

The top favorite seems to be the Northwood pieces, which are well marked with a capital N within a circle, usually at the bottom of the piece. Fenton signed his pieces in script, and these are being reproduced today by the Imperial Glass Company of Bellaire, Ohio, which is still turning out the product. Early Imperial glass was marked with a cross, the eight letters of its name appearing two to a section. Newer Imperial pieces are signed with a G superimposed on an I. The most popular colors in order of preference are purple, blue, green, orange, yellow, and marigold. White carnival glass is quite rare. You will find that most of this glass is really inexpensive in value. Search for deep cut, well-colored quality pieces if you want to collect carnival glass.

Depression Glass

A new phenomenon in the collecting world is "depression glass," so called because it was popular during the 1930's. In the past, most depression glass ended up in the dump or at summer

Until recently, depression glass was neglected as a collectible. It was given this name because it was sold in abundance during those years. Produced in many colors and patterns, most of it was made by the Jeanette Glass Co., Indiana Glass Co., Hazel Atlas Glass Co., Imperial Glass Co., MacBeth Evans Glass Co., Hocking Glass Co., United States Glass Co., and Heisey Co. Production was centered in Pennsylvania, Ohio, and West Virginia.

cottages, since no one thought it would ever be worth anything. It languished in the shadow of more exotic glass, and was being sold by auctioneers for 25 or 50 cents a boxful simply to get rid of it. The mania for collecting anything brought prominence to depression glass very recently, and the prices for it are now off and running. The high prices reached by the finer older glass have created the demand by those with limited funds. This glass was made by the Jeanette Glass Company, Indiana Glass Company, Hazel Atlas Glass Company, Imperial Glass Company, MacBeth Evans Glass Company, Anchor-Hocking Glass Company, United States Glass Company, and Federal Glass Company. Production was centered in the Pennsylvania, Ohio, and West Virginia areas, as it was with carnival glass. Depression glass is very brittle, so odd pieces such as butter dishes, handled pitchers, cookie jars, and even ashtrays are not common. American Sweetheart is the most desired pattern as more was made. Red is best, blue second, and pink least desired. Blue Madrid made by the Federal Glass Company is in short supply because they were not able to produce the exact blue wanted. Most depression glass was made in the "mold etched" process which was unique to the period. However, some was made by the "chip mold," paste mold, or even handmade process. The latter techniques were a holdover from the carnival glass period in which some of the finer pieces of relatively inexpensive glass were produced. Many glass patterns were given names, such as Old Cafe Lace, Lace Edge, Miss America, Queen Mary, Colonial, Coronation, Rouletter, Hobnail, Oyster and Pearls, and the like. A good reference book for this type of glass is listed in the bibliography.

Contemporary Glass

Many are concerned about the advisability of collecting contemporary glass. This is fine as long as proper documentation of artists and makers is provided. Experience has shown that most antiques change hands at far greater value if the name of the maker is known. The hours spent on research to document old

Contemporary glass designed and made by the Nekker brothers of Israel has a satin sheen and boasts a slight iridescence.

Robert Bryden, owner of the Pairpoint Glass Works in Sagamore, Massachusetts, is one of the few remaining master craftsmen in glass. After the old Pairpoint works closed in New Bedford in 1958, he went to Europe to teach glassblowing. He reopened the Pairpoint Works in 1970 to make special glass which is being avidly collected today.

unrecorded items could be spent in other pursuits, so the information should be recorded now for future generations. Some concerns do not mark their pieces, and I do not recommend collecting their output. Some companies may sign them with their name, but not with the name of the artist—again, the artist's name is most important. Several people may be involved in the making of one glass piece—be sure you get the names of all those who worked on the piece, or do not buy it. You will realize the wisdom of this if you are concerned with the future interest in and value of the piece. If value is of no concern to you, buy what you please, but realize that you have actually done the piece an injustice by not permitting future owners to know its origin. If paper labels are provided, keep them on the piece since they are valuable for documentation. Do not put your glass in the dishwasher, just clean it with a damp rag and dry it carefully. Not long ago, a broken Tiffany bowl with the paper label intact sold for $45 at an auction. The label will undoubtedly find its way to the bottom of an unmarked bowl which may be Tiffany in order to raise its value. As with most antiques, those items which are American made will have the most value in the future, so it is best to collect contemporary American glass. Buy rejects, samples, and closeout pieces from concerns where handwork is still in process. The oddity and small flaws which caused rejection will often command more interest and value as time goes on.

ART GLASS REPRODUCTIONS

In the late 1950's and early 1960's, foreign glassmakers began turning out remarkably good reproductions of early art glasses, such as millifiore, burmese, amberina, and peachblow. Many reproductions were made in Murano, Italy, some in Portugal, and some in other countries such as Japan. Unknowing buyers would often bid high prices at auction for such pieces, possibly learning later what they were. The work is hand done, and some of it is quite good, though it should not be equated in value with the old pieces. Once the general public realized what was going on, sales in such reproductions slumped. Since art glass reproductions have been off the market for a few years, there is new interest in them as collectable items, as they represent a form of period handwork which is quite good. Since the pieces are shorter in supply now (though they are not antiques in the general sense as some are still being made), prices are going up and stabilizing on such reproductions. This work frightens appraisers, because much of the work is good and added age will only make it more difficult to separate the reproductions from the really old pieces.

Glass Oddities

Many whimsies were made from glass, since this was an easily worked material and colors could be used at little extra cost. Canes, penny banks, pipes, toys, candy holders, darning balls, animals, birds, floral displays, and the like poured from the factories. Some say this was the result of extra glass being used up at the close of the day by workmen who made such trinkets as gifts to families and friends. You must judge these items on their interest and workmanship, and on whether they are pleasing and desirable. It is not necessary to spend huge sums of money for them—you should enjoy them for the artistic artifacts they are.

PAPERWEIGHTS

Paperweights are an important facet of glass collecting, since they represent an art form which demands good workmanship and are usually pretty and functional. Many fine weights were made overseas, especially at Bacarrat, Clichy, and St. Cloud in France, but some weights on a par with these were made in America. Most of the large glass factories employed paperweight makers, but this effort must have been concentrated in New England. Both the Boston and Sandwich Glass Company and the New England Glass Company were well known for this work. The Pairpoint works in New Bedford and some works in New Jersey (such as the works at Millville) contributed some elegant pieces.

Many private makers have been at work, and some of the contemporary pieces are commanding more money than the old ones. Domenick Labino of Grand Rapids, Ohio; Charles Kaziun of Brockton, Massachusetts; Ronald Hansen of Mackinac City,

Paperweight mold of fruit-wood in which the weight shown was made. The mold is by Johnny Gentile of Morgantown, West Virginia, and the weight is by Joe Kopcych of Bridgewater, Massachusetts.

Bottles are classed into groups, such as flasks and liquors, figurals, bitters, medicinals, and commercials. A Warner's Safe Kidney and Liver Cure made in Rochester, New York, by a man who used to sell safes and later went into the bottle business, using the safe as his trademark, is shown at left. A fish bottle in which cod liver oil was probably packed is shown in the center. A Drake's Plantation Bitters in which a patent medicine was sold is shown at right. All are made in amber color. (Photo by Eastman Kodak)

At left is an imported paperweight of a type which is coming into the country today from China. In the center is an end o' day type, most likely New England from the last quarter of the nineteenth century. At right is a rare French sulfide weight with classic figures.

Michigan; and Johnny Gentile of Star City, Morgantown, West Virginia are among the contemporary makers whose works are being studiously collected at this time. There are a lot of handmade weights coming to America from the Orient and Europe—some quite good, but all must be judged on the quality of the design and workmanship.

Some weights are referred to as having sulphide interior decoration. This is merely a porcelain design or figure of some sort imbedded in the glass. The difficulty of molding the decoration into hot glass without destroying it is what gives these weights interest and value.

Glass Bottles

Bottle collecting is the second most popular hobby in our country today, next to coins. Since most bottles are made of glass, they represent an important part in the history of this manufacture. Bottles were made as early as 1608 (when

Sherds of glass dug from the foundations of the Boston and Sandwich Glass factory. They reveal that the company was a maker of common production bottles for industrial use, ink bottles, and other shapes and forms not heretofore known to have been made at this works. (Ray Barlow)

Jamestown was settled), and many interesting ones are being made today. Pre-revolutionary American-made bottles are rare. Most American bottles of that era came from overseas, primarily from England and France. During the seventeenth century, bottle and window glass houses were set up in many places in this country, but no documented pieces have been found. Some eighteenth century pieces have been located, with enough documentation to land them in museums and great collections. After the Revolutionary War, the American glass industry expanded quickly, and there are many examples which have survived and are available to collectors. Bottles are divided into categories—there are historical flasks, bitters, medicines, and figurals. Early flasks were free blown, but by the early part of the nineteenth century most were being blown into wooden or iron molds so that designs would appear and uniform sizes would result. The early blown mold bottles are quite plentiful which is amazing when you realize how fragile and brittle the old glass is. As the settlement of the country moved rapidly west the glassworkers went with it, and as a result there is much good glass in bottle-form made throughout the nineteenth century. This is quite desirable today, and a directory of early glassmakers appears on pages 110–112.

Perhaps the most desirable bottles are early nineteenth century historical flasks with good color. Bitters are rising in value, but good figurals portraying our early political and national heros are already well up in price. Design, color, and condition are most important. Foreign bottles are not of great importance in American collecting, unless they are of extreme age. Recent Indian digs have uncovered seventeenth and eighteenth century English and French bottles, which have considerable value as they were used by the Indians and our first settlers. Wrecks of old ships off the coasts here and in the Caribbean have long held old bottles which are being brought up by divers every year. Bottle auctions are held throughout the country, and help set the prices by which bottles are bought and sold today.

Bottles are of great interest as a collectable, since you can dig them from the ground at no charge. Diggers will spend weekends tracking down old dumps behind farms in the country, and even

Covered glass sweetmeat dish in canary yellow. Although the dolphin feet, shells, and color have roots in Sandwich, Massachusetts, this dish is a product of the Portieux Glass Company of France from the third quarter of the nineteenth century. The rosette at the bottom is a mark of this company.

Silvered glass (which is often called mercury glass) was popular during the third quarter of the nineteenth century. A silver nitrate solution was rinsed on the inside while the glass was warm. All pieces have a double wall and were sealed at the bottom after silvering. Silvered glass was often painted or etched with acid for decoration. (Currier Gallery of Art, Manchester, New Hampshire)

hunting in old town dumps. The bottles have lain buried for years, so all you have to do is arm yourself with a shovel, pick, and hoe and you are in business. A first aid kit, gloves, and high boots are also necessary. Snakes are common around old dumps, so be sure your legs and hands are protected. Poison ivy is a hazard, so you must be prepared with medication for it. Above all, obtain permission to hunt from the landowners, as some are quite touchy about having their ground dug up. Some bottle collectors attend building wreckings and ask permission to search the foundations, cellars, and walls for hidden bottles. Many good bottles are found while a backhoe or bulldozer is digging a cellar for a new building or cleaning up the debris from one just torn down. A cement layer and his crew, while laying a sidewalk for me, once reinforced the concrete with the many beer bottles which they emptied on a hot day and threw into the mix. These will undoubtedly be the subject of much conjecture when they are dug up someday.

Mary Gregory was a decorator at the Boston and Sandwich Glass Company. She is known for her paintings of children on glass, inspired by Kate Greenaway, whose children's books were popular in the nineteenth century. Although this panel is similar to the work she did, it must be judged by the rules followed by most collectors for Mary Gregory glass:

    (1) The central figure must be a child.
    (2) Only one arm should be visible.
    (3) One leg should appear shorter than the other.
    (4) The child must be standing or sitting in a patch of fog or clouds.
    (5) There should be terns at the front and rear of the picture.
    (6) The painting must be all white.

This panel does not meet all the requirements, so it would not be judged as her handiwork.

Early Glass Manufactories
in the United States

Amelung, John Frederick—See New Bremen Glass Manufactory.

Bakewell & Ensell—Pittsburgh, Pennsylvania, 1808–1882; operated under various partnership names; *Bakewell & Pages; Bakewell, Pears & Bakewell; Bakewell, Pears & Co.*, etc.; glass of all kinds including art and pressed.

Boston and Sandwich Glass Company—Sandwich, Massachusetts, 1825–1888; Deming Jarves; all types of glass, including early pressed glass.

Boston Crown Glass Company—Boston, Massachusetts, 1793–1829; Robert Hewes and others; window glass, bottles.

Boston Porcelain & Glass Manufacturing Company—Cambridge, Massachusetts, 1814–1888; George Blake, Thomas Curtis, and Jesse Putnam; glass, stoneware, porcelain. In 1817, became the *New England Glass Company*. Originated amberina, pomona. Prolific in the art glass period. Moved by final owner, Edward Libbey, to Toledo, Ohio, in 1888.

Brooklyn Glass Works—Brooklyn, New York, 1823–1868; full range of glass items. John Gilliland. Moved in 1868 to Corning, New York, to become the Corning Glass Company.

Cape Cod Glass Company—Sandwich, Massachusetts, 1858–1869; under direction of Deming Jarves. Operated 1869–1881 by a Dr. Flowers. Cut, pressed, and decorative glass.

Chelmsford Glass Works—Chelmsford, Massachusetts, 1802–1839; Jonathan Hunnewell and Samuel Gore. Window glass and bottles. Moved to Suncook, New Hampshire, in 1839 and operated there until 1850.

Cincinnati Glass Manufacturing Company—Cincinnati, Ohio, 1814–1822; Isaac Craig. Bottles, window glass.

Dorflinger Glass Works—Greenpoint, Long Island, New York, 1858–1865; Christian and Christopher Dorflinger. Also, White Mills, Pennsylvania, 1865–1918. Cut and colored glass; table and decorative wares.

Glassboro—New Jersey, 1781–1824; started by members of the Stanger family.

110

Granite Glass Works—Stoddard, New Hampshire, 1846–1872; bottles and flasks.

Hewes, Robert—Temple, New Hampshire, 1780–1782; window glass and bottles.

Jersey Glass Company—Jersey City, New Jersey, 1824–1860; established by George Dummer. All types of glass.

Kensington Glass Works—Philadelphia, Pennsylvania, 1771; advertised with the name of Thomas Dyott after 1824. Changed to *Dyottville Glass Works* in 1833. Operated under various ownerships into the twentieth century. Noted for historical flasks and bottles under Dyott's ownership.

LaBelle Glass Works—Bridgeport, Ohio, 1872–1900; pressed and flint glass.

Mantua Glass Works—Mantua, Ohio, 1821–1829; bottles, flint glassware.

Marlboro Street Works—Keene, New Hampshire, 1815–1850; Henry Rowe Schoolcraft and Timothy Twitchell. Historical flasks, bottles, tableware.

McKee & Brothers—East Birmingham, Pennsylvania, 1850–1890; J. & F. Mckee; all types of glass.

Millville, New Jersey, Glass Works—founded 1806 and still in business. Originated by James Lee. Originally produced window glass and bottles. Acquired by Whitall Brothers in 1844 and became *Whitall-Tatum Company.*

Mount Vernon Glass Company—Mount Vernon, New York, 1810–1844; bottles, flasks, flint glass, historical flasks, etc.

Mount Washington Glass Company—South Boston, Massachusetts, 1837–1869. Moved in 1869 to New Bedford, joined with Pairpoint Silver Company. Closed in 1958. Reopened by Robert Bryden as *Pairpoint Glass Company,* 1970, Sagamore, Massachusetts. Glass of all kinds. Originated burmese, peachblow, rose amber.

New Bremen Glass Manufactory—Frederick, Maryland, 1784–1795; started by John Frederick Amelung. Noted for engraved glass.

New Geneva Glass Works—New Geneva, Pennsylvania, 1797–1807; Albert Gallatin and others. Window glass, bottles, tableware. Later moved to Greensboro.

New Hampshire Glass Factory—Keene, New Hampshire (North Works), 1814–1855; window glass.

Pitkin Glass Works—Manchester, Connecticut, 1783–1830; Elisha Pitkin and Samuel Bishop. Originators of Pitkin type flask; also made bottles and tableware.

Pittsburgh Glassworks—Pittsburgh, Pennsylvania, 1797–1886; James O'Hara and Isaac Craig. Window glass, bottles, holloware.

Portland Glass Works—Portland, Maine, 1863–1873; lamps, tableware, colored glass.

South Stoddard Glass Works—South Stoddard, New Hampshire, 1850–1873; bottles and historical flasks.

South Wheeling Glass Works—Wheeling, West Virginia, 1835–1880; flint and colored glass.

Stiegel, Henry William—Manheim, Pennsylvania, 1764–1774; noted for enameled, decorated, and colored wares.

Stoddard Glass Works—South Stoddard, New Hampshire, 1842–1850; Joseph Foster. Mostly bottles and flasks.

Suncook Glass Works—Suncook, New Hampshire, 1839–1850; moved from Chelmsford. Window glass, tableware.

Vermont Glass Factory—Salisbury, Vermont, 1813–1842; in 1842, became the *Lake Dunmore Glass Company.* Bottles, flasks, and holloware.

Willington Glass Company—West Willington, Connecticut, 1815–1872; bottles, flasks, and holloware.

Wistar, Caspar—Salem County, New Jersey, 1739–1780; window glass, bottles, and holloware.

Zanesville Glass Manufacturing Company—Zanesville, Ohio, 1815–1851; holloware, bottles, and historical flasks.

Glass Glossary

Agata—A mottled effect obtained by spraying alcohol or other chemicals onto the bodies of colored glass.

Amber—Amber colored, very popular during the last part of the nineteenth century into the twentieth.

Amber (Rose)—Basically, an amberina made by the Mount Washington Glass Company.

Amberina—An art glass, most popular during the last part of the nineteenth century, believed to have originated at the New England Glass Company. Shaded from ruby to amber by including gold in the glass metal, which would turn amber first and then to varying hues of red as more heat was applied.

Amberina (Cased or Plated)—An inner core of glass which is most often fiery opalescent creamy white, covered with an amberina exterior. Most glass in this style is ribbed.

Art—A general term used to describe the many vari-colored fancy glasswares of the late nineteenth century.

Art Deco—The period between 1920 and 1940. Artistic work was done as well as the inexpensive work now called carnival and depression glass.

Art Noveau—The period between about 1895 and 1915, characterized by the iridescent colorings and Oriental shapes. Leading makers were Tiffany, Lalique, Galle, etc.

Aurene—A product of the Corning Glass Works, attributed to Frederick Carder. Most often in a blue shade with gold iridescence. Twentieth century.

Baccarat—High quality French glass manufacturer, still in business since early in the nineteenth century. It is well known for its paperweights.

Blown three mold—Glass hand blown into a tri-divided mold, found in vertical ribbed patterns; diamond quilting, gothic, sunburst, and fluted. Some geometric. Early nineteenth century.

Bryden—Robert Bryden, last manager of the original Mount Washington-Pairpoint Glass Works in New Bedford, closed in 1958. Reopened the Pairpoint Glass Works at Sagamore, Massachusetts, 1970.

113

Burmese—Shaded pink to a lemon yellow. First made in the 1880's at the Mount Washington Glass Works, New Bedford, by Frederick Shirley. Most often found in a satin finish.

Cameo—Glass which has been dipped into another colored glass (or "flashed") then cut in cameo relief.

Carnival—An inexpensive iridescent glass first produced by Frank Fenton in Newark, Ohio in 1907. None was made in New England. It received its name as a result of being used as prizes at carnivals and fairs.

Clichy—A French glassworks at Clichy, dating from the early nineteenth century. A maker of fine paperweights.

Coralene—Art glass with frosted crystal decoration.

Crown Milano—Made by Frederick Shirley at Mount Washington Glass works. A satin finish ecru colored glass, decorated with flowers and gilding. 1880's.

Cut glass—Usually heavy lead crystal with designs cut into it by a spinning abrasive wheel. The Mount Washington Glass Company is considered by many to have made the best in the world. The most brilliant period for this product is 1890–1910, when it was the height of fashion.

Daum—During the last half of the nineteenth century, Antonin and Auguste Daum worked at Nancy, France, with Emile Galle. Their pieces are usually signed "Daum-Nancy."

Depression—A name given to the inexpensive colorful glass made during the Depression, and often given away at theatres as an incentive to go to the movies on slow nights. It was used as premiums, and also sold at the five and dime stores.

Durand—Victor Durand worked 1925–1932 in Vineland, New Jersey, and produced colorful glass in both art noveau and art deco styles.

Etched—A reference to inexpensive glass which was decorated by lightly etching it with a spinning copper wheel.

Favrile—Made by Louis Comfort Tiffany in the first quarter of this century. The word is taken from the German word "faber," which means color. It can be any color, with iridescent tints and highlights.

Flashed—Flashed glass is made by dipping a clear body of glass into a liquid mixture of colored glass. This is bonded by heat to create a coating which may be cut or etched to reveal the clear glass beneath.

Galle—The master French glassmaker of Nancy, France, Emile Galle is noted for his art noveau glass and cameo glass.

Gunderson—Robert Gunderson was plant manager of the Pairpoint Works in New Bedford from 1939 to 1952. Glass made there during this period is often referred to as Gunderson glass.

Iridescent—A name applied to any glass which has an iridescent shine which is created by chemical processes. It was made in imitation of early Roman glass which had absorbed minerals from the soil while lying buried for hundreds of years.

Kew Blas—Gold iridescent glass made at the Union Glass Company in Somerville, Massachusetts. Late nineteenth century.

Lalique—Rene Lalique, France, first quarter of this century. Worked in art noveau styles; with pressing, cutting, frosting, cameo, etc.

Lutz—Best known for his threaded glass and other art glass work at the Boston and Sandwich Glass Company. Worked also for Dorflinger and the Mount Washington Glass Works, mostly during the third quarter of the nineteenth century.

Mary Gregory—Ruth Webb Lee documents her as a decorator at the Boston and Sandwich Glass Company at Sandwich on Cape Cod, Massachusetts. She is believed responsible for copying the Kate Greenaway figures and translating them into decorations, all in white, on art glass.

Mother of Pearl—A satin finish glass with design worked into it, created by Joseph Webb in 1885 in Beaver Falls, Pennsylvania.

Mount Washington—The Mount Washington Glass Company was formed by Deming Jarves in 1837 for his son. It was later moved to New Bedford. The name has been synonymous with the name Pairpoint since 1894 when the two companies merged, the latter originally being the Pairpoint Silver Company.

Pattern—Glass which is pressed mechanically into a mold is called pattern glass. This was first done by Benjamin Bakewell in Pittsburgh in 1825, and was improved at the Boston and

Sandwich Glass Company in 1827.

Peachblow—That made by Hobbs and Brocunier in Wheeling shades from rose to yellow. That made at the New England Glass Works shades from a rose-red at the top to white at the base. The latter is also called "Wild Rose," and was first made in the 1880's.

Pigeonblood—Known to have been made by Hobbs and Brocunier. It looks ruby in color until it is held to the light, which causes the color to change to an orange-yellow.

Pomona—Made by Joseph Locke at the New England Glass Company. It is a clear glass with etched pattern, having amber staining and often blue cornflowers for decoration.

Portieux—A noted concern of the nineteenth century at Portieux, France. Identified by imprint of name and later by a rosette design, generally at the base of the piece.

Quezal—Named after the exotic Quetzal bird of South America whose brilliant plumage it resembles. Made in 1916–1918 by the Quezal Art Glass and Decorating Company in Brooklyn. It features deep colorings and iridescence, much in the manner of Tiffany. Most is art noveau in style.

Rubena Crystal—First made by Hobbs and Brocunier. A ware which shades from red to clear.

Rubena Verde—A ware which shades from red to yellow.

Sandwich—Common name given to items made at the Boston and Sandwich Glass Company, Sandwich, Massachusetts, 1825–1888.

Satin—Glass which has been bathed in hydrofluoric acid to give it a soft, satin finish.

Spangled—Generally, a cased glass which has been colored with design and fragments of metals such as gold to make it sparkle.

Spatter—Made by rolling hot glass over broken bits of colored glass to incorporate them into the body of the piece.

St. Louis—A firm which had its beginnings in the seventeenth century in France. Noted for its pressed glass and paperweights.

Stained—Glass is often colored by staining it while hot. Much pressed glass is colored this way.

Steuben—The famous works still operating at Corning, New

York. Well known for its handmade clear glass.

Threaded—The best known artisan of this style is Nicholas Lutz, who worked at the Boston and Sandwich Glass Factory. The glass is threaded and striped in the Venetian style.

Tiffany—Louis Comfort Tiffany was an American pioneer of art noveau designs and iridescent glass. He worked beginning in 1878, and his plant continued working until 1933, the year of his death.

Vasa Murrhina—The Vasa Murrhina Art Glass Company operated in Hartford, Connecticut, during the art glass period. This glass sparkled with imbedded mica colored with gold.

Venetian—A term given to the delicate styled glass which has been made in that region of Italy since the fourteenth century.

Waterford—Originally operated at Waterford, Ireland, between 1783 and 1851. It was reopened in 1947 as the Waterford Glassworks.

Chapter 4

Ceramics

If anyone had to select the earliest collectible which was in an art form as well as functional, he would have to name ceramics. The art of fashioning clay into usable vessels is as old as civilization. Ancient man learned to shape readily available clay into useful objects, and then harden them in the sun. He learned to make them hard enough to withstand heat, and also that such heat hardened them even more. He learned later that with the addition of crushed flint or other stone he could make a very strong body which would withstand rough usage. The final step in early ceramics was the discovery that after glazing the clay vessels would no longer soak up water, and that liquids could then be stored in them for indefinite periods.

The simplest glaze was that of a clay which had a lower firing temperature than the body clay. This would be mixed with water and then slipped (or poured) over the vessel and fired, leaving a clear hard coating which was bonded to the surface by the intense heat. Metal glazes were then perfected, lead being the most preferred and the most dangerous. Lead was mixed with a liquid clay mixture, and after firing provided a very luminescent surface, though dangerous, if food or edible liquids were stored against it any length of time. The lives of our ancestors were undoubtedly shortened immeasurably by the amount of lead used in household ceramics, plates, and other cooking utensils. Tin was often used in glazes, as were iron filings, zinc, copper, and other minerals and metals that would contribute a hard surface or color to the make.

A later technique involved the use of common table salt. This would be thrown into a kiln during the last minutes of firing. As it vaporized, it would be deposited on the clay bodies, providing a hard sheen, rough with imperfections.

119

Americans are inclined to collect simple redware, a name attached to those products made of simple red clay, and stoneware, which is most often made of light colored clays reinforced with flint or other hardening material. Both products are still made today, some by kilns still operating in the fashion they have used since the nineteenth century, and some by craft potters who are working both in traditional and contemporary motifs.

It is interesting to note the technique of making simple stoneware, and I quote one such recipe which was popular in England and America early in the nineteenth century. "Tobacco-pipe clay is beaten much in water; by this process, the finer parts of the clay remain suspended in the water, while the coarser sand and other impurities fall to the bottom. The thick liquid consisting of water and finer parts of the clay is further purified by passing it through hair and lawn sieves of different degrees of fineness. After this, the liquor is mixed in various proportions for various ware with another liquor of the same density, and consisting of flints calcined, ground and suspended in water. The mixture is then dried in a kiln; and afterwards beaten to a proper temper, it becomes fit for being formed at the wheel into dishes, plates, bowls, etc. When this ware is to be put into the furnace to be baked, the several pieces of it are placed in the cases made of clay, called seggars, which are piled one upon another, in the dome of the furnace. A fire is lighted; when the ware is brought to a proper temper, which happens in about 48 hours, it is glazed by common salt. The salt is thrown into the furnace through holes in the upper part of it, by the heat of which it is instantly converted into a thick vapour; which, circulating through the furnace, enters the seggar through the holes made in its side (the top being covered to prevent the salt from falling on the ware), and attaching itself to the surface of the ware, it forms that vitreous coat upon the surface, which is called its glaze."

The formulas for the more sophisticated wares, such as porcelain, bone china, soft and hard paste, Queensware, and the like, are much more complicated, but all ceramics begin with the basics noted above. A once-popular glaze was a shining black which was made up of 100 parts of lead, 18 parts of crushed flint,

Early English combware with simple decoration, made in the late seventeenth and early eighteenth centuries. (Roger Bacon, New Hampshire)

One of the first ceramic products to be beautified by a metallic glaze was copper luster. Although the old pieces are of interest, reproductions of them have hurt current values.

Artisan shaping a bowl cover on the turning wheel at the Vienna Porcelain Manufactory, Vienna, Austria.

and 40 parts of manganese. With such ingredients, the glaze must have helped in the spoilage of foods. Most manufacturers today use fritted, body sheen, or soft glazes which are made up of basic clays with nothing to affect any food stored next to them. You must be careful in purchasing clay artifacts from underdeveloped nations as some may be coated with the dangerous lead glaze. It was not until the 1820's that experimentation resulted in glazes made with no lead, but they were expensive at the time and did not come into general use on stoneware until a decade or two later.

The art of ceramicmaking in Europe was confined to the most basic work in earthenware when the Pilgrims settled this country. The secret of porcelainmaking lay locked in the Orient, and it was not until the later seventeenth century in France that making porcelain was attempted with much success. You may use this as a simple definition: If one can see through the body, it is porcelain; if it is opaque, it is earthenware. The first porcelains that bore any resemblance to those from China were turned out at Rouen and St. Cloud in France. However, it was not until 1708 that Johann Freiderich Bottger perfected a true porcelain body by the use of kaolin and the petuntse clays which had been an Oriental secret for so many centuries. It was not long before potteries copying Boettger's formula and techniques were set up both on the continent and in England, and the vast ceramics industry was born. To attempt to discuss the industry before that time would hardly be worthwhile as little of that production can be found today, either here or overseas. It is enough of a project to concentrate on what can be found and collected today. There are actually many more fine types of ceramics from all over the world in America today than there were at the turn of the century. The importation of such antiquity did not reach great heights until after World War I, when American affluence climbed. Before then, most homes were equipped with relatively inexpensive dinnerware made by some concern in this country, and little accent was noted in antiques collecting. Lucky was the bride who received a complete service of French, English, or German dinnerware, as this was the ultimate gift. Much of this has survived, but hardly enough to satisfy the demand on the part of collectors who want something old and of good quality. We were fortunate that the makers continued to turn out the same patterns in open stock for many years so that replacements were easy to obtain. Today, you must most often scrounge about in shops and shows looking for needed items to fill out a set, since many patterns have been discontinued in favor of more contemporary designs.

Early American Ceramics

An American experiment in porcelainmaking took place in the 1740's, when a clay called "unaker" was found in Virginia. Without sufficient moneyed clientele to support it the project went out of business, but not until it had established a very unique link with the mother country. The clay was so pure and perfect that all through that century it was shipped to England, and much of the desired output of ceramics there was made of American raw material.

Inventories of estates in eighteenth century America reveal little or no fine china, except in the homes of the wealthy. Tea drinking was not really popular until the time of Queen Anne, although tea is known to have been imported as early as the 1660's. Ceramic tea sets were in demand after her time, and most wealthy homes were equipped with at least one. The poorer people were still eating from wooden or pewter plates and vessels. Perhaps our first recognized potter was John Pride of Salem, Massachusetts, who was registered as early as 1641. A brickworks was established in nearby Danvers as early as 1629, but there is no evidence that eating vessels or plates were made. I could provide a relatively good list of seventeenth and eighteenth century potters, but it would do little good to collectors as little or none of the production can be documented today. Fortunately, some stoneware bears the imprint of makers' names and often bears the name of a commercial concern for whom they might have made it. Most noted among these are the Remmy and Crolius families of New York City, who imprinted their names, as well as that of Manhattan Wells, which was near the site where

Mid-nineteenth century redware covered pot from New England. The shape is very good and the workmanship is quite refined. It is glazed inside and out, but no attempt was made to decorate it.

The last output of the Pewabic Pottery, started by Mary Chase Stratton in Detroit early in the twentieth century. This location has since been taken over by Michigan University as a working ceramics location, where classes are given.

Ceramics at the Vienna Porcelain Manufactory waiting their turn to be decorated and fired. They are turned by hand on a wheel, with some parts (such as covers and handles) being molded.

Well-decorated stoneware two-handled jug made by Chapman, Upson, and Wright, manufacturers in Middlebury, Connecticut.

Mid-nineteenth century shaving mug from Maine, with good design and proportions. Redware items like this are rare because they are fragile and are easily broken.

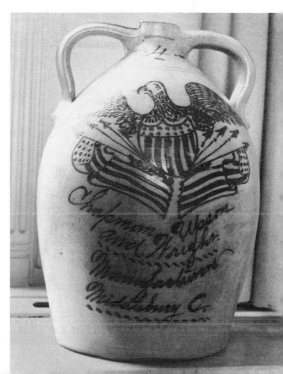

they worked. The wells were the water supply for the city. If you find marked stoneware, you can document it from books listed in the bibliography, as space does not permit a complete listing here. Needless to say, any eighteenth century work is very desirable. Of course, the best area in which to look would be the thirteen original colonies. However, the area which includes New Jersey, Pennsylvania, New York, and New England is the prime place to look, as their output was the greatest during those times. Unmarked redware and stoneware has value if the shapes and workmanship are good. The decorated slipware made of red clay and then handpainted throughout the northern colonies has now become highly collectable. Some of these pieces have reached the high three figure price range and have no place to go but up.

Regional Types

Let us examine the most desirable pieces to locate in the various types made. There is evidence that a delft type ware was made in this country in the latter part of the seventeenth century and well into the eighteenth, but none has survived. Inventories of the period tell of the blue and white ware copied after the fashion of its European counterpart. This type of decorated earthenware originated in Ireland. Dutch traders hauled clay from there for the makers in their own country, and brought with them some gaily decorated tin glazed ware that caught the fancy of those on the continent. The Dutch copied the style and are generally credited with originating it due to the large output from Delft, whose name was eventually attached to it. Delft was made in other countries, including the Lowlands, Germany, France, and England. The first American redware was unmarked, but as the eighteenth century progressed the Pennsylvania Germans began coloring their pieces with designs and sayings, and some were well-signed by their makers. Added to this was the technique of sgraffito — the scratch carving which is believed to have originated in the Commonwealth of Pennsylvania. Designs were created in such ways as carving the original clay body before firing, filling the indentations with a coloring agent, and

Etruscan majolica pitcher in a shell and seaweed pattern made in the 1880's by Griffin, Smith, and Hill of Phoenixville, Pennsylvania. This is the most desirable majolica.

Rare stoneware crock stamped "J.E. Norton, Bennington, Vt." Pictures of buildings are not common on such stoneware, and are therefore highly prized.

Mug by left-handed Russell Henry of Birdsboro, Pennsylvania. Henry digs his own clay, fashions his own shapes, and then decorates them by painting before firing. Made in 1969, this piece reflects the mood of the times—the eagle bears the words "Flower Power" in its pennant. Henry's shapes are strong, his decorations are folk art in themselves, and his awareness of our times makes him quite contemporary.

Pennsylvania stoneware collected in the Amish country near Lancaster. Decorated items generally have more value. (Folk Art Museum, Witmer, Pennsylvania)

Mid-nineteenth century Chinese celadon vase. The feet enhance its proportions and appearance.

then glazing and firing it. The carving might also be done after the glaze was applied, with the coloring added using a colored glaze. For protection, painting was done under a glaze which was later fired. Tin glazes were popular at the time since they could be colored themselves, lending a better look to the piece. Though most of this work seems to have turned up in Pennsylvania, it is known that this technique was copied throughout the colonies. Perhaps you can trace the origins of such pieces through design, as the Pennsylvania motifs are quite regional in their look.

However, you must be careful in your attribution, since much simple ware was shipped in from other countries, notably England, during these years. Fragments have been found at many historic sites in this country, and their documentation has led back across the ocean, even though most people would think that such simple wares were most likely made in the colonies.

As clay refining methods improved, potters grew more sophisticated in their work, and much thinner and very functional wares appeared including shaving mugs, drinking

Late nineteenth century Oriental Imari covered dish in an unusual shape. Decorated in orange, purple, and gilding, this style originated in Japan. It is believed that the gaudy Dutch and Welsh ceramics of the nineteenth century were inspired by Imari decoration.

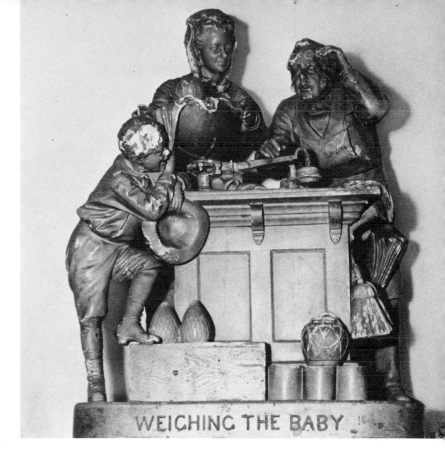

A group of plaster figures made by John Rodgers of New York City in the mid-nineteenth century. He created over two hundred designs from situations in real life and gave them great appeal. "Weighing the Baby" pictures a puzzled mother and grocer as Junior tugs down on the scale in the foreground of the group.

WEIGHING THE BABY

mugs, milk pitchers, and batter jugs. The bean pot made its appearance early in the nineteenth century in both redware and stoneware. This work is being done today, and with the knowledge of old recipes and methods of firing, all of us are exposed to the possibility of buying a recently made piece which has been aged quite quickly through the use of chemicals. There is no known easy way to tell the old from the new, but science can prove the age of an item if a fragment is examined. Most of you will not want to go through the expense of this, so you must familiarize yourself with the "look" of old redware by searching it out in museums and collections and doing a lot of studying. There is no formula that I can put into print to help you. So far as collecting is concerned, you should look for pieces documented with dates and makers' names. Next in importance are those pieces with good folk art decoration, with animals, birds, and people being the most popular. Color must be good and condition is very important. Many a cat, dog, or chicken has been fed from old redware as it fell from popularity, and many pieces have suffered as a result.

American Stoneware

The American stoneware industry did not take hold until after the Revolutionary War. Eighteenth century production is noted and some of it is cataloged, but there is little likelihood that one can find much of it today, except in the better shops which make a specialty of ferreting out such pieces for discriminating customers. Most pieces are preserved in museums or historical societies, as well they should be. After the turn of the century, production was increased to the point that much ware was exported to other countries. Accounts of American manufacturing for 1828 reveal that stoneware was one of our major exports. Knowing the frugality of people in other lands suggests that some early nineteenth century stoneware could very well be turning up outside America, so if you are a traveler it behooves you to be on the lookout for it. Designs were created by sgraffito and by direct painting under the glaze, or with colored glazes, most often in cobalt blue. You can easily determine the most valuable pieces by the following simple rules, which of course must have their exceptions. Shapes and forms are most important, as well as good workmanship. Decorations may be graded for importance as follows: at the top of the list will be pictures of buildings, most often farmhouses and the like; next in rarity are those of animals and fish; followed by birds; floral designs; and finally those with unidentifiable designs or no decoration at all. Age is helpful, regardless of decoration, but most people collect these pieces only as examples of early folk art.

Rare pieces like large water coolers, footwarmers, batter and switchel jugs, and funerary urns command much interest regardless of decoration, since they are difficult forms to find. You must realize that such stoneware was made well into this century, and that as recently as the 1920's concerns were still using them in marketing products such as molasses, vinegar, tea, jams and jellies, chemicals, and other liquid products. By today's standards they look quite old, and most acquire a good patina after lying unused in cellars and barns for many years.

The kiln needed to mass produce such items had to be quite large and this limited the number that were set up in America. If a

American porcelain made by William Ellis Tucker of Philadelphia, 1826–1838. The pitcher in the center is a commemorative piece dated 1831. The center urn shows transfer work done by Tucker. The other pieces are hand decorated with floral motifs resembling Sevres work. (Hammerslough Collection, William Penn Memorial Museum, Harrisburg, Pennsylvania)

Bennington ware. Top, left to right: flint enamel change cover; "Swiss Lady," used to hide returning change at a bar; scroddled ware tulip vase; blue and white trinket box; scroddled ware slop jar; parian porcelain trinket box; scroddled ware tulip vase; flint enamel spoon holder. Bottom, left to right: blue and white cottage vase with applied grapes; Rockingham pedestaled vase; scroddled ware book flask; lamp with Sandwich clam broth glass front, flint enamel baluster pedestal, and Rockingham step base; another cottage vase. (Bennington Museum, Bennington, Vermont)

kiln was used for salt glazing no other glaze could be fired in it, as the residue of salt from past firings would make it impossible for other glazes to stick to the bodies. Fuel for the kilns and availability of clay were important and both often dictated the location of a business. Richard Carter Barret (Director of the Bennington Museum in Bennington, Vermont) relates that farmers from the Bennington area traveling to sell their produce in Troy or Albany were encouraged to return loaded with clay from any cellar hole being dug along the way, since they could sell the clay to the potteries in Bennington. The clays of New Jersey are world famous, and were shipped just about everywhere—at first by boat and ox cart, and later by rail and ferry. Colored clays will not necessarily remain the same hue after firing. Some blue clays are known to turn red, and some green clays turn black. Tobacco-pipe clay was favored for delicate pieces and was much in demand.

Naturally, the first fuel was wood. Coal was adapted for this purpose after the Revolutionary War. As early as 1827, a railroad was built in Carbon County, Pennsylvania, to haul coal down to the ferryboats which plied the Delaware River to Philadelphia. After the discovery of oil wells in Pennsylvania at mid-century, oil was successfully used as a fuel for kilns. Mary Chase Perry Stratton first used electricity for firing during the late 1800's at her Pewabic Pottery in Detroit. Gas was employed where available, and to this day natural gas is very much accepted.

Ceramic makers are still experimenting with glazes in an effort to come up with something new. One potter frequents a local junk yard to retrieve ashes after the dealers have burned the tarred coatings from old electric and telephone wire. Mixed with a clear glaze, these ashes create an unusual effect on his pottery. Other potters use manganese and manganese oxide, and still others work with tin, zinc, copper, and other minerals which create an illuminating effect. The greatest artisans are those who combine a talent for design with skill in painting on their pieces. Perhaps the most noted craftsman in this field is left-handed Russell Henry of Birdsboro, Pennsylvania, whose artwork is as compelling as the shapes and forms he spins on his wheel. The contemporary mood has crept into ceramics, too, and modern art blows hot and cold as far as current appreciation is concerned. Time will prove its aesthetic value.

American Porcelain

America was quite late in developing good porcelain for sale to the public in any quantity. The first firm on record is that of Bonnin and Morris of Philadelphia. Some of their output has survived, but there was very little made, which accounts for the fact that it is not regarded as a collectable. The next successful effort was that of Dr. Daniel Mead in New York City about 1812. His work was on a par with that of the Europeans, but again little was made. The first really successful porcelain maker was William Ellis Tucker, who produced ware as early as 1825, and though perhaps not on a par with its European counterparts, Tucker's work survives today as the most collectible of the early work in this area. The plant survived under various partnerships until 1838, and during that time produced much ware which has survived. Tucker imported workmen from France; hence the French look to his work. You might mistake his pieces for the contemporary Sevres in color, shape, and decoration. Not much Tucker china has turned up on the open market in recent years. The Hammerslough collection of Tucker china at the William Penn Memorial Museum in Harrisburg was acquired piece by piece in Pennsylvania, New Jersey, and Delaware years ago. Very little of it was marked, as many companies during that era were willing to let the public think they might be buying a foreign made product, since most buyers felt that the best work was not done in America. For identification: Tucker bodies have a greenish tint to the white; the gilding has a purplish tint; the pedestals on vases and urns are never fully painted and often turn up at the corners, and the top surface of the pedestal is always white, but some decoration or gilding may be on it. Some of the Tucker workmen also signed their pieces with their initials. Edwin Attlee Barber's book *Marks of American Potters* (listed in the bibliography) will provide you with the complete listing, as well as that of other potters and potteries in this country.

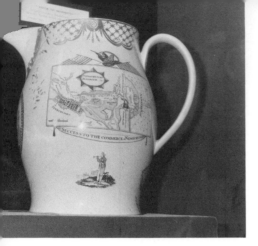

Interesting Liverpool transfer pitcher bearing the inscription "Success To the Commerce of Newburyport." The map of this Massachusetts port harbor is most unusual and gives great value to this piece. English, around 1820. (The Mariners Museum, Newport News, Virginia)

English ceramics made before 1842 usually carry the name of the maker and bear either the design designation or title of the transfer print used for decoration. The print shown is on the bottom of a brown and white platter made about 1840 by the firm of J. & J. Jackson of Staffordshire, England.

Richly designed long-handled Rockinghamware pitcher made at the U.S. Pottery Company in Bennington, Vermont between 1847 and 1858. It is marked on the base with the 1849 Fenton stamp. Representative of the fine work done at this pottery, it features deep molding and good color. (Bud Foster Antiques, Wexford, Pennsylvania)

Historical blue plates are fun to collect, but they are expensive if you collect only those from the first series made from 1820 to 1840 by several concerns in Staffordshire, England. An English product of the later series done between 1884 and 1892 is shown above. It bears only the inscription "Ye Olde Historical Pottery" on its base.

This porcelain Indian Brave is a contemporary work by the Royal Doulton Company of England. Made in limited edition, the value is expected to rise as time goes by.

Regimental stein made in Germany in 1907 for an infantry regiment. It lists the officers and men of the company to which its owner belonged and mentions its exploits. The figure at the top of the lid indicates the branch of service; if a cavalry regiment, it would be a man astride a horse, etc.

Another maker of porcelain was Smith, Fife & Co. of Philadelphia, who were in business about 1830. Some pieces bear a marked resemblance to Tucker's work, and it has been learned that one moulding concern supplied both potteries. It is also known that professional modelers would sell their designs to more than one company. Other modelers might have worked for several different concerns, causing a great similarity in the work produced.

David Henderson was involved in the creation of the Jersey City Pottery Company in 1829 and the American Pottery Company in 1833. The American Pottery Company was operated under different ownerships until 1892, but not until it had created a prodigious amount of good pottery and porcelain which is prized by collectors today. The company pioneered in the use of transfer printing in America, and much commemorative work was done.

John Norton established a pottery at Bennington, Vermont, in order to make jugs in which he could sell his cider. His stoneware business soon outdid his cider business, and he expanded to take care of the demand for his wares. The pottery continued to operate in the hands of his family through most of the century, turning out a variety of functional and decorative pieces. His son-in-law, Christopher Weber Fenton, opened the United States Pottery Company in 1847 and continued in business until 1858. Fenton hired the great English modeler, Daniel Greatback, who turned out designs for many animal figures and other decorative pieces which were made in both the brown colored Rockingham-ware and the pure white parian. Rockinghamware is reputed to have originated at the estates of the Earl of Rockingham in England, and found much favor in both England and America. Many American concerns turned it out, but that from Bennington seems to be the most desired. Parian was made in ceramic imitation of a marble from the Islands of Crete and Paros that was popular for carvings of busts and figures.

The Copeland-Spode works in England is credited with being the first to make parian early in the nineteenth century. It is a pure porcelain which is unglazed on the exterior to give it the feel and look of marble. Richard Carter Barret gives the many clues

Twentieth century art pottery vase made by the Roseville Pottery, Zanesville, Ohio, with the graceful sweeping art deco style which is becoming popular today.

Well-decorated porcelain urn by William Ellis Tucker, Philadelphia, 1826–1838. (Hammerslough Collection)

necessary in identifying Fenton's production in his book *How to Identify Bennington Pottery* (listed in the biblography). They include such tips as looking for crude grape designs as opposed to the more refined and smaller English grapes. The soil at Bennington also contained much iron pyrite, and despite screening black specks will show in the white body, while the English pieces are relatively free of this. In Bennington Rockinghamware, you must be able to put your little finger under the dog's neck on a hound handled pitcher. In pitchers from other makers, the hound rests his chin on his paws, leaving no room. Bennington dogs and cows were molded with ribs and throat folds either visible or felt, whereas others were smooth. In a cow creamer, the eyes must be wide open and the nostrils a pronounced half moon shape, while folds in the neck and ribs must be very evident. These few tips point up how much there is to learn.

It was not until the 1880's, when Lenox set up shop in New Jersey and Castleton went into business just above Pittsburgh, that America enjoyed any long lived production of fine porcelains. Most collectors will agree their output is on a par with that of the rest of the world as far as quality is concerned. Both concerns are still in business, and are engaged to do many custom presentation pieces by the White House, as well as making dinner services for the president's home. However, collectors have not yet taken to collecting these porcelains as antiques, perhaps because most of the patterns are still being made and do not possess any aura of age and early workmanship.

There are many other American potteries which made their mark with very good production, and I have listed them at the end of this chapter along with the glossary. Most of their production is well marked, which makes identification easy. You must approach ceramic collecting with a definite set of rules to follow. Since much of the collectible American production was made during the period of industrial growth, you are faced with the problem of determining if you will be content with machine-made items, or if you will zero in only on those items which were handmade or custom modeled and hand decorated.

Art Pottery

This brings us to the art pottery era, which arrived shortly after the Civil War. Located mostly in the Pennsylvania, Ohio, Indiana, and West Virginia areas, the art pottery concerns developed lines of specialty and decorative pieces, glazing them in many colors. Flowers and fruits were popular, with most designs molded in relief. Much of the production was good and much was shoddy, yet this type of production continues to this day, with many lesser quality pieces commanding attention as collectables. Most of these items were made in earthenware, but some of the better companies turned out porcelains. Majolica was and still is quite popular. A ceramic whose origin is lost in history, majolica has an obvious Mediterranean influence, and some say it originated at the island of Majorca. The early wares were tin enamelled and brightly colored. The American potters carried on this tradition, and the best and most desired were made in Phoenixville, Pennsylvania, before the turn of the century. Labeled "Etruscan" or "Etruscan Majolica" with the initials G, S, and H superimposed, it was made by Griffen, Smith, and Hill from 1879 to 1894. Though the European production of the period was of good quality, it is the Etruscan which has the value because it is American. The names of the Rookwood, Weller and Roseville, Knowles, Taylor and Knowles, Homer Laughlin, and East Liverpool Potteries are well known to collectors, as all of these were located in Ohio and spread their wares throughout the country. The most prolific potteries of the era are noted at the end of this chapter.

Art pottery need not be old to be in demand. Some of the most sought after was made by Hugh Robertson at the Dedham Pottery, near Boston. This plant began production as the Chelsea Ceramic Art Works in 1866, and closed its doors in 1948. Even its late production has skyrocketed in price. The Dorchester (Mass.) Pottery is still operating—continuing a tradition begun in 1894 by Charles Henderson. Its present-day output is limited, yet all of it is worth more than the list price the minute it leaves the plant when the kiln is emptied on Thursday morning. It is the quality and handwork which makes this pottery so desirable—it does not need age to enhance it. Another contemporary pottery was started in 1901 in Colorado Springs, Colorado, by Artus van Briggle, who had been a decorator at Rookwood. He went west because of his health, but died shortly after opening his business there. It continues today, turning out well-moulded handmade items which are being collected by those who know that such items will be much in demand if production ever ceases. This *can* happen—witness the demise of the Pennsbury Pottery in Morrisville, Pennsylvania, which closed its doors in 1971 after having been in business about 20 years. Its story is typical of the many small enterprises set up to provide an interesting quality product which surrender slowly to competition from within this country as well as from overseas. Since Pennsbury is a current collectible which has not yet entirely disappeared, and one about which little is known, I feel it is of enough importance to devote space to.

Pennsbury Pottery was started by Ernest Below, who had been a ceramics engineer at the Stangel Pottery in New Jersey. His mother served as the designer and was responsible for the Pennsylvania "Dutch" motifs which were so successful. His father worked creating shapes in ceramics. Most was cast in a browntone background which made the hand-painted artwork stand out. Local housewives and school girls were trained to decorate the ceramics. The plant started with eight people and grew to employ between forty and fifty at the time of its demise. Clay came from Tennessee and Georgia and was mixed with flint and other ingredients. The plant originally used six different clays, and then narrowed it to two or three. Glazes were fritted, body sheen, and soft. Complete dinnerware sets and gift items were popular. The pottery started with sculptured birds but found these hard to sell in the face of competition from Japan.

Pennsbury Pottery will be remembered best for its commemorative work. The pottery made ashtrays for Electrolux, dishes for railroads, plates for fraternal organizations and churches, mugs and ashtrays for nearby Washington Crossing State Park, and just about anything demanded by clubs or organizations for presentation at annual meetings and the like. The rarest item of all is a single plate made for presentation to Walt Disney when he attended the opening of the Walt Disney School in nearby Tullytown. It has never turned up, and its whereabouts is unknown even to the Disney Archives in California. There are mugs for Historic Fallsington, and another great rarity—scenic plates made for the last steam engine run on the Reading Railroad. The tray for this set had the engine picture on it, and only 3,500 plates were made to be given to the passengers. The rooster was a popular design as it symbolized happiness. Pennsylvania hex symbols and designs with Amish figures were popular with the tourists. The pottery burned down shortly after an auction was held to dispose of the remaining ceramic pieces. All the machinery and dies were destroyed, making it highly unlikely that this pottery will ever be reproduced, and therefore causing a great interest in it.

This story may be repeated many times over throughout the country. You have to examine the work of such small potteries to determine its quality. If it is good, collect it. Quality will always command interest and good prices in the future. If the pottery goes out of business, it can only heighten the interest in its work.

Imported Porcelain

Europe and the Orient represent the other sources for most of the ceramics to be found here. Though America lagged in porcelain manufacture, we were not hesitant in importing it from those countries which made it well. The Winterthur Conference Report of 1972 reveals how limited such trade was before the Revolutionary War, in that very little china appears in the inventory of estates through the seventeenth and eighteenth centuries. Archeological digs along the coast from Virginia to Massachusetts have unearthed fragments of all kinds of pottery and porcelain which reveal a great deal about their origins. As would be expected, china from England predominates, but it was limited to those who were wealthy. Researchers have been able to pinpoint the area in England which the sherds came from. In one dig at Plymouth, Massachusetts (which reflected the period between 1760 and 1835) they uncovered eight plates, eight chamber pots and three bowls in delftware, three mugs, a bowl, a teacup, teapot lid, a saucer and plate in white salt-glazed stoneware, an agateware bowl, a slip-decorated redware pitcher, four slip-decorated redware chamber pots, three redware crocks, five smaller redware bowls, and one Whieldon-type teapot. The predominence of chamber pots is puzzling, but they must have been considered more essential than dinnerware through those years.

In the September, 1891, edition of *Scribners* magazine, Alice Morse Earle wrote of her experiences as a *China Hunter in New England*. She bemoaned the fact that there was little early work to be found. She stated that Bow, Chelsea, and Derby wares were seldom seen in old New England homes, "nor have we found specimens of the better class of Wedgwood's manufactures in any great numbers." The demand for the better Wedgwood ware was great in England, so little of it was sent to America.

English Porcelain

The ceramics factory at Bow is considered to be the oldest in England. It was located in the eastern section of London. Some of its product was stamped "New Canton" because the buildings were in the Chinese style. Bow is thought to have been founded as early as 1730, but its first patents for making porcelain using Virginia unaker clay were taken out in 1744. Bow led in the production of the first bone china, made with the addition of powdered bone ash, and is also credited with turning out the first china with transfer prints done under the glaze.

The Chelsea factory was established about 1742 and made fine porcelain which was the counterpart of the best from Europe. A Huguenot refugee brought his knowledge to this plant and enabled it to copy the best French work. William Duesbury (owner of the Derby Works, also in London) purchased the Chelsea enterprise, and at one time owned the Bow Works as well. This creates a real problem in identifying the output from these plants, as molds were interchanged and workmen might work in one or more of the plants, taking their designs with them. You must rely on the markings of these pieces to aid in identification. The bibliography lists books which will help.

Problems in Attribution

Even pieces which are well-marked are subject to suspicion because of imitators and the fakers of the nineteenth century. Quite notable in this respect was the firm of Mssrs. Samson and Company of Paris, which went into business in 1845 and worked late into the century. The company usually produced wares of the eighteenth century and marked them with original marks, and this can confuse the average student of ceramics today. In the eighteenth century most potters in England were still working with soft paste bodies, using a mixture of powdered glass and clays. Samson reproduced porcelain, and this might have been made from the Oriental formula of China clay and Kaolin, or from the Spode formula which included bone ash and good china clay.

A shelf of stoneware decorated by Charles Hill at the Dorchester Pottery in Dorchester, Massachusetts. This is contemporary work, but it has been made in the same manner since the business was started in 1894. Dorchester pottery is a fine collectible today.

Ceramic figural bottles such as the penguin colored in blue and orange against a white background, shown above, are popular. This one contains the Moscow New Year's drink and is sold in Russia and the other iron curtain countries.

Blanc de chine figure with the all nations mark, Kuan Yin, about 1675–1750. The molding is sensitive and the workmanship is quite good. These white porcelain figures are being reproduced today, so you should examine your prospective purchases carefully.

You must arm yourself with information on how to tell the two apart. Hard paste does not warm quickly to the touch. If there is a chip on a soft paste piece, its open surface will appear glassy. A glaze on soft paste can wear away, whereas a glaze on hard paste will survive almost intact over many years. An enamelled decoration on soft paste will sink into the ceramic but it will remain on the surface of hard paste.

Nicholas Sprimont, a French silversmith, brought the Chelsea Works to the attention of the ceramics world in the 1740's, but his methods and ideas were hardly English. You will have to do your homework to learn to differentiate the Bow, Meissen, St. Cloud, or Chantilly blanc de chine from that made in the Orient in the eighteenth century. Samson's work in the nineteenth century just adds more confusion. Fortunately, by the nineteenth century most firms in England had themselves well established, and were contemporary enough so that others did not attempt to imitate them or copy them in later years. By the middle of the century, each company's work and markings were so distinctive that we have little trouble in accurate attribution.

During the eighteenth century, English makers were copying the best Chinese designs, as these were popular. Adding this to copying the porcelain bodies makes determining the country of origin quite difficult even for experienced students. Some of the early Bow, Worcester, Newhall, and Caughley are so similar to the Chinese work as to cause problems in correct attribution, even as far as country. A concern at Lowestoft gave its name to a great deal of what must have been Chinese export porcelain. History records that some potteries acted as importers and exporters as well as makers, and sold both native and export chinas. It seems likely that Lowestoft was one of these, attaching its name to both, and this has helped to cause this attribution.

China was made to order in both the Orient and England, and it is likely that much was made for the wealthy in America. Alice Morse Earle tells the story of a Miss Leslie, the sister of a great painter, who ordered a dinner service made and decorated for her in China. She directed that a coat of arms be placed in the center of each plate, and made a drawing which she pasted in the center of a specimen she had drawn. She wrote "Put this in the middle" under the coat of arms. When the service arrived, she found on every piece not only the coat of arms, but also, carefully written and fired in, the words "Put this in the middle." I wonder at the whereabouts of this set today.

Commemorative and Historical Ware

After the Revolutionary War, English potters were quick to forgive political differences in return for American business, and a lively trade was begun, with commemorative and historical wares shipped here in great quantities. The art of transfer printing had been brought to perfection in the 1770's by Thomas Turner, who was the first to turn out complete dinner services in this manner. Artists were sent to America to paint or sketch scenes of prominent buildings, landmarks, or landscapes. These scenes were immediately transformed into transfer prints for china. Famous military and naval engagements were also portrayed, along with portraits of famous men and ships who did the British in during the war. These enjoyed a rise in popularity until the War of 1812. Interest was renewed in them after this war, and between 1820 and 1840 a great amount of historic china entered the country. Blue was the most popular color, but much was also done in other colors. Items with a lot of detail, such as ships and rigging, were most often done in black against a cream or off-white background. Most of the black and white transfers are referred to as Liverpool transfers as they came from this port. The blue pieces are commonly referred to as "historical blues" since most portray a place, event, or person of American historical importance. Another series of the blues was done as a revival during the 1890's, but these blues are clearly marked to document their age. Even these later blues are assuming some importance now. You might do well to collect the blues being made today by such firms as Wedgwood for historic homes, churches, and the like, as these will be among the collectibles someday. Some which sold as souvenirs as recently as ten years ago for two or three dollars are commanding up to ten dollars right now, because they were made in limited editions.

WEDGWOOD AND SPODE

Names like Wedgwood and Spode are known even to the casual observer, as a lot has been written about these two famous concerns, both of which are still operating. The Wedgwoods were involved in pottery making by the end of the seventeenth century, but it was not until Josiah took command in the mid-eighteenth century that Wedgwood developed into a respected manufactory responsible for much of the best ceramics available. Both Josiah Wedgwood and Josiah Spode served as apprentices to Thomas Whieldon, who is credited with making the popular tortoiseshell ware. Wedgwood is now operating in a huge new plant in Barlaston, and Spode is located at Stoke-on-Trent. Both are located in Staffordshire County, which had 150 potteries at work within its borders in 1766. Staffordshire was occupied by the Romans at the time of Christ as there is abundant clay and plenty of firewood available. Also, the fog and dampness which plague southern England are not as evident in Staffordshire, and this is quite important in manufacturing ceramics since humidity affects glazing and firing. The term "Staffordshire" is generic when referring to chinas made in the county. It could have been used by any or all of the potters. The term is now used by collectors and dealers as a quick reference to the area of origin of the china in question.

CREAMWARE AND PEARLWARE

There are other terms which should be explored. Creamware (or Queensware, as it was called later in the eighteenth century) is simply a yellow lead glazed ware popular from about 1750 to 1820. Wedgwood is commonly referred to as the originator, but this is an uncertain attribution in light of the fact that others were making it at the same time. Ivor Noel Hume tells us that nine out of ten creamware pieces were unmarked and probably no more than one out of a thousand was dated. Pearlware is a whiter composition which came into favor at the turn of the century, and often decorated in oriental motifs.

ROYAL DOULTON, ROYAL CROWN DERBY, AND MINTON

Space does not permit an examination of all the English concerns which contributed so much to the development of the industry. However, I will examine the history of one concern which is still operating in order to show the numerous changes it has undergone. Sir Henry Doulton was the second son of John, founder of Doulton and Company in the late eighteenth century. Sir Henry was a creative Victorian potter, and during his lifetime outstripped his competitors in the production of such industrial wares as air-tight jars for storing food and tobacco; screw-topped food warmers and bottles; and architectural terracotta statuary and tiles used by many London architects. An example of this work is the lion outside Waterloo Station. Doulton concentrated on industrial ware until 1862, with the exception of some stoneware Toby jugs and mugs which were shown at the International Exhibition of 1862. Following this was an association with the Lambeth School of Art, which designed salt-glazed vases and jars with simple incised and colored decorations along with terracotta statues, portrait heads, and medallions. In 1877, Sir Henry purchased a works at Burslem, Staffordshire, and began to manufacture decorated earthenware and bone china. Most of the china collected today stems from this late nineteenth century production.

Another important potter was Thomas Minton, who began his career as an engraver apprenticed to Thomas Turner. Minton supplied Josiah Spode with printed designs for his wares for a short time, and then opened his own plant in 1796. It was not until 1824 that he made his reputation in the field by turning his production to forms influenced by the then popular Sevres factory in France. One of the most important techniques developed by Minton was the Pate-sur-pate, brought from France by Marc Louis Solon, acknowledged master of this art form. Pate-sur-pate, meaning body on body, is an expensive and frustrating method of decoration developed from the original Chinese technique. Solon went to work for Minton in 1870, and, though it was imitated, Minton was the only firm engaged in turning out this art product. Spectacular models were produced showing the prevailing influence of interest in Sevres China of the Louis XV style, Grecian influenced parian figures, Chinoiserie designs, and an overriding opulence of decoration. The Minton concern was later purchased by Doulton as the second member of the triumverate which makes up Doulton today.

The third member of the Doulton triumverate is the oldest. Royal Crown Derby has been in continuous operation since 1756, when an agreement between Andre Planche, William Duesbury, and John Hatch made them partners. Duesbury insisted on thinner potting than was prevalent at the time. This work, along with the finer enameling used, attracted the attention of George III, who conferred the right to use the crown as a factory mark. The ware then became known as Crown Derby, and by the end of the eighteenth century, Crown Derby was the leader in the English fine china industry. Early in the nineteenth century the factory passed into the hands of Robert Bloor, a former clerk. He introduced the highly colored Japanese or Imari decorations for which Crown Derby became famous. Much of the production of this period was actually of inferior quality and could be listed as seconds.

By 1877 a new company was formed, and the management of the Derby Crown Porcelain Company set about recovering its reputation. By 1890 the excellence of the wares and the favored Japanese decorations had come to the attention of Queen Victoria, who permitted the pottery to change its name to the Royal Crown Derby Porcelain Company. It was the only pottery permitted the honor of using the Royal and Crown designations in its name. Also in 1890, Desire Leroy left Minton. His raised gilding, white enamel painting on colored grounds, and delicate floral and bird studies are uniquely beautiful.

The three great potteries, Royal Doulton, Royal Crown Derby, and Minton are now all part of Doulton and Company. It is currently engaged in producing a collector's series of many types of modeled human and animal figures, some of which are selling in the four figure price range. Fine modeling and fine coloring are featured in these collectibles for tomorrow. The tradition of great work done by three separate concerns is obviously still very much alive in the consolidated company of today.

Modeler at work at the Wiener Porzellanmanufaktur Augarten, better known as the Vienna Porcelain Manufactory, founded in 1718. The parts of intricate statuary are molded separately and then joined by a skilled craftsman. The modeler shown is at work on a model of the Marly Horses, originally done by Guilliam Cousteau.

Collectors are fortunate the English provided a good marking system for their nineteenth-century ceramics. Until 1842, pieces were often identified by the name of the pattern or design, and either the name or initials of the maker, and, at times, the location of the factory. Between 1842 and 1883, the "diamond" mark, which enables us to pinpoint the day the piece was made, came into use. In the corners of the diamond are numbers or letters, which, by consulting charts, reveal the day, month and year, as well as the class of ceramic, and the lot number from which it came. In 1867, this was modified with a clue that can be helpful. If one sees a letter of the alphabet at the top point of the diamond, he knows the piece was made before 1867; if there is a number at the point, it came after 1867. Beginning in 1884, a numerical marking system was used, with a combination of numerals following the prefix (Rd. or Rd. No.). The number is the clue to the year the item was made, up to 1892. In that year, because of a law passed here, the country of origin was stamped on items imported here. However, one must examine each piece for other clues as to age. Much has been brought here by immigrants or imported by dealers that does not have the country of origin marked because it was not required for sale in Great Britain.

French Porcelain

Another country which competed for American business was France, whose famous factories at Rouen and St. Cloud date back into the seventeenth century. Very little of the Rouen production has survived, although it is known that a reasonably good European porcelain was first made at Rouen. This porcelain was soft paste, and most was decorated in blue. The St. Cloud production is documented by pieces marked as early as 1697, decorated in Japanese and other oriental styles, with gilding featured. Another factory was founded at Chantilly in 1725, and produced wares which imitated currently favored oriental designs.

SEVRES

One of the most prominent works—Sevres—had its humble beginnings in Vincennes. It was in operation there from 1738 to 1756, when King Louis XV took it under his patronage. He allowed the formation of a new company which was moved to Sevres to undertake the making of soft paste porcelain. Most of the Sevres production from 1753 to 1756 carries the same markings as that of Vincennes. In 1761, the formula for making hard paste porcelain was acquired, and this made up the bulk of the company's production thereafter. The concern used the double L as a mark from 1740 on. From 1753 to the time of the revolution a date letter was inserted. After 1802, the Sevres markings were done in red, with a date abbreviation used between 1818 and 1834. After 1834, the full date was used. On the orders of the Nazis, a special edition of 80 small plates was turned out in 1943 to commemorate the reuniting of the French and German lands by Hitler. I wonder about the location of these today. Sevres was one of the most imitated potteries, and it trained some fine craftsmen who later joined other concerns, bringing with them skills unsurpassed anywhere.

LIMOGES

Another famous name in French porcelain is Limoges. A

pottery was formed in this town as early as 1771, and as many as 35 different concerns were eventually located there. You will see such markings as Elite, JP or J. Pouyat, Guerin, JPL, Aron and Valin, Pierre Tharaud, and perhaps the most famous of all, Haviland. David Haviland, an importer from New York, established a plant at Limoges in the 1840's and provided his own outlet for the product in America. This high quality porcelain caught the fancy of the American public, so much so that Haviland Limoges was once considered a necessary wedding gift for the well-to-do bride.

German Porcelain

Americans have always held ceramics from the Germanic regions of Europe in high esteem. After the origination of porcelain in Dresden by Bottger and the creation of the famed Meissen works there, the secret soon spread throughout the area, so that by 1718 it was quite well known. The names of Meissen and Dresden are synonymous with respect to ceramics, and both are similarly marked. The work was greatly imitated by other concerns in Germany in the nineteenth century, and Samson imitated it in Paris. Although he was required to mark his pieces to show they were reproductions, he got around this nicely by stamping the original marks beneath the glaze, and putting his mark on the glaze where it could be rubbed off at will, in the same manner that paper labels used today to identify country of origin fall off so easily. There were many other great porcelain manufactories in Germany, but none captured the fancy of the American buyer as much as Dresden. As a result, little of their production is found in America.

Although very good work was done, the production from potteries elsewhere in Europe had little impact in America. People have a fetish for collecting not only good work but good names as well, and if the supply of an item is not sufficient, they will lose interest in trying to locate it. Scarcity can hurt collecting by lowering the price, quite contrary to the idea that if something is rare it is more valuable.

CHINESE PORCELAIN

There has been much speculation as to the feasibility of collecting Chinese porcelains in the light of recent efforts to expand our trade with the People's Republic. This country had its doors closed to the western world for over twenty years, and the interest in Oriental artifacts steadily increased during that time. There has been some feeling that the market would be flooded with shipments of all kinds of antiques, as such a large country must surely have antiques going back to its earliest civilization. Since the Chinese worker, under Communism, is unable to amass the wealth needed to indulge in collecting, it would be logical to assume that many artifacts would soon be finding their way to western countries in search of dollars and other hard currency. If the markets were flooded with such merchandise, it would again be logical to assume that the law of supply and demand would drive down the prices of existing treasures outside China and provide an unsettling effect on collecting them. However, in the opinion of those who deal in such antiquities, this is not going to happen. Years ago, the great capitals at Anyang and Loyang were stripped of their antiquities, with most of these finding their way into western museums and providing the basis for some of the world's finest collections of this art. When the railway system was expanded in China in the early part of the century, many lines were run through old cemeteries. When the graves were dug up for relocation, all sorts of worldly possessions were found with the bodies, having evidently been buried with them for their trip to the unknown. The easy sale of such items led to grave robbing everywhere and since then grave robbing has provided many antiques for the western world.

China developed the earliest porcelain industry, and until its wares were duplicated in Europe, much fine porcelain was sent there in trade. This trade continued throughout the rise of the porcelain industry elsewhere. Chinese trade with Europe began in earnest early in the seventeenth century, but it was not common in America until after the Revolutionary War. America began sending clipper ships directly to the Orient, bypassing the necessity of transshipment through England. You can assume that most of the Oriental ware collected today came to America after 1800. This is the period when Canton blue earthenware and porcelains from Nanking, Fukien, and Canton first made their presence felt. The popular five color Chinese export porcelain, often called Rose Medallion, is known to have arrived in America as early as the 1790's, yet the bulk of it appears to have arrived after 1850 during the height of the Chinese-American trade. Little or no green colored celadon arrived in America until after the War of 1812. You must be careful in purchasing the pure white blanc-de-chine figures (whose history goes back many centuries) as they are being reproduced quite well today. Imari ware (first made in Japan in blue and orange with gilding) is now being reproduced in China with remarkable fidelity. It is still being handmade and hand decorated, and this guarantees that quality pieces will rank high as collectibles in some future generation.

When Chiang Kai-shek left the mainland to occupy Taiwan, he took with him the palace treasures from Peking. Since then the People's Republic has been trying to replace them with similar items in order to restore the old palaces to their original dignity. There are agents from the People's Republic buying items all over the world for return to China, and their buying offers keen competition to anyone interested in Oriental artifacts. There is no indication that markets throughout the world will be flooded with Chinese antiquities, since there really is little of fine quality or value left to export. No one looks for a drop in prices for such items. Some of the best will undoubtedly continue to rise in price in spite of the new "open door."

Determining Age and Authenticity

There are no set rules for determining the age and authenticity of early ceramics, but the following pointers are offered as an aid. You must remember that no one rule can guarantee authenticity—you must inspect many features and all must check properly before attribution can be made. A simple clue is the wear on the bottom of any pieces which must rest on a table or shelf. If the piece is old, this wear will show through roughness, wear of the glaze, or small chips and cracks. Many early ceramics become crazed with age, and this is difficult to reproduce. Items fired in kilns before the middle of the nineteenth century will often show the marks of the tripod on which they rested in the seggar so that the heat could flow evenly around them. These are called tripod marks, and there are usually three which pierce the glaze on the underside of the dish out toward the rim. They will show up as three dots. There may be a triple dot at each point—this is almost always a guarantee of age. Contemporary pieces are still being fired on tripods, so this clue is not always constant. I have seen tripod marks on Doulton pieces whose other markings put them as being made after 1892. However, a piece without tripod marks should not be evaluated as being made before 1850.

Painting designs on the clay bodies, then glazing and firing was the most popular technique used in all countries back to the eighteenth century. However, some pottery was painted over the first glaze, and then reglazed and fired. A good clue to early handmade pottery value is that, generally, the more colors used, the higher the value. In the early days, each color had to be painted on, glazed, and then fired, which was a time-consuming process. Some plants used the technique of painting with colored glazes which would then be fired, doing away with the extra steps color usually demanded. Such glazes were used at the Fenton works in Bennington, therefore they are still brilliant today.

Some people feel that a piece must look old to be old, but on the surface many Chinese porcelains several hundred years old look like they were made just a few days ago. This is a tribute to the superior formulas and ingenuity used by the Chinese artisans. However, most ceramics will show their age up to a point; it is up to you to evaluate how old a piece is if there are no markings or other identification to help you. If you are concerned about age, and are not satisfied with the determination of age either from the person from whom you are buying or from your own analysis, leave the item alone. A "lost" treasure can sometimes be a headache you really don't need.

Ceramics Glossary

Basalt—A black stoneware made by mixing iron ore byproducts with basic clay.

Belleek—A delicate porcelain which originated in Ireland, characterized by its sheen and fragility.

Biscuit—A moulded clay item before its firing.

Bone China—A clay mixture that includes powdered calcined bone powder to strengthen it and give it a porcelain-hard quality.

Caffette—A clay container which holds unfired bodies in a kiln.

Calcine—A technique for baking metals, stone, bone, or other materials to reduce them to powder before mixing with clay or a glaze.

Ceramic—A generic term for items made from clay and fired to hardness.

China—A generic term used to describe tablewares and decorative items made from clay and other ingredients.

Chinese export—The ceramic wares which arrived in Europe and America from the Orient in the eighteenth and nineteenth centuries.

Clay—Fine grained earth made up of hydrated silicates of aluminum, which forms a paste with water and can be molded and fired to hardness.

Creamware—A cream or ivory colored pottery which originated in England in the eighteenth century.

Delft—Originated in Ireland as a white tin-glazed blue and white decorated earthenware. Received its name from the city in Holland which made and popularized it. Made also in England, Germany, and other countries.

Dresden—The home of the original porcelain in Germany, discovered by Johann Freiderich Boettger.

Earthenware—Simple opaque ware made of clay and requiring glazing to offset its porosity

Enamelling—Decoration of ceramic bodies before firing with paints made from various substances.

Flint enamel—A pottery enamel which is made by calcining flint stone into powder, then mixing it with liquid glaze.

Glaze—A transparent or colored coating put on ceramics before firing to offset their porosity.

Graniteware—A very hard earthenware toughened with calcined flint stone.

Greenware—Clay products in their unfired state.

Ironstone—Patented by Mason in England in 1813. Usually a thicker, very tough earthenware; mostly in pure white with impressed or raised decoration.

Jasperware—Barium sulphate is added to clay to produce a nonporous hard body akin to porcelain. It is easily colored. Wedgwood is best known for working with it.

Kaolin—A fine clay used in the making of porcelain.

Kiln—An oven in which clay products are baked to hardness.

Lowestoft—A name often applied to Chinese export porcelains of the eighteenth and nineteenth centuries as late as the 1890's. It is believed that Lowestoft originally imported wares from China and reshipped them under its name from East Anglia, England.

Lusterware—Any ceramic body glazed with a metallic compound which will give it luster and shine.

Majolica—Originally an Italian redware which was colorfully fired with tin glazes. It became a product of practically every country with minor variations.

Meissen—Synonymous with Dresden, as the wares were made at the Meissen plant in Dresden, Germany.

Parian—An unglazed porcelain originated early in the nineteenth century as a poor man's imitation of Parian marble.

Petuntse—A form of feldspar which was mixed with clay to make various ceramics, including stoneware and porcelain.

Porcelain—A hard translucent ceramic which originated in China.

Potters wheel—A whirling device on which clay objects are formed by hand.

Queensware—Another name for creamware.

Redware—Made of red clay and glazed when needed to cancel its porosity.

Rockinghamware—A name given to the brown and mottled colored wares reputedly originating at the estate of the Earl of Rockingham in England in the eighteenth century. Much is referred to mistakenly as Benningtonware, a reference to the community in Vermont where a lot was made.

Salt glaze—An inexpensive quick glazing achieved by throwing salt into the kiln during the final moments of firing—the vapours then depositing on the bodies.

Seggar—Clay holder inside a kiln which holds the green clay for firing and protects it from direct heat.

Slip—A simple glaze made by mixing clay with water and slipping or trailing it on the piece to be protected.

Stoneware—A very strong earthenware which has the strength of porcelain and does not require an inside glaze to make it impervious to water.

Transferwares—Transfer printing on ceramic bodies by the use of paper decals or transfers.

Underglaze—A reference to the painting or other decorating done on ceramics before glazing and firing.

Vitreous china—A strong earthenware body with an almost glasslike shiny glaze.

Chapter 5

Silver and Pewter

It was not until the twentieth century that much attention was paid to American handmade silver. Those who owned old silver thought most of it was made in England, since not much research had been done on early makers in this country, and names and touchmarks gave no apparent clues. Late in the nineteenth century Professor Woolsey of Yale suggested that more research should be done, and this was followed at the turn of the century by a book prepared by N. W. Elwell which had forty pages of photography of both American and English silver. In 1906, The Museum of Fine Arts in Boston mounted the first exhibition of American silver, featuring silver which had been identified as to maker. The Museum of Fine Arts held another display in 1911, at which over a thousand pieces were shown. Since then, many books have been written and much information has been assembled, and several large museums keep permanent collections on display.

It would seem that the great centers of silvermaking in the eighteenth century were Boston, New York, and Philadelphia, and many apprentices were trained in the shops. The craft then spread into the smaller cities and towns, and some really sophisticated country work has turned up to rival the urban centers. Unfortunately, the English withheld supplies of silver from the colonies in order to keep their own craftsmen busy, which held down production here. There was much melting down of coins and surreptitious buying of stolen metal from prize ships captured by pirates and others. A great deal of Spanish silver from the mines in Mexico and South America found its way into the hands of American silversmiths as booty from battles at sea. Pieces were made to order, and in most cases the buyer would bring his own metal to the silversmith who would be paid for his efforts by retaining a percentage of it.

159

The English Heritage

America owes its heritage in silvermaking to England, as the early craftsmen came from there already trained in the most progressive techniques. Silversmiths were regulated by the crown as early as the thirteenth century, with stiff penalties for those who attempted to defraud the public. Until then, most work had been done in gold, primarily for royalty and the Church. A goldsmith's guild had been formed to police its members, and to upgrade the quality of work by providing for an apprentice system in order to train craftsmen properly. Some of the great early work was done in monastaries, since ecclesiastical gold and silver was in great demand for communion services, salvers, crosses, and candlesticks. A marking system, instituted in 1477, required that a leopard's head, with or without crown, had to be stamped on every piece which met the weight of 22 shillings to the pound. Two years later, the date letter was required on every piece, and this makes it possible to document the year the piece was made. The silversmiths began stamping their pieces with touchmarks for identification at about this time. Most people were illiterate, so these marks were important. The touchmark might be a flower, horse's head, star, moon, or some other recognizable object which was registered in the maker's name. In 1560, the sterling standard of 92.5% pure silver (with the remaining 7.5% being alloy) was passed to unify the production to a single standard. At one time, the crown varied this percentage to 95.8% to discourage the practice of melting coins in order to

Mustard pot in silver with a blue glass liner by Myer Myers, New York, 1723–1795. This is an example of a rare piece of silver executed quite tastefully. (Museum of Fine Arts, Boston)

George II silver coffeepot made in the second quarter of the eighteenth century. English silver is beautifully made, but it commands less money here than its American counterpart. (Sotheby-Parke Bernet, New York)

Sturdy silver tankard by Jeremiah Dummer, Boston, 1645–1718. Early American silver resembles the English because its makers were mostly English immigrants or had been trained by English craftsmen living in the colonies.

Plated silver tea set made by the Forbes Silver Company of New York City. Footed pieces such as these are worth more than those which rest flat on the table.

reclaim the metal for other uses, but in 1719 the old standard was revived, and it remains constant to this day. In 1784, all gold and silversmiths were required to pay a duty to the crown for every piece produced, and the head of the reigning monarch was stamped on the piece to signify that the duty had been paid. This rule remained in effect until 1890, so you can quickly place silver in this time span if such a stamp appears. In addition to the touchmark, makers began putting their names or initials on their work as a further mark of identification.

Some leopard heads bear a crown—these were evident from the earliest days of the guild until the mid-eighteenth century. Some have a striking resemblance to a lion, and records show that this stamp was approved in the middle of the sixteenth century.

Reproductions

Most buyers of silver realize that this sort of marking system is not without its hazards, as fakers have been at work to turn it to their advantage. It is not too difficult to cast a die in the exact mold of an early touchmark, and then impress it on a later piece whose style and workmanship will not give it away. Another trick is to cut an authentic hallmark from a lesser piece and insert it in a more important one to increase its value. The marks from a spoon can be imbedded in the bottom of a teapot, as silver is quite malleable and this work can be done well enough to fool the naked eye. However, such fakery can be detected by the use of lights and close examination. Another method is to breathe on the suspected piece—the moisture will reveal any reconstruction work. Experts who study shapes and forms can readily tell if there has been any tampering. Not long ago, a fine pair of candlesticks with marks of a mid-eighteenth century maker were sold as his work. However, he worked in a period when the style they represented could not have been made. Needless to say, the smarter dealers offered no bids at the auction. You would not expect to find Federal period styling done by a maker quite prominent in the rococo period which preceded it, especially when none of his known work reflects such design.

You must acquaint yourself with historical facts, since they will often help provide clues as to age and quite often to country of origin as well. Silver teapots were not made before the third quarter of the seventeenth century—tea was not a common drink until the restoration of Charles II to the English throne in 1660. Any claim that a teapot was made before this time must be regarded with suspicion. Sugar was not in common usage until the end of the seventeenth century, so the earliest sugar bowls cannot be dated before then. Cream was first added to tea during the Queen Anne period and so creamers came into vogue at that time. As a rule, these were not necessarily made in sets, and the teapot, sugar bowl, and creamer were not required to look alike. It was not until the end of the eighteenth century that making all the pieces in a set became the rule. Tea caddies and tea boxes did not make their appearance until the time of Queen Anne, and coffee was accepted as a drink only a few years earlier. Although coffee had been known in England from the middle of the seventeenth century, there is no evidence of silver pieces made then to accommodate it.

Sheffield Plate and Electroplating

It was not until the eighteenth century that much silver was made for those whose station was below that of royalty. As England's trade with the world increased, so did the affluency of her traders, and they soon became patrons of the arts and crafts. At first, production was limited to functional items such as tankards, mugs, pieces for tea and coffee sets, and other tableware. A later development in production that was to have a far reaching effect was the creation of Sheffield plate. Named after the community where it was popularized, Sheffield was made as a "poor man's" silver. The process is simple—less expensive copper sheeting is sandwiched between two thinner layers of silver and the layers are bound together by heating and rolling.

This lesser metal is then shaped to the desired form, with the seams hidden by pure silver, soldered and hammered where needed. As Sheffield ages and wears, the copper shines from

Silver caster made in the late eighteenth century by noted patriot Paul Revere. His name is stamped clearly on the side. (Sotheby-Parke Bernet, New York)

Plated silver teapot made in the late nineteenth century by the Pairpoint Silver Company, New Bedford, Massachusetts. The handle is wood to provide insulation. Good plated silver is being collected today.

beneath, giving it a rosy look. Most collectors feel that it should be left this way, as it is this sort of patina which gives it authenticity and charm. Others feel that replating by modern methods will not harm it, but will improve it instead, since it will be returned to its original look. It is not known that Sheffield was made in America, and any that is found is almost automatically attributed to England.

American entry into the manufacture of less expensive silverware occurred when the electroplating technique was developed in the 1840's. A body of a lesser metal such as copper, brass, or white metal is dipped into a silver solution. When electricity is short circuited within the solution, it deposits its contents on the body. To provide the necessary thickness for wear, each piece was dipped several times, and was marked "triple plate" for three dippings and "quadruple plate" for four. This process continued until the 1890's when the method of dipping was improved to the point where only one dipping was required to deposit the necessary coating on the base metal. The public had been conditioned to the name "quadruple plate" as a term for the best in plated ware, and rather than risk loss of sales with reference to a single plate, the old designation was used until World War II. After the war the term "silver on copper" was introduced, and most plated ware is so marked today. The English counterpart to this production is marked "E.P.N.S.," which translates to mean electroplated nickel silver.

Early American Silver

Robert Sanderson of Hampton, New Hampshire (1608–1693), is credited with being the first of the New England silversmiths. With his partner, John Hull, he turned out early work on a par with that made in England. Sanderson moved to Watertown, Massachusetts, in 1642, where he and Hull later made the famous

Silver bread basket made by Daniel Christian Fueter, New York around 1765. The decoration of this delicate footed piece enhances its beauty and value. (Museum of Fine Arts, Boston)

pine tree shillings which became coin of the commonwealth at the time. Sanderson's three sons (Joseph, Benjamin, and Robert) all followed their father's trade, and all worked in the making of church plate, much of which has survived. To attempt to list the many makers who worked in the seventeenth and eighteenth centuries would take many pages, and we are more interested in those who achieved some sort of fame and in reviewing the work that was done.

Silversmiths were known to have done a great deal of work other than turning out pieces of church or tableware. Some smiths engraved the plates from which money was printed. Others turned out sword handles, belt buckles, coins, buttons, card boxes, and other necessities of the day. Fortunately, since most American silversmiths were of English birth or descent, they marked their pieces well, and because of this we know the origin of the pieces and can note regional differences in style and workmanship. Silver knives were used during the seventeenth century, but spoons did not make their appearance until the end of it. Forks are rare, even in the eighteenth century, since the soft silver did not lend itself to rough usage. The English made Sheffield forks, but few or none of these were manufactured in America. In the early part of the eighteenth century, American silversmiths did not copy the style of the tall English teapots, preferring the lower ones in the pigeon-breasted Queen Anne style. Even these went out of fashion during the third quarter of the eighteenth century, when tea urns became the standard. Most of these urns were built with warmers underneath, and some had a place where a piece of hot iron could be inserted to maintain the heat. The basic style was low pots for tea, and tall pots for coffee and chocolate. Ceramics makers later evolved a pattern for the latter which had the spout at the top for easier pouring. It is not known why the silver makers retained the spout emerging from the center of the pot, as chocolate is a heavy liquid and can clog the spout. Chocolate arrived in England in the mid-seventeenth century, about the same time as tea and coffee. You can easily tell a chocolate pot from the early period, as most were made with a removable piece at the top where a stirring rod could be inserted. The English pots may have this device, but it does not appear in American colonial work.

Tea caddies were popular—the name coming from the Malaysian word meaning pound, with reference to the amount packed in a container of this size. Tobacco was another product which came into favor in the mid-seventeenth century, and boxes were made to hold it. Snuff became quite popular during the time of Queen Anne, and snuff boxes became fashionable. Silver spice boxes (or nutmeg boxes as they were often called) came into vogue in the eighteenth century, so one might season his food properly while traveling. Sugar was a very expensive luxury in England until the end of the seventeenth century, when the demand for it to sweeten hot drinks resulted in greater imports. It came in loaf or chunk form, so sugar boxes were made to house it with proper decorum for the fancy table. Tongs and cutters were added to the inventory of silver wares to handle the chunk sugar. One of the American colonial makers of sugar boxes was John Coney of Boston (1655–1722), who trained a very important Huguenot apprentice, Appolos Rivoire, the father of the noted Paul Revere. The Revere silver is cataloged *Revere I* and *Revere II* for identification.

Dish crosses which served as trivets to raise heated dishes from the table are rare in American made silver. Marrow spoons were common in England, but not here. Chafing stands are rare in both countries; they were generally quite small in order to accommodate small silver pots. Ladles, wine siphons, andirons, chandeliers, sconces, and frames for looking glasses were not common products by American silversmiths.

Nineteenth Century American Silver

The great interest in American silver has all but depleted the available supply for the common collector. Today, you must wait for the liquidation of an estate where there are no heirs, or where money is more desired than old silver. Until recently, nineteenth century silver was not much in demand, but as the rarity of early work increased, so did the interest in later work. Actually, there were many silversmiths doing hand work until the Civil War, as this industry was not affected by the industrial revolution until the 1840's when the method for electroplating was discovered.

Paul Revere and his son worked in Boston until 1818. The increasing Chinese-American trade also brought with it a Chinese export silver of very good quality. A great deal of this silver came into America during the nineteenth century; yet it has been only recently that sufficient research has been done to make identification possible. Much of it is stamped with English hallmarks, since the Orientals were great imitators of anything which was successful.

French and Huguenot Silver

There is a new interest in early French silver today, but very little is available here. Actually, many of the styles popularized in England in the late seventeenth and early eighteenth centuries were created by Huguenot craftsmen who left their country after the Edict of Nantes had been revoked, again denying them freedom from religious persecution. Among those who fled to England were the forebears of Paul Lamerie, who was destined to become England's most noted maker. Other Huguenots who had a great influence were Peter Platel and Anthony Nelme. The workmen who were not affected by the Edict of Nantes continued to work in France, turning out the same quality of work as that made in England. However, there is not much French silver in America, and the eighteenth century silver so desired by all is in great demand in France. Noted English craftsmen of the late eighteenth century include Matthew Boulton (1728–1809); Paul Storr, who began his work in 1792; and members of the Batemen family, which included two lady silvermakers, Hester and Anne.

American Plated Silver

After the Civil War, plated silver came into its own. The war industries were geared to making items out of metal, and when peace came they turned their efforts to everyday items. Victorian styling was still very much in vogue, and highly decorated work began to appear since the machines made mass production possible. In the hand era (before 1840) decoration was applied by chasing or engraving the outside of the piece, or by hammering it from the inside against a mold in what is called repousse. The highly figured pieces were stamped out in sections and then soldered together and plated. This type of work is popular to this day, although the designs have changed. Some experts feel that when these pieces are replated they do not have the look of the originals of years ago, but this is quite easily explained. After dipping, the early makers would have each piece polished ready for the trade, usually with a substance that would turn black with use. This was allowed to remain in the cracks and crevices in order to highlight the raised shiny surfaces. A man who had worked at a silver factory before the turn of the century gave me this information. It is unlikely this technique would be duplicated today, especially if the public knew how it was done.

There is a fad today for collecting old silver pieces and having them stripped to reveal the base metal, which can be copper, brass, white metal, or even steel. The pieces were often made of combinations of different metals, with copper forming the places where there is less stress, and other metals used for feet, handles, finials, and spouts. This rule also applies to those pieces which were plated in nickel and, later, chromium. You should look for interesting forms, as this is most important in determining the value of such items.

Period Designs and Decoration

Decorating silver is an exacting art, and there are several ways in which it was done. Perhaps the first technique was engraving, which is done with a sharp tool which removes the metal where it is cut. The term "bright cut" is used to define cutting which is deep and often undercut so that there will be more brilliance as it reflects light. Chasing resembles engraved work, but it is done with a tool which impresses the design, removing no metal. Repousse is done by hammering a body of silver from the inside to produce a raised surface with a shaped decoration. A gadroon or fluted decoration around rims was very popular. Some pieces, such as feet, handles, spouts, and finials, were cast and then joined by silver soldering to the main body. Polishing with a jeweler's rouge erases the markings of such joined work.

The term "coin" or "pure coin" was adopted to signify the content of the pure metal, which was 900 parts to 100 parts alloy. This came into general use in the 1830's. The term "sterling" was adopted from the name of a group of German craftsmen known as the "Easterlings" who migrated to England early in the fourteenth century. Their work in refining silver to its pure standards prompted a royal edict which set forth their formula as the law of the realm. However, it was not until after the Civil War that the term was much in use in America, so if you see the word "sterling" stamped on a piece, you will know that it was most likely made after that time.

You can trace the design of silver easily, as it followed the tastes in furniture. Pieces were made to compliment room settings of furniture, and with such a clue you can reasonably ascribe the period of its manufacture. In the eighteenth century, silversmiths worked in pure forms, with little thought to fancy design or decoration. The Queen Anne period brought with it grace and elegance in curves and a delicate style which was reflected in all the decorative arts. The mid-century styles of Chippendale influenced the arts with their rococo decoration. This became especially popular after the excavations in Greece and Italy, which created a revival of interest in classical decorative forms. After the Revolutionary War, the austerity of Hepplewhite brought a return to dignity, expressed through straight lines and less embellishment. What is known now as the Federal style was quite popular well into the 1830's, after which the machines began to erode the quality of silver work. The gaudy productions of the Empire and Victorian periods were in keeping with the furniture of the day and, like the furniture of that time, have only recently been accepted on a wide scale for collecting. Until now, no silver collector would have allowed any nineteenth century silver made after 1830 into his collection. Recent studies into the decorative arts have revealed that much silver was still handmade after 1830, and regardless of style, it represents the craftsmanship of the times. Rather than being made by individual small shops as in the past, large factories were set up to take care of the growing demand for the product at the time of America's great industrial growth.

Collecting American Silver

There is one very good reason for accepting nineteenth century silver, and that is the scarcity of earlier pieces. Unless you have unlimited funds, you cannot reasonably collect the early work. The shortage of early work came about because of several reasons. First, there was limited output of eighteenth century American work because of a shortage of metal. At the time of the Revolution, many Tories, still loyal to the Crown, returned to England taking whatever they could, and if they owned silver it was the first thing they took. Much silver was donated to be melted down to help pay for the war effort. In the course of the war, the English also besieged many cities along the American coast. When they received no cooperation from the colonists in supplying them with food or other needs, they would stand their battleships offshore and demolish the community. This resulted in the wholesale destruction of many of our native decorative arts. When the British captured a town, the first thing the soldiers stole was the silver, since it was wealth that could be picked up and carried away.

Today, much nineteenth century sterling is purchased for its scrap value. You will find it difficult to match pieces in a flatware set, and very few people wish to set a table unless the service is complete. There is at least one silver company which will make some pieces on order (Towle). A check with your local jeweler will help determine if he can get pieces from other concerns. There are some dealers who specialize in selling odd silver pieces, so if you have patience and get around to shows you may be able to select items you need.

The thin coin silver spoons which obviously were made in abundance during the early nineteenth century are still quite plentiful. Most are well marked, and a book such as Seymour Wyler's *Old Silver, English, American, Foreign* (Crown Publishers) is quite helpful in identifying makers. Collect spoons of native or regional interest to you. Spoon racks are handy for display. After polishing coin silver pieces, rub them with ordinary flour to remove the excess polish and to give them a sheen which will not tarnish quickly.

Commemorative and souvenir spoons in sterling are quite common, and represent an interesting facet of collecting. Friends touring foreign countries can acquire some for you, and you can begin a collection on your own by purchasing them new or old from dealers. When such a collection comes up for sale it will reward the collector well for his efforts, as long as the pieces are varied and difficult to acquire unless one travels a lot.

There is much contemporary silver being collected for investment purposes, and there is no doubt that most of it will increase in value. The price of the raw metal will rise with the economy, and if the work is good, of artistic quality, or in a limited edition to make it rare, contemporary silver can represent a good investment. Many mints are turning out plates, coins, statues, and the like with a published assurance that only a limited number will be made. However, you must remember that any machine-made item can be reproduced at any time in the future, and there can be no guarantee to protect you against reproductions. The best investment is in old handmade work which cannot be duplicated. Buy the contemporary silver if you like it, but remember that there is only a chance that it will acquire some importance in the future, and do not depend on it. A magazine entitled *Acquire* is now being published in New York, and is devoted exclusively to information about limited edition work in all fields of the decorative arts. The magazine *Silver*, published in Vancouver, Washington, is an excellent reference work on old silver.

A popular item in the voluminous Chinese-American trade of the nineteenth century was silver, which is of quite good quality. Until recently, there has been little interest in it, but perhaps this is because it was not readily identified. English hallmarks were put on much of it, leading buyers into believing it came from England. However, you will find Oriental designs on such pieces, and this is a good clue to their origin. Not enough research has been done on Chinese silver, so there is little advice I can give you. However, the simplest clue is that if the British hallmarks cannot be traced to a maker there, you should carry your study further with the help of silver dealers and appraisers to determine if it came from the East. The Museum of the China-American Trade in Milton, Massachusetts, has assembled many pieces for study, and you are advised to examine this collection. You will note that the quality is different—the pieces look heavier and the work is not as well defined as its English counterpart.

American Pewter

In the eighteenth century, a shortage of tin plagued the American pewter makers. They were entirely dependent on exports as there was no established source in America at the time. Plenty of English pewter was shipped in to take care of the demand, and this in effect helped provide the material for some American production. Pewter is composed primarily of tin, with the basic formula being 90% tin plus 10% antimony, copper, or other alloys. Lead can be added to give it weight, and this is a good clue to Continental pewter since American and English pewter is lighter in comparison. It is felt that the lead content helped to promote the poisoning of food and led to the slow illness of many of its users. Fortunately, American makers used little or no lead in their production. Since pewter is soft the pieces would not survive, and they would be taken to the local pewterer, who melted them down in order to recast the metal into new pieces. As payment for his services he would retain part of the metal, using it for his own new production. This practice helped diminish the available supply of eighteenth century pewter, since so much of it was melted down. The Revolutionary War also helped to create this shortage, as much plate was melted down for bullets. Pewter cannot withstand high temperatures, and any piece coming in contact with excessive heat will be damaged or destroyed instantly. A lot of the early production must have been lost in this manner.

Following the lead of the silversmiths, the pewterers were conscientious in marking their handmade pieces. Those pieces which were cast in molds were less likely to be marked. Other makers would not mark pieces, hoping to mislead the public into thinking that they were buying imported pewter which was considered to be of finer quality.

The availability of eighteenth century American pewter is quite limited. Serious collectors have been buying it for years and, along with museums and historical societies, they have locked up most of it from the general trade channels. An estate will occasionally come up for sale with such early pieces, and prices seem to skyrocket every year as the demand exceeds the supply. There are books providing identification of makers by name and touchmark listed in the bibliography, so there is no great mystery in identifying pewter. You must be careful of fake touches as these will crop up from time to time, but they are the great minority, so do not worry too much about it. Pewter has not been considered a valuable commodity until recently, so there has been little reason to doctor it. Until now, most pewter has gone to serious buyers who would recognize any alteration, and there has been little incentive for fakery. Now that public acceptance has broadened for the product, it is only natural to assume that some unscrupulous people will attempt to take advantage of those with limited knowledge, so the danger is now more present than ever. You should only rely on competent dealers for advice. When an estate is settled, you may also buy with relative safety, as the collector put his stamp of approval on the piece just by owning it. If an auctioneer suspects that later work has been done on an item, he will gladly give you the benefit of this advice if you ask him during the pre-sale inspection.

Unmarked Pewter

There is much unmarked pewter that could be American, and it is being bought up by those who hope for a magic formula which will someday unlock the secret of its origin and add to its interest and value. Some pewter appears with an eagle touch, which would seem American but is as yet unidentified as to maker. It is best to invest in pieces which are identifiable, and to put little money in those which are not. Some collectors feel that the rolled edge of a plate or dish could signify country of origin—if it were rolled on the top side, it would be English, and if rolled underneath, American. There is little to support this theory, as it is generally accepted that most early American pewterers were trained in England, and it is most likely that they practiced their trade with the techniques they learned originally. Measurements are no clue, as these would be comparable. Shapes and forms were similar as well. You must rely on touchmarks and names for proper identification.

Machine-made Pewter

Almost every community had its resident pewterer. The pewterer might have been no more than a reworker of metal who had equipped himself with molds into which melted down scrap could be poured. Craftsmen who worked with the hammer and primitive lathes were in the minority, and it is this handwork which brings the top dollar today. Mechanization began creeping slowly into industry in the mid-1790's, when Josiah Wedgwood introduced machinery which speeded up his production in ceramics, but it was not until after the War of 1812 that such progress made any great impact in America. The approximate date used for the beginning of the industrial age is 1830 and coincides with the deterioration of all the decorative arts, pewter being no exception. By this time a harder metal called Brittania was in general use. Developed in England during the eighteenth century, the Brittania formula does not seem to have come into general use in America until after 1820. By 1830, most work was in Britannia, and by 1840, most was machine-made. Some work was done by molding, and other work was turned out individually on lathes powered by steam or water. Wooden forms were created in the sizes of dishes or bowls wanted, and these would be fastened in a lathe with a sheet of Brittania held against them. As the mold and metal were spun, the artisan would hold a steel tool against the metal, molding it to the wooden shape. The piece would then be removed and finished at the workbench, where rims could be worked, and feet, handles, spouts, and the like could be added by soldering. Some very collectible work was done during this period, and though not as valuable as the earlier production, it has found great favor with collectors who must settle for second best. Actually, much desirable production was done as late as the 1880's, especially in the newer parts of the country, where artisans worked with less sophisticated tools for a longer period.

A collection of American pewter with most of the pots made during the Britannia period (post 1830). These are judged by marker and form, but condition is also important.

Another unusual pewter touchmark with a reverse N. No explanation is known for this, although the piece is known to be eighteenth century English work. (William Penn Memorial Museum, Harrisburg, Pennsylvania)

Unusual touchmark in pewter which was used by some eighteenth century English craftsmen to suggest that their work was done in London. The first O was stamped as a Q so that the piece would not be an outright forgery.

Pewter communion set by Johan Christopher Heyne who worked in Lancaster, Pennsylvania about 1750--1730. He is regarded as one of America's foremost pewterers. (William Penn Memorial Museum, Harrisburg, Pennsylvania)

Points of Identification

There are some rules that must be observed in collecting pewter. If the word "pewter" is imprinted on a piece, it is much too new to be collected. You must look for recent solder work on legs, spouts, covers, etc., as some pieces have been remade. If the pewter is quite heavy, and its markings give you no clue as to country of origin, judge its weight against that of lead. If the lead content is high, it is most likely European. Condition is very important and repairs, which are usually visible, injure value greatly. If the product is black and scaly with age, do not attempt to clean it yourself. This work should be done by those equipped for it. Good cleaning requires dipping or scouring with such materials as hydrochloric acid, and this can be dangerous work. It must be done under ideal conditions in a well ventilated area. The acid must be neutralized at the proper moment—so that not too much metal is lost, and so that the touchmarks remain distinct. You will find that pieces such as the large chargers are oil impregnated, which makes cleaning quite difficult. It is best to steer away from pewter in this condition. Avoid pewter which has been highly polished, as most collectors want it to retain a soft patina. It has been argued that the metal was originally shiny and that restoring it in this manner should not hurt it. Maybe this is true, but you must recognize that others may not share this opinion, and that the majority of buyers want pewter to have an aged look, if possible. You may have difficulty in selling the shiny product, and therefore it is not a good investment.

You should refer to any flat piece less than nine inches in diameter as a plate, and any nine inches or greater in diameter as a dish. The latter may also be referred to as trenchers or chargers, as these are old English names for serving dishes.

There are some production techniques which should be noted. Casting pewter in a mold would often leave pits and hollows in the metal. These would be filled with a soldering iron using scrap pewter metal or solder. The piece would then be placed in a lathe and "skimmed" by holding a sharp tool against it, shaving off any rough spots and raised imperfections. A spiral mark would quite often be left from this process and it will still be visible. Pieces which were completely hand hammered are most desired, and this work can usually be noted at the booge, which is the curved raised wall at the bottom of plates and dishes. The hammer marks will be most visible there.

An early porringer can often be identified by the method in which the handle has been attached. The body would be formed and then a mold for the handle would be held against it in proper position. The body would be hung over an anvil or other support during this process, and protected from contact with it by a wet rag or burlap. When the hot pewter was poured into the handle mold, it would melt and fuse with the body, but the body would also soften enough to absorb an imprint from the cloth on the inside at the point where the handle was attached. This "crosshatching," as it is called, indicates the manner in which it was made.

Little engraving or chasing was done on pewter in this country. Some European work was decorated in this manner. It is noticeably absent on church communion services, as most of these must have been presentation pieces. However, unlike silver, pewter presentation pieces were rarely marked.

Oriental pewter has been imported for a long time, but it is of poor quality with a heavy lead content. Some work which is mistaken for pewter might even be made of a white metal which colors to resemble it greatly. The weight of the piece is a clue to its contents—you must learn to "feel" pewter as well as look at it.

Forms in pewter are important. Items with interesting shapes make ideal shelf and decorative pieces, and are most in demand. Tankards, chargers, whale oil lamps, porringers, sets of measures, posset cups, salts, tea caddies, tea and coffee pots, candle holders, and tureens are ideal items. Rare items like wine funnels and pumps, brandy warmers, barber's basins, chamber pots, and other medical items may be in short supply, but are also in short demand. Some enthusiasts like to collect church pewter, such as the beakers, salvers, and flagons used for communion, but these are rare since most churches have disposed of theirs by now.

Pewter should be more decorative than functional, so it is those pieces with beauty of design and great handcraftsmanship which command the highest interest and prices. Proportions and workmanship are vital, but the most important feature is identification with a maker. Some experts feel that Americans pursue this too much as a prerequisite to collecting, and that the piece should stand on its own merit, regardless of maker. This is high idealism, and the collecting fraternity is not yet ready for it, so unless you have money to burn, do not get too involved with unmarked pewter.

Woodenware in kitchens gave way to pewter early in the eighteenth century, both in America and abroad, but a century later pewter suffered a decline in the face of competition from the expanding ceramics and glass industries. Its final ignominy came after the 1850's at the hands of the silver platers who used Britannia bodies for their wares, covering up the metal which was once so important to the well-being and economy of the world. Collectors who recognize the forms are having these pieces stripped of their blackened and fading silverplate, restoring them to greater interest and value. Much of the early Reed and Barton silverware made in Taunton, Massachusetts, during this period could be plated Britannia.

Chapter 6

Brass, Bronze, Copper, Iron, and Tin

Brass, bronze, copper, iron, and tin are base metals which have always been used for functional items and decorative objects. Less exotic than gold and silver, they do not command anywhere near the same prices. You must not get too excited about collecting objects made of these metals, as there is little made from them which is documented as to maker, and the danger of reproduction is always present.

Brass

Brass is an alloyed metal made of copper and zinc. The proportions of each in the mixture determine the hardness of the brass, copper being the softer metal. It has been known since ancient times, so there is a history of brass work with which to compare the more contemporary pieces. There are only a few items in brass collectible in America which have any monetary importance, such as weathervanes, signed fireplace equipment, some unusual candlesticks, firemarks, lighting devices, and some warming pans. It is not an impressive list when compared to the other decorative arts, and this is due to the lack of documentation on makers and the possibility of reproduction. A common collectible is candlesticks, but you can purchase seventeenth and eighteenth century pieces (mostly English or European made) for less than three figures. Lanterns, buckets, apple butter kettles, whale oil lights, most andirons, fenders, tools and screens for fireplaces, and other small decorative objects will most often fall beneath the three figure mark. A hundred dollars is not much to pay for a piece of antiquity, when you consider the astronomical

181

prices being paid for furniture, glass, pewter, silver, ceramics, and the like. A simple redware decorated dish can command up to a thousand dollars, but there are very few pieces of brass that can equal that, no matter how exotic they are.

Most of the eighteenth century brass you find will have originated in England. There was very little American manufacture which can be documented, and we know that very little was made because of the shortage of materials. Some good Continental brass has arrived, and more is being imported today than ever before. The Mediterranean countries are a good source of brass, as a lot is being discarded by housewives there who are turning to teflon and stainless steel for cooking. They are tired of polishing brass, and they are quite happy to relinquish this role to the American housewife, who will in time realize that it can be a chore. Dealers tell me that more brass is sold to men than to women—men will take it home as a gift, but will rarely participate in cleaning it. The abundance of the product along with the shortage of help to take care of it is a contributing factor to the lack of interest in brass as a collectible. You must survey your needs and your desire to clean it before buying.

The problem of reproduction is present, as there are workers today still turning out products which have an eighteenth and early nineteenth century look. Banging a piece up a bit, charring it over a fire, and allowing the iron handles and fittings to rust a little can create an aura of age that can fool the neophyte. You have only to visit a country like Holland to see the tremendous amount of this work going on. The once popular coal hods with Delft handles are now a drag on the market: the sale of the new has hurt the old.

There are several good makers of weathervanes and lighting devices whose works age rapidly in the out-of-doors. Some are antiqued with chemicals to give them a good aged look, and once they have been used for several years it is difficult to separate them from the truly old, especially if the pieces were cast in sand molds. The roughness can fool you, so you must know from whom you are buying before investing much money.

There is a lot of trinket collecting in brass. Snuff boxes, military buttons, telescopes and binoculars, sextants and octants, ship's clocks, cuspidors, horse related items (hames, stirrups, brass handled buggy whips), early belt buckles, cigar cutters, stencils, and drinking mugs are popular. Powder and shot holders from the Revolutionary War have value. Whale oil lamps are rarest of all, as most were made of glass, tin, or pewter. Those with interesting shape and proportion are most desired. Look for signed fireplace equipment, as some makers were diligent in this.

Brass beds, which really contain little brass, are of interest today. The bedsteads were made of steel and brass plated. The only pure brass might be in the decorative balls, finials, or other decorations. Brass alone is not structurally strong enough to support weight. You can use a magnet to check the sections: if the magnet clings to the metal, it is steel; if not, it is most likely pure brass.

Typical memorabilia which can be found at shows and flea markets, left to right: a lantern marked "Peter Gray, Maker, Boston"; a brass cuspidor used at the now-defunct Crescent Hotel in Waterville, Maine; a German cooking stove in brass and iron.

Bells come from every country in the world and are made in all materials, so collecting them is easy. However, you must really search to find exotic ones like these.

Brass whale oil lamp from New-buryport, Massachusetts, about 1830–1840. An unusually fine example, it has a delicate font, molded pillar, and dolphin handle. The base was spun and attached by soldering. This is the best type to be found in brass.

Men make the best customers for brass and copper items such as this samovar and cooking pot with burner—after all, it is their wives who end up cleaning them. Imports from the Mediterranean countries have lowered prices on many items made of brass and copper.

Iron stove plate with the imprint of Wilhelm Stiegel, 1758, Lancaster County, Pennsylvania and made at his Elizabeth Furnace.

Iron lawn dog of the type made late in the nineteenth century by Janes, Kirtland Company of New York City. Not many of these were made, and few have survived, but they are interesting.

Tin boxes with original paintings and stenciling are very good items. Their origin can be determined by the type of decoration used. Found in Maine, these are suggestive of the work done in the Westbrook area in the second quarter of the nineteenth century. The smallest is two and a half inches long.

Brass bells are popular, though most do not command much money. A special bell-metal was formed with the introduction of tin to the mixture, and most bells are made of this. Paul Revere is noted for his bells, and if you find one bearing his stamp of manufacture, you are indeed fortunate. However, ordinary school, dinner, and farm bells are relatively inexpensive. Sleigh bells of brass or bell metal are most in demand, but excellent strings are still in the less than three figure category. Some are chrome plated, so you should use a magnet to check the metal if you are not sure.

Much ecclesiastical brass was turned out in the shape of candlesticks, candelabra, votive light stands, sanctuary lights, crosses, and even entire altars. Some is sold surreptitiously on the open market, but much is sold legitimately. A transfer to a new church structure will often attract donations of new church artifacts, and the old may be sold to benefit the treasury. However, some pastors in Europe have recently been liquidating church brass to dealers in order to raise funds for operation. Over the years, many churches have received numerous donations of objects which have fallen into disuse or disrepair, and rather than continue storing them, will clandestinely dispose of them. Since a great disturbance was raised over this procedure several years ago, most of it has come to a halt.

Brass candlesticks are quite common, including those dating back to the eighteenth century. There are earlier ones from as much as two centuries before which have come to America in recent years. Most were made in England, though you will find Flemish design in some early pieces. The early ones may have a spike or pricket on which the candle could be imbedded for support. However, these went out of favor with the appearance of the socket modified by the pushup stem beneath, which allowed one to advance the candle upward to make full use of all of it and made for easier cleaning. The dripless candle was unknown in the early days, so all holders had a drip pan to catch the residue, which could then be recast into a new candle. The bases of candlesticks are no clue to their age—they will be found in square, round, oval, octagonal, and hexagonal shapes, and perhaps in many others as well. Some collectors have stated that a good candlestick would have been made in two sections with a screw assembly to tighten them together. This work was often done in the seventeenth century, and the holders would certainly show their age to confirm this. You must be careful not to confuse these with holders from the Orient which were made in great abundance in this manner in the last century and into the present one. You should accept this screw base as a sign of recent rather than old manufacture 99% of the time. When whale oil became popular about 1820, candleholders were pressed into service to hold oil lamps which featured a candle sized peg at their base so that they might be inserted into a candleholder. These are called "peg lamps" and may sometimes be found in brass, though glass was used most often.

Perhaps the most reproduced forms in brass are the chamber candleholders and candle chandeliers. The former are still being turned out all over the world, with many coming from the Orient. You must understand that 90% of the world's population is still lighted by candle or oil, and that these chamber holders are very much a part of present-day culture. The chandeliers are being made for historical societies and others who are restoring old homes to their original elegance. The early ones were mostly from England, so the reproductions have the same look and are quite well done. You would have to examine them closely to tell the difference. Candelabra were popular, though few early ones are found today. You will do just as well by locating contemporary reproductions of these as they are faithfully done and in good taste. I might note that at the Peterhof Palace of Elizabeth, Empress of Russia, near Leningrad, a hundred people were employed each evening just to light the candles, replace them, and put them out at dawn. The many candelabra and chandeliers necessitated this large work force.

Door knockers in brass are quite popular. They are reproduced in great quantities today, and as they age it becomes difficult to tell when they were made. Present-day sand casting leaves rough marks and impressions similar to those found on the old ones. Knockers gained popularity in England in the eighteenth century and were brought to America to become part of the popular culture. The eagle, lion, horse, and dog were popular motifs.

Rams, flowers, dolphins, and even clenched fists were also included.

Furniture knobs and other pulls were fashionable as early as the seventeenth century, and were designed in keeping with the styles of the day. Brass was most popular for these, though some may be found made of other metals. It was not until the Chippendale period that large backplates became popular, and these were made in what is called the wing style. The Federal period featured oval and often rectangular (with cut out corner) plates. Toward the end of the Federal period, pull knobs in brass or wood were fashionable, and these continued into the Victorian period. You cannot fault a chest or other piece of furniture for having new brasses, so long as they are sand cast and have the look of the old, but you must be sure they are in the same period with the piece.

Brass was used for inlaying furniture, with spectacular results. This art reached its pinnacle in France and Italy. Andre Boulle (1642–1732) worked under the patronage of Louis XIV, and succeeded in turning out work which is the epitome of this form. There was a revival of this work in the early nineteenth century, but none is known to have been done in America. Ormolu mounts of brass were popular at this time, and were used as decoration at corners, feet, and handles. This style was most popular in France and Italy, but some work was also done in England.

Brass locks and keys are popular, no matter what country they come from. The door locks are used in restorations, and the padlocks are used as decorative items. Locks for furniture did not become popular until the middle of the eighteenth century. Some of these locks are stamped with the names of makers, which will heighten interest, if not the value.

You will find skillets, shoehorns, tobacco boxes, sundials, snuffers, spirit measures, spoons, trivets, and weights and measures in brass. You must judge these on their interesting qualities and condition. Repairs to brass are quite visible, and they must be in good taste and not offensive. Warming pans sell reasonably, but are of interest. They are judged by their pleasing proportions, condition, and above all by the beautiful or unique pierced design in the cover. Almost all warming pans found in

America came from England, though some must be from other countries. There was little or no manufacture of these pans in America. Handles have often been replaced, so you must judge the condition of it at the time of buying.

Bronze

Since bronze is a close cousin to brass, I might note that there is tremendous interest in the decorative arts which use this metal. Notable are the bronze figures, most of which were done in France and even Russia. The signed bronzes are most popular and valuable. Subject interest is paramount, and those with animals in action are quite desirable. Those with a solitary figure standing are least desired. The bronzes which depict motion of man or beast are among the best. You must be sure of the metal before investing, as many famous renditions have been reproduced in various other alloys such as spelter, which is a cheap metal with a high zinc content, or even white metal, which is about the cheapest iron-based substitute you can find. White metal contains iron, tin, albata, electrum, argentine, and other metals of lesser nature. A class of bronzes done during the Renaissance in Italy is quite desirable, but it is unlikely that you will find any here. Also, these bronzes have been reproduced over the years, making attribution very difficult. Little or no serious bronze work was done in this country. The bronzes to which Tiffany attached its name were most often done in France or Russia.

Copper

Copper has a close kinship to brass. Being a soft metal, it is easily formed, has good color, and can withstand the heat of cooking and other abuse. About all that can be said for brass can be said for this metal. However, there are some exceptions. Horse ornaments, bells, door knockers, fireplace equipment, warming pans, and candleholders are scarce in copper. It was used a great deal in the making of cooking utensils, which were then tinned on the interior so food would not come in contact with the copper. Brass must have seemed more like gold, hence its greater popularity. Actually, copper could have been used to make just about anything in metal. There were specific uses for it, especially in weathervanes, copper and shot pouches, canteens, daggers, knives, and ale warmers. Less spectacularly, it was used as a sheathing for wooden vessels as early as the mid-eighteenth century. Along with brass and bronze, it was used as a base for cloisonne, champleve, and enameling.

Copper was not favored as it turns green with age and attrition, and therefore requires more care than brass or other metals. Food could not be cooked or stored in it, nor did it have the strength of other metals for use in heavy tools. It was used in coinage, and perhaps here one will find its greatest value.

Disc music player of the nineteenth century. There are table and floor models and some that operate only by inserting a coin, intended for use in public places.

Cherry pitter made by Goodell and Company, Antrim, New Hampshire during the nineteenth century, which still works well today.

Pole arms are rare in America and most of these are in museums and private collections, having been brought here years ago. (Schuller Museum of Arms and Armor, Laconia, New Hampshire)

Iron

Iron was the metal most readily available to the American colonists, as huge bogs were discovered right in New England. Bog iron was found in the area around Plymouth and throughout what is now called the greater Boston area. Saugus was the home of the first iron works (dating back to 1636) and the location has been fully restored to its original condition for all to visit. The original pounding hammer was found beneath many layers of earth, and has been re-installed to pound iron today. Bog iron is found in marshes or even at the bottom of lakes and ponds. The Saugus marshes and locations in Braintree and Needham yielded much iron. The ponds in Gilmanton, New Hampshire, were rich in a pure ore. Salisbury, New York, was the site of early ironmaking, as were many locations in Pennsylvania. Ore was mined in those states, and right after the Revolution, coal was used to melt it. The Pennsylvania Historical and Museum Commission has restored some ironmaking locations including those at Hopewell Village, near Reading, and the Cornwall Furnace, near Hershey.

Since iron was readily available, it was used for just about everything where a strong metal was needed. Kitchen pots, pans, and utensils, carpentry and husbandry tools, weapons, horse equipment, lighting devices, door locks, hardware of all kinds, and nails and spikes were all products of pre-1800 manufacture. After the turn of the century, machines came into their own and coal became readily available to all who wanted it. This resulted in a tremendous expansion of America's iron and steelmaking facilities. The center of the business shifted toward the Pittsburgh area as both iron and coal were available there in great quantity. Birmingham, Alabama, became a center for steelmaking, and supplied the South during the Civil War. I would need several volumes to discuss everything that was made in iron and steel since then—much of it right through the art deco period which is being collected today. The items mentioned above are collectible from the eighteenth century on.

IRON BANKS

The nineteenth century brought with it a changing technology, and after the Civil War the inventive genius of America was turned loose. This was a period when factories turned from war production to making goods for consumers, so all sorts of gadgets and tools made their appearance. Many are quite interesting and form the basis for numerous collections today. Notable in this respect are the iron banks, both mechanical and still, which have risen very high in value. Some have reached the five figure price range, which far exceeds anything made of metals other than silver, pewter, or gold. You must learn what is most desirable for you. Those banks which are mechanical and scarce are hot items. All have been cataloged, and the collectors are always on the lookout for some with which to round out their collections. You should stay abreast of the activity at auctions and shows to inform yourself of values, since they change continually. Early in the 1930's, the *Book of Knowledge* brought out a series of reproductions of mechanical banks and so labeled them on the bottoms. Though they are not original, these have assumed a good collecting value today. Reproductions are made in Japan at this

Advertising tin is very collectible, since there are many varied items from each generation. Color and condition are most important.

A tin bathtub which predated the built-in model. They are often stenciled and used as room planters today.

Nineteenth century tin baking oven used in front of the fireplace. A rotisserie spit inside is turned by the handle on the right, and a bottom shelf holds pans for baking.

time, some being quite good and some easily told from the old, the paint jobs being the first clue as to age. It is difficult to duplicate the old worn paint. You should never repaint an old bank of any kind, as it will harm its value. Rust may be cleaned off of old banks, but they should not be repainted.

Still banks (those which perform no function other than to accept money in a slot) have assumed importance, since they were made in interesting shapes and some have approached the rare status. Many people are collecting new banks in iron, and as these are often made as special items in limited editions for banking institutions and others, they will have their own importance and increased value in time.

Many iron banks are being made by the John Wright Company of Pennsylvania, and are being done in exact reproduction of earlier banks. As long as a present-day bank is of iron, it can have some value in the future, but you should steer away from plastics, pottery, or other materials. Some of the old tin banks are quite important, and in recent years there have been several new versions which have been made and which have already acquired a good value. Condition is important in judging all banks.

Collecting armor of this type is next to impossible today, and reproductions are being made to satisfy the demand. (Schuller Museum of Arms and Armor)

Fire lighting pan with striker and flint from the late nineteenth century, found in Maine. The pan is tin and the striker is steel.

Appealing tin candle sconce, initialed "J.B." The floral cutout at the top makes it interesting.

Iron lighting devices have soared in value recently. Both floor and table models of old rush holders and candleholders are of importance. There is one glaring problem, however, and that is in determining the age of iron artifacts. I have seen excellent reproductions aged in a hurry via salt and manure piles—a year or two of this unorthodox treatment can fill iron with pits, rust, and lines which can fool experienced eyes. When someone tells me a piece of iron is old and that he knows it is merely by examination, I am quite suspect about his qualifications as an appraiser. I feel that too much money is being paid for "eighteenth century" iron, as I knew a blacksmith (now deceased) who could duplicate it in a year. Hang on to your money before investing great sums in old iron. You may be joining the ever growing club of losers. Buy only that iron which has documentation if you are spending a great sum.

Tin

Until recently, tin languished in the role of an inexpensive commodity as far as collecting was concerned. Even the Historical Society of Early American Decoration, Inc., founded in the memory of Esther Stevens Brazer, gave little impetus to collecting tin for a long time. Decorating tin is now a great and rewarding pastime, and more attention is being given to this poor man's metal than ever before. Decorators are looking for interesting shapes and forms on which to paint their designs, causing an upsurge in prices. You can see the patterns and research material accumulated by Esther Brazer at the Bump Tavern in Cooperstown, New York—part of the Farmer's Museum complex.

Early American decoration may be divided into the following classifications: stencilling on tin and wood, country painting, gold leaf painting, lace edge painting, freehand bronze, glass panels, and Chippendale painting. The Guild has established specific categories of craftsmanship for the execution of techniques found in each. Chapters of the Society are set up in all the New England states, with the exception of Rhode Island, and in New York, New Jersey, Maryland, Illinois, and Pennsylvania.

Tin is an important base for decoration as many country items were made from it. There were many noted early decorators such as the Butlers in upstate New York and Zachariah Stevens at what is now Westbrook, Maine. Their work, along with that of others, many unrecorded, has enabled students to classify the decorations as originating in specific regions. Tin items with existing old decoration have climbed quite high in value. Those pieces which are not decorated but are just old items used about the kitchen and home are climbing in value as artists compete with each other for unusual pieces to decorate. This is a very rewarding area of collecting. You can take classes in decorating techniques, either painting or stencilling, and make yourself a good income by buying, decorating, and selling old tin items.

Artists like Peter Ompir in Sheffield, Massachusetts, and Mona Rowell of Pepperell, Massachusetts, have already created a legion of fans who buy everything they can turn out in the way of decorated wares. Tin is very prominent in their work.

Chapter 7

Folk Art and Wall Decorations

It has only been in the last few years that there has been any great appreciation of what we term "folk art." Folk art encompasses what can be considered the work of relatively untrained hands—items created by people who saw a need for a product and simply made it, or perhaps even invented a tool or kitchen aid to do a particular job in the days when one could not go to the local discount store and buy one. Some items are functional and some are decorative, but collectors today look at them in light of the latter, as most have aged and acquired a patina that endears them to the aesthete. Folk art items were made in all materials, but mostly in those which were easily available around a farm or average home. Though some bear the style of pieces made by city craftsmen for the carriage trade, most do not incorporate the quality which is turned out in the hands of those trained and skilled in their endeavor.

Some people refer to folk art items as "primitives," and this is not necessarily an accurate description. There is a marked distinction between the work done by untrained hands and the work done by an uncivilized people. The term "primitive" could be more accurately applied to the workmanship done at the earliest stages of civilization when man first gathered crude tools and materials with which to work. This term should represent the beginnings of any art movement and the work done during this period. "Folk art" is a better definition of work done by a civilized people who were simply untrained in the particular field of creation or decoration in which they engaged. There are many natural artists who have a flair for quality—in form, proportion, workmanship, and beauty—and are able to express it with little or no training. These self-taught artists need not necessarily be lumped together with those whose early civilizations gave them

197

little preparation or incentive to do this work. The term "primitive" is used loosely to indicate some early work done in this country, and though it is not totally objectionable, neither is it totally accurate.

There is no area in America in which such work was not done, so you have the entire country in which to collect. The greatest concentration of items has been found in the New England and Pennsylvania areas, as both were quite prolific in industry, and both had substantial populations. The traditions of the British Isles are quite evident in the New England work, and those of the Germans, Dutch, and Swiss in Pennsylvania. The influence of the Dutch, and later the French, is felt in work from New York State.

Wood Carving

The greatest interest lies in wood, as this is a material which has always been plentiful, is easily worked, and can be carved or decorated in many ways. Many kitchen items such as dishes, bowls, butter molds, tableware, rolling pins, funnels, boxes and baskets, dough boxes, pails and buckets, sugar tubs, dippers, spatulas, washboards, and dish strainers were turned out in abundance.

For the farm chores, the man of the house would turn his talents to the production of milk pails, churns, stools, watering troughs, fruit baskets, apple driers, herb driers, winnowing sieves, eel traps, bean flailers, kegs for rum and cider, water kegs, feed pails for horses, etc. The well-equipped home would also need a large (spinning) and small (flax) wheel on which to turn out the needed fibres for clothing. The more fortunate lady would have a full-sized loom to make cloth, but others were content with lap looms. Some carvers turned out swizzle sticks used to stir the drink, which is a mixture of ale and beer. Along the coast, you will find decoys carved to assist in the hunt. Wooden weathervane figures are common wherever metal was at a premium. Small boxes of all kinds are quite popular, and those with carving or painted decoration are most desirable, as they reflect the industry of the man with his knife or other carving tools, and the lady

Native art from various sections of Africa is in great demand. Good carvings such as these (done in wood, soapstone, and other materials) show the work of untrained artists who had good ideas and innate ability.

A hand blueberry picker is shown on the left, next to a basket holder which was strung round the worker's neck to make it possible for him to pick with both hands. Found in Maine, these artifacts are typical of many one--of-a-kind items made by American craftsmen for use by their families.

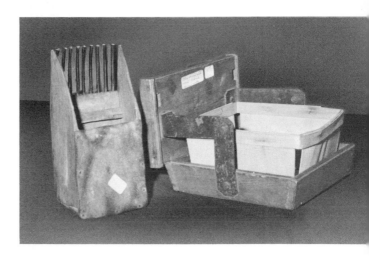

An unusual footed basket made by the Shakers at a colony in New Hampshire. The tapered handles woven into the basket are a sign of their work.

carefully adding the flowers, leaves, and pictorial decoration to the effort with her brush and quill.

Some of the greatest work in carving was done for sailing vessels. Huge figureheads fastened to the prow were a must on every ship, and these were often rather exotic ladies as well as important historical figures of the times. Since it is our national symbol, eagle carving was practiced just about everywhere, and those who did this work are well recorded. Charles Bellamy, a native of Kittery, Maine, maintained studios both there and in nearby Portsmouth, New Hampshire. His doorway eagles are very much desired today, although his work ranged all the way to the huge twelve foot bird carved to be put on a vessel made at the Portsmouth Navy Yard. The ship is long gone, but the eagle survives at the marine museum at Newport News, Virginia. Bellamy's work is well recorded, and the greatest collection of it is probably at the Shelburne Museum in Shelburne, Vermont.

Another noted carver was Wilhelm Schimmel, whose rather primitive eagles are in great demand in his native Pennsylvania as well as elsewhere. Schimmel was what is often described as an "itinerant" artist, who often did his work in return for meals and lodging. His eagles have quite a rare quality in their bold cutting, and you will almost know one instantly once you have seen some others with which to compare your example.

Carved wooden work must be in good condition. Age takes its toll, and those pieces which have not survived well may have little or no value. Old wood which has been repainted has been hurt as far as the collectors are concerned. It is better to leave the faded decoration than to try to renew it. Evidence of new saw or chisel marks make a buyer suspicious. Above all, the piece must be interesting and reflect an attempt for quality on the part of the maker. Those pieces which are signed, and they are infrequent, can have greater value, if you can document the maker as to the time and place where he worked. Assembling information about one maker can enhance the value of all his work, so long as it is of good quality.

In recent years, a large amount of wood carving which falls into the folk art category has been imported, especially from Europe and Africa. These items are finding favor here, as their American

Well-carved butter prints, which are numerous and varied. These are from the Folk Art Museum, Witmer, Pennsylvania.

Rare wooden charcoal warmer with holes drilled in it to allow heat to escape. This one has a tin lining to hold the coals, but most were made completely of tin with wooden framing only.

A collection of food choppers, wooden bowls, and other kitchen artifacts which were gathered and photographed by Mary Earle Gould many years ago. Miss Gould authored several books on early antiques.

counterparts have risen greatly in price, and in some cases can rarely be located for sale.

Scrimshaw and Sgraffito

Another form of carving is done on bone or ivory. If the work is done on materials which come from sea creatures, it is called scrimshaw—if the materials are from land animals, it is usually referred to as engraving or sgraffito work.

Powder horns, knife handles, and sword scabbards and handles were extensively decorated in this manner. Using a pointed tool, the workman incised the lines in the decoration he wanted, then rubbed ink, powder, or other colorings into the crevices, making them stand out in relief against the white substance of the bone or ivory. Actually, bone and ivory work seems to predate the work done on marine materials, as horn carving was popular during the eighteenth century. Items of Revolutionary War vintage are especially good, and work on war-related items continued well through the Civil War. Many soldiers filled their idle time by making gifts for family and friends, as well as by decorating their own possessions.

The term "scrimshaw" is believed to have originated from the Dutch word, *Scrimshander* which is a reference to a lazy fellow. In reality, the men who did this work must have been talented and it is believed that they actually competed with each other to turn out the best works of art. Such objects may not necessarily have been made only aboard ship. Most of the work we collect today was probably made during the first three quarters of the nineteenth century, after the American merchant marine enlarged to take care of our world trade. Listed as materials are teeth from sperm whales, whalebone only or lower jaw of the sperm whale, baleen (the tough straining fibre masses in the mouth of the sperm whale), woods available on ships from all over the world, as well as mother of pearl, abalone shell, and coconut shell. Whales' teeth might be found as large as eight inches long, hollow, and about two inches wide at the base, tapering to the point.

The work was begun by scraping the teeth or bone with a knife or sandpaper, then scratch carving it with a steel needle. A whaling ship held up to thirty men, and would quite often remain at sea for two years. One can only guess at the amount of scrimshaw that returned with them. When ships are portrayed, you should notice how the flag is flying, as it should be in the direction of the wind, and the men on board should also be portrayed in some activity. If a picture is done, it should have a frame around it. English scrimshaw may be judged by the length of the teeth—they are often up to ten and one-half inches long. The English flag can also be noted, and they carved more strongly than the Americans. Scenes from *Godey's Ladies' Book* were often reproduced. If possible, you should collect teeth in pairs, and they should point in opposite directions, being matched from opposite sides of the jaw. Some teeth may feature pictures in frames in daguerrotype fashion, others may be inlaid or painted. Patriotic teeth and those which commemorate the death of famous people like Presidents, with angels, tombstones, and the like are important. One tooth pictures a barber giving a haircut to William Henry Harrison—on the other side, it reveals that it was cut too short, and that the President caught cold and died. Other collectible teeth are those with harbor scenes of ships or even the sailor's home in the background. Memorial or mourning teeth might feature a lady leaning on a tombstone with space left for the name of the sailor when he passed on. Others feature women and children weeping. Teeth which are carved in relief such as one found showing a man kissing a girl's foot are important. You may also find architectural scenes of buildings done from prints.

There is also a long list of items which were made from these materials and then decorated, such as small carved boxes, sewing baskets and implements, jagging wheels, crimpers, bodkins, sewing needles, candleholders, swifts, dolls and beds, rolling pins, chess figures, chess boards, napkin rings, canes, shoe horns, door knobs, magazine racks, dippers, water kegs, billy clubs, bird cages, and even rope bed tighteners.

Since there is an embargo on killing whales, it is only natural that even the reproductions of this work being done today will eventually rise in value. However, you will notice that most new work lacks the dexterity in penmanship as well as the determination, follow through, and bold strokes which characterize the old.

Very rare and valuable is the "Susan's tooth," which features a picture of the ship *Susan,* and was done by one man who lived in Nantucket. It is early work (about 1820–1830) and only about a dozen have been found. You might look for the signed work of William Parry of New Bedford, who was active in the 1930's, as this is perhaps the best of the contemporary work.

Indian and Eskimo Artifacts

Indian artifacts have soared in price, and most of them are not really very old. New England is not a good place in which to collect these, as few have survived. Most Indians left this area by the time of the Revolutionary War, so New Englanders must content themselves with broken sherds of pottery, glass, arrowheads, and some metal items which have been located in burial grounds. None of the Indian cloth, baskets, decorated bone, or ivory has survived in this area. Pennsylvanians have been able to come up with some later objects, but it is in the far West that most collecting can be done. The best collection in the East is at the Hershey Museum in Hershey, Pennsylvania, and you can learn much from this about what there is to collect and what to look for. The far West has many museums devoted to early Indian culture, and if you travel there you will be in the heart of the good learning and collecting area.

When the Indians migrated from the East to escape the oncoming whites, they took everything with them, often even the bones of their ancestors, who were dug up, bagged, and reburied at their new homesite. Although some old items are found throughout the country, the newer pieces are commanding much more attention, especially those which were made in this century.

The Eskimos make up a part of the native population of Alaska, and their work is assuming new importance, even that which is very contemporary. The Canadians have assembled the best collections of Eskimo art and have sent exhibitions of it

Innuit (Eskimo) owls carved in green stone, 1957. These were made on Cape Dorset, a peninsula above Hudson's Bay—an area where art instruction is highly unlikely.

throughout this country and Europe. Eskimo carvers are known to have strong skilled hands. They work with ivory, bone, and stone, creating vibrant human and animal forms which radiate a strong sense of life. It is believed that the Eskimos originally carved for religious reasons or for tribal chiefs who often gave gifts to other leaders. The changes in their lifestyle are noticeable in the work they do today. Although there are many regions of the Canadian and Alaskan arctic where life is similar to what it has been for centuries, there are other areas where civilization has brought with it a different approach to artistic endeavors. There are the purists who say the twentieth century Eskimo carver has gone commercial, changing from ethnological inspiration to the inspiration of the dollar. The Eskimos have even created cooperatives to market their work through a central agency, which does smack of commercialism, but you must remember that life near the North Pole is difficult and dollars hard to come by. If we are to condemn them for commercialism, we might as well condemn Toulouse-Lautrec, Wilhelm Schimmel, or John James Audubon, whose work often went for groceries and spirits to replenish their souls.

Eskimo work is referred to as "Innuit," which means "the people." The carvers attempted to portray their immediate lifestyle and that of people about them, often working with a soft stone which is found in abundance in the Arctic. They created works around the shapes of the chunks as they were broken from the ground. The forms of nature helped inspire much of their output. If you wish to collect Innuit, go to Lapland, Iceland, Greenland, or Alaska. Other than that, make the acquaintance of a serviceman who might someday be stationed at the Dew line or

Sculpture Inuit, an Eskimo carving from Povungnituk on the eastern shore of Hudson's Bay, Canada. Executed in grey stone, bone, and skin by Joe Talirunili in 1964. (Canadian Eskimo Arts Council)

some other remote hardship duty post. Give him your shopping list and the amounts that you wish to pay. The contemporary work is a very good collectable at its present prices—do not hesitate to buy a lot since it can only rise in value.

Contemporary folk art from the U.S.S.R., painted by Taisa Voronetskaya of Leningrad, which has been shown in many exhibitions of work from that country. (USSR Ministry of Culture)

Russian Native Carving

If you like carvings and know someone going to Russia, ask them to obtain some of the artistic soft stone and bone carvings which come from the Ural Mountain area. The first record of stone work being done is in the eighteenth century, when the deposits were discovered on the mountain banks of the Irgina and

Sylva rivers. The stone is found in many colors and is excellent for artistic carving. Peasants of the Perm Region began to make Easter eggs of white gypsum and selenite, picture frames, flower petal shaped ash trays, and even platters. They imitated the forms of porcelain articles and wood carvings. When the decorative arts declined in Russia in the late nineteenth and early twentieth centuries this work all but halted. However, there was a revival in this art form in the 1930's, and today the Russian government encourages this carving as it brings in hard currency from other nations and is a highly desired Russian export. The animals carved in the soft stone are beautifully done and on a par with the best you can find anywhere.

Bone carving in Russia has a more ancient history, as it dates back to the tenth century. Bone carvers of the Moscow Palata were quite famous in the seventeenth century. In the eighteenth and nineteenth centuries, the Kholmogory craftsmen in Archangel province began turning out intricate pieces, such as bone caskets and little cases and boxes, and doing much fretwork and adornment with carvings of men, flowers, and animals. The pieces were often colored to heighten their beauty. In the second half of the nineteenth century, craftsmen from Tobolsk turned out miniature mammoth bone sculptures, drawing on animals and birds for their inspiration. Some of these were brought to this country by immigrants, and some are being shipped here today by dealers who are picking them up all over Europe and Asia. These little-known collectibles are sleepers in American collecting today.

Weathervanes

Early weathervanes are often classified in the folk art category. Not many wooden ones have survived, but those in tin, copper, and brass represent ingenuity on the part of the makers. You may find them utilizing the figure of a horse, man, fish, driver and sulky, locomotive, feather, building, bird, deer, other animal, or just about anything which could have excited the maker's imagination. It would be difficult to grade the designs as to quality, since the figure alone is not sufficient for judgment. The size, condition, and material from which the weathervanes are made is important, as well as their age. Those with bullet holes are not as desirable as those in pristine condition. Some are dimensional, with filled out bodies rather than just sheets of material, and these are more desirable. One of the most impressive of these is a huge ram which once graced the Amoskeag Mills in Manchester, New Hampshire, and is now displayed at the Currier Gallery of Art in that city.

Horse-drawn fire engine weathervane made by Cushman and White, Waltham, Massachusetts. (Henry Ford Museum Collection)

Rare horse, sulky, and driver weathervane figure found in New England. This one is from the nineteenth century and is molded in dimension. (Abby Aldrich Rockefeller Collection, Colonial Williamsburg)

When old weathervanes are taken down, they are often injured since the iron rod on which most are mounted is cut. The rod usually comes down through the ceiling of the cupola and is imbedded in the floor to give the weathervane strength and stability. Rather than disturb the roof, removers will often cut the rod just above it and this does not help in its resale.

The weathervane was the farmer's trusted friend in predicting the weather. A South wind in the Summer meant fair; if the wind shifted to the East, it brought rain. West winds meant fair all the year around. If the wind blew cold from the North when a storm cleared, it meant that the storm had backed up and would come again. A northeast wind brought a storm which usually lasted three days, and a southeast wind brought one of lesser duration.

If I were to calculate the rarest of the vanes, I would list these—sulky and driver, fire engine, locomotive, centaur, and oddities like the minister in a long coat riding a high wheel bicycle. Geese are rare, roosters are common. Plows were popular, along with horses, dogs, sheep, and cows. Some vanes were even gilded for fancy homes. Fine reproductions are being made today, and these are quite acceptable for use on an old building. The price of the old weathervanes has risen so much that perhaps a new one is a much wiser investment at this time. After all, most people cannot tell old from new when they have the item in their hands—if it is perched on your roof, forty or fifty feet away, perhaps they will never know.

Rare locomotive tin weathervane figure from New England, molded in some dimension. Many weathervane figures are cut flat. (Abby Aldrich Rockefeller Collection, Colonial Williamsburg)

Paintings

EARLY AMERICAN

"Primitive" paintings, birth, death, wedding and mourning certificates are often referred to as folk art. Again, those which were done by a relatively unprofessional artist may well fall into this category—one which is perhaps used more as a means of communication regarding important events. Paintings or wall decorations of this type are nothing more than a pigment of some kind applied to a surface which may be cloth, wood, ceramic, glass, or just about anything which suits the artist's fancy. Until recently, all paintings featured a subject of some sort—a face, figure, building, landscape, animals, or other central theme. Even those of a primitive nature had a theme which is recognizable to us today. The Pennsylvania German *fractur* is an excellent exercise in calligraphy, and early examples are quite important and valuable today. Practically every family had a member who was responsible for making up the certificates which documented important events, like birth and death, and most were done in colorful fashion with floral or other decoration adding a touch of beauty. Other sections of America had their artists working in this fashion as well, but the *fracturs* are more plentiful and might be easier to find.

After the mechanical printing presses took over (about 1830–40) hand work began to disappear, and the printed certificate took its place—gone was this native bit of talent which is so highly prized now. Good collections may be seen at the Ephrata Cloister, the Farm Museum at Landis Valley near Lancaster, and at the William Penn Memorial Museum in Harrisburg.

The eighteenth and nineteenth centuries brought with them many itinerant artists who decorated walls and furniture as well as painting portraits of members of a family. It has been said that some artists would prepare bodies on canvas during the winter months and that during the good weather they would travel to homes, attaching heads to the bodies, since this speeded up the work. Eric de Jonge, chief curator at the William Penn Museum, questions this, citing that no unfinished body pictures have ever turned up to confirm this tale. He feels that no woman, especially, would want to be painted in any finery other than her own.

In family portraits, it was not uncommon for a new baby to be added to an old picture as the artist made his rounds from year to year. Many old portraits such as these are unsigned, but there is new interest in them. Their value is measured by the ability of the artist, the interest he conveys, and the condition of the work. Years ago many such pictures were thrown away and the frames were adapted for other use. This practice has driven the price up on the remaining pictures. Of special interest are groups of people engaged in some activity, such as a battle, party, band concert, or some other facet of life, whether peaceful or brutal. Some pictures are painted on materials as common as a mattress cover, but do not worry about this as it may enhance the value.

Early painting by J.O.J. Frost, with the title written in: "The First Road from Marblehead to Salem." It is typical of work by untrained artists, but is still valuable as an example of early art. (Sotheby-Parke Bernet, New York)

Mourning pictures are in great demand, even though they are morbid in content. They represent a native folk art form, and many were done by hand.

Folk art on the panels of a chimney breast over the fireplace in an eighteenth century home in New Hampshire. Layers of paint were removed to reveal the work, which had been preserved in good condition.

WHITE MOUNTAIN AND HUDSON RIVER SCHOOLS

The eighteenth century produced little or no American landscape work. The settlers were surrounded by the beauty of the outdoors, and did not need to capture it to bring into their homes. Without photography, portrait painting flourished as a means of preserving the images of family and friends. Early in the nineteenth century, America's cities grew, making the great outdoors more remote, and a great desire for landscape work flourished. The industrial age brought with it teeming cities, tenements, and pollution from smokestacks, and even the factory worker attempted to bring some of the outdoors into his home via a painting or even a print. Men like Thomas Cole and Alvin Fisher went to the top of Mount Washington to paint as early as 1825—beginning what is now referred to as the White Mountain

William Harnett was the leader of the *trompe l'oeil* school of painters who created the illusion of reality in still lifes. His "Still Life with Three Castles Tobacco No. 2" is pictured. (Sotheby-Parke Bernet, New York)

Mid-nineteenth century Hudson River landscape, unsigned, has the important attributes required of a painting of the period: good workmanship, people, animals, steam vessel, sailing vessels, horses, and house with a barn. It is valuable because of its quality, even though it is unsigned.

Unsigned mid-nineteenth century Hudson River landscape. People, animals, and sailing vessels add to its value.

"Mountain of the Holy Cross, Colorado," painted by Thomas Moran, has been copied and reproduced at great length. Moran was a favored landscape painter who worked in both the East and the West.

Portrait by John Singer Sargent, noted nineteenth century Boston artist. Framing the children with lilies gave the scene a complete look of innocence and wonder. (Sotheby-Parke Bernet, New York)

School of painters. Their New Hampshire landscapes created a great impression, and soon artists were seeking out places of beauty to capture on canvas. The Hudson River area gave birth to a school of painters who did fine landscape work, and it was not long before many painters headed West to capture the mountains and scenery there. These were schools of realism in that the artist attempted to faithfully portray a scene with no attempt to alter it. This is a photo-technique that has gradually been challenged by succeeding generations. Such men worked well into this century, and are well-documented in the books listed in the bibliography. A good rule to use is that if an artist does not appear in the books, he has not arrived as far as collecting is concerned. These two schools of painters are highly desired today, and prices are rising on their work every year. You would do well to invest in works by known American artists of this period who are recorded, as they represent perhaps the finest investment in antiquity today.

Investment in European paintings by unknown artists is hazardous, as years ago (as well as today) paintings were turned out almost on a mass production basis. If the artists are not regarded highly enough to receive acclaim in their native countries, they do not represent a good investment. Many travelers buy such oils on trips, hoping they have uncovered an artist who someday may be famous. You should buy these unknown Europeans for enjoyment alone, and invest in the American paintings for enjoyment as well as future reward.

BARBIZON SCHOOL

When landscapes came into fashion early in the nineteenth century, a group of artists began painting scenes in places like the Black Forest near Dusseldorf in Germany. The French picked this up in their forests at Fontainebleau, and both efforts resulted in what is termed the Barbizon School of painting. It is characterized by dark foregrounds, lighter backgrounds, and a central theme which draws one's eye, giving a great effect of three dimensions. This school served as an inspiration to many American painters who came to Europe to study. Corot, Daubigny, Millet, and Rousseau are among those who painted during this period.

IMPRESSIONISM

Impressionism followed the Barbizon School, and was pioneered by men like Monet, Renoir, and Cezanne. These artists created their atmospheric impressions of nature by breaking up the lines of light and substance to give a rather dreamy quality to their work. Impressionism was not readily accepted either in Europe or in America, and it was not until the Art Institute of Chicago hung some Impressionist works in the 1890's that any measure of appreciation was shown. At the time, the Institute was the target of many critics who felt the work was quite inferior, and today it still tries to protect its reputation for being first in the exhibition of new works in order to live up to its late nineteenth century success. Impressionism is quite popular today, with the work of some artists selling in the millions.

CUBISM

Picasso revolted against Impressionism with a form generally referred to as Cubism. This is a technique of breaking down and taking apart forms of nature. It has a geometric quality which reshapes known forms to the ideas of the artists, and is not bound by any rules of conformity to accepted forms. There have been few successful practitioners of Cubism, with Picasso remaining as the leader and the best known. Though other styles have succeeded it, some work in Cubism is still being done.

THE ASHCAN SCHOOL AND SURREALISM

The twenties brought with them the Ashcan School, which was nothing more than a realistic portrayal of life in the city. The street or alley scene usually contained the inevitable waste receptacle which gave this school its name. Much of this is good art, and the supply is quite limited. Though it was not appreciated very much at the time, values on this school have risen a great deal today.

A new idea was also brewing, at the same time: Surrealism, or super realty. Its goal is to liberate man's unconscious personality from the chains of reason and inhibition, and its best known exponent is Salvador Dali. Surrealism could well be called a partner to Abstractionism, and utilizes shapes, forms, and colors which have no counterparts in nature. Though this school has its investors and afficionados, it has not yet taken the country by storm, and only time will tell if it can repeat the successes of early styles which had to wait years before being appreciated. Dali is a wealthy man, but money alone does not determine the quality or longevity of a style.

EXPRESSIONISM

One type of painting may appear in any period. Expressionism is a revelation of the personal emotions of an artist, and may be traced throughout his lifetime. El Greco, the noted Greek who made his fame and fortune in Spain, was a very religious man. All of his figures, whether human, imaginary, or natural, are elongated toward heaven as if in search of a Divinity. El Greco's work is easily identified because of this personal expression. Van Gogh's work clearly reflects his tormented passion as he painted before, through, and after his period of madness. When you can see a complete showing of his work such as the one some years ago at the Guggenheim Museum in New York, you can trace his emotions quite easily as you view the successive canvases.

MODERN ART

Unfortunately, there has been little painting of great renown which has been done since the Depression. The period spawned a group of artists who lived mostly in major cities, some living on funds from the WPA, which granted them survival and freedom to work, but much of what they turned out was revolutionary with a Bolshevik tint. Communism was being preached everywhere as the solution to America's economic problems, and artists naturally reflected this. Some Depression art is being collected today and touted as great art, but in my opinion, you should be very careful before you invest in it.

The period which followed World War II brought with it perhaps the greatest era of mediocrity in the history of art. We have been subjected to rather amateur work in most of the arts:

painting, sculpting, ceramics, and even music. There are those who have found a formula for becoming rich by thrusting upon the public the most devious and garish work in an attempt to be so different that they stand apart from everything else. These practitioners have succeeded in luring supporters to their work, whether it is good, bad, or indifferent. The most tragic consequence has been that museums and galleries are lending their space to exhibit this work regardless of quality. Some analyze this as the "Art Institute syndrome," in that the museums do not want to be left behind again as they were in the exhibition of Impressionism, and therefore will exhibit just about anything today. It is a situation which will reverse itself in time, since new young artists are coming along who will have nothing to do with such mediocrity. A new school of realism is already at work throughout the country, and the small exhibitions at crafts festivals and fairs reflect this.

On examination, you must concede that to achieve the workmanship necessary to the Realist, Barbizon, and Impressionist schools, one must be an accomplished painter, since these are the most challenging and difficult styles to do well. Those who indulge in the action school (which is nothing more than what appears to be paint thrown at a canvas) and those who paint in geometric forms are just exhibiting to us their inability to really do anything with a brush and canvas. Those who attempt to interpret a mess of gobbleygook as projecting a message are being rather demagogic in relation to good art. Creating good art makes demands on the ability, time, and patience of the artist. Those works which can be splashed out in five or ten minutes in kindergarten fashion certainly do not meet this test. All the explaining in the world cannot compensate for this, any more than all the talking in the world can improve the quality of a piece of furniture ground out by machine in Grand Rapids, Michigan in the 1920's. When you invest in modern art, you must judge the work on its quality—good taste, good design, and good workmanship. The minute you stray away from this, you are gambling. Those who gambled on Picasso years ago have made out quite well, but he is an exception—how well can you pick the exceptions today?

At a talk with college students, the noted cartoonist Al Capp was asked, "I look at a Picasso painting and I think it is garbage. How can I learn to appreciate art?" Capp replied, "You understand it well, it is garbage." Which prompted a further question, "Who determines that a Picasso painting is worth five hundred thousand dollars?" Capp's answer was, "The dealer who just paid one hundred thousand for it." This proves that the price of art is relative to those who appreciate it, and also depends on who owns it. In the hands of a well-known person, some oils are valuable, but if you own them, you may have long trying days to dispose of them at any price.

MARINE PAINTINGS

Marine paintings are what the name implies—scenes of ships at sail, in a harbor, or docked. America had many fine marine artists dating from the eighteenth century all the way into the twentieth. Those done by accomplished artists will have value as is the case with most art. Condition is important and the scene portrayed has

Fitz Hugh Lane (1804–1865) was one of the greatest marine painters. This scene of Boston harbor shows the exquisite attention to detail which marks his work. (Museum of Fine Arts, Boston)

a bearing on the value. The better artists are listed in the books cited in the bibliography, and those of the earlier period usually command better prices. Scenes of ships should include men in action on board, and the introduction of whales, sea gulls, or other marine life is important. Flags should fly, preferably American. Size is quite important, since most collectors like large marine paintings because of their panoramic quality.

There are many English and French marine paintings which turn up in this country, and these are quite well done. Again, those by famous artists are of importance in America. The next most important school of marine painters flourished in Chinese ports during the last century. Artists would often paint the sailing vessels which dropped anchor and sell the finished products to the captains. Some of these were probably exported to America as part of the active America-China trade. The background of an Oriental city with an American ship in the foreground makes for quite an interesting painting, and you are well rewarded in collecting them.

HISTORY AND CARE OF OIL PAINTINGS

Let us trace briefly the history of oil paintings and their care today. Western painting was influenced by the Greeks and Romans. They used tempera, a simple recipe containing either a whole egg or just the yolk mixed with gelatin made from parchment skin. The first mention of oil colors appears in thirteenth century German manuscripts, but these were not very good, as a proper solvent had not been developed. Alchemy soon brought forth turpentine, and varnish was created from resin boiled in linseed, poppy, or walnut oil. Painting was done on wood or parchment, and gold leaf would often be applied by a jeweler. Early painting was featured on horse ornaments and carriages. Portrait painting soon became quite popular, followed by landscapes.

Conservators and scholars can tell much about a painting by thorough examination. Photographs, x-ray, infra-red, and ultra-violet lights are employed to check layers of painting, signatures, ground color, and canvas to determine age and authenticity. They can discover repairs, addition of new paint, loss of old paint, and even sketches beneath the paint from which the artist worked. Total examination involves measurements, as no picture is supposed to be reproduced in the exact measurements of the original, and most of these are well catalogued. The expert can judge the age of the canvas, frame, ground layer, and picture layer of paint, along with the surface coating used for protection. He can tell old oil since it becomes translucent with age. You must be familiar with an artist in order to compare a picture with his known works. You should be versed in the language and literature of the country of origin, as a great deal is related by the time span and subject matter of a painting.

Paintings deteriorate slowly; they are usually brittle and fragile. It is best not to touch a damaged area with your fingers, apply a self-adhesive tape to a tear, or try to protect the surface with a blanket or wrinkled papers which can exert pressure on the painting surface. Dust is detrimental to canvas, and the reverse of a painting should be protected with a stiff board or paper which is *not* in contact with the surface itself. Paintings suffer from extremes of dryness and humidity, and a uniform 45% relative humidity is best. Paintings should not be hung in sunlight or over radiators or fireplaces.

Above all, do not attempt to clean paintings at home. Old remedies such as rubbing bread or a sliced onion over the surface to clean them are taboo. Do not use a detergent or any soap in attempting to clean a canvas. Special solutions are employed by conservators, and these range in varying strengths and solubil- ities. Each solution must be tested on the painting before use to make sure it will not lift the original paint with the dirt. The canvas is cleaned bit by bit with a small cotton swab (often as small as a Q-tip) in order to carefully make sure there is no change in pigment strength or vulnerability to the solution being used. This is an art to be practiced by the professionals, so leave the cleaning to them. At home, an occasional light dusting or gentle wiping with clear water on a damp rag is permissible once a painting has been restored properly and a protective varnish coating applied.

You must also realize that the professional has the proper materials if any repairs to tears in the canvas are required. The paint formulas used by the original artist have been catalogued so that the expert can match them exactly for touchups and restorations. This is important if the work is to be done properly. If the painting is worth saving, have a professional save it for you.

Engraving

The first plates from which prints were made were wood engravings, which produce what are now called wood-block prints. This work had been done in Europe for many years, but the first recorded American artist in this medium was John Foster of Boston, who did a likeness of the Reverend Richard Mather.

"The Horse Shoc Fall, Niagara With the Tower" is a fine early print engraved by R. Brandard from the mid-nineteenth century painting by W. H. Bartlett. Since it shows a tower which is no longer there, this print explains the interest in prints and paintings which preserve scenes long since gone.

Where the artist wants a white space he carves out the wood, leaving the remaining surface to receive the ink. Printing is done by rolling the paper over the inked block. This crude work has great appeal, as well as being an early form of the art of reproducing likenesses. Many newspapers and periodicals relied on woodcuts for printing pictures right into the nineteenth century.

Line engravings were made in eighteenth century America by cutting or incising a design or picture on a soft copper plate by means of a sharp tool. Paul Revere made many of these, including his famous "Boston Massacre." This cutting is known as "intaglio" work, in that the lines are cut into the plate. Some plates were done in "relief," where the engraving is left raised above the plate. Printing is done by putting ink into the cut lines, wiping the plate clean, and then rolling damp paper against the surface on a press and forcing it into the lines where it picks up the ink. The work was later done on steel plates, as copper was quite soft and could not make as many impressions as the harder metal. This technique was developed about 1820, so steel engravings may all be dated after that time.

Early English prints which feature horses and wagons or coaching scenes give an accurate account of life in the early days. Dated 1825, this one has the quaint touch of a dog riding as passenger, with his eyes registering alarm at the rapid speed.

Stipple engraving is done by impressing a design in dots rather than lines. An artist coats a plate with wax, and then stipples through it to the metal beneath. Acid which does not penetrate the wax is then spread over the plate, eating out holes in the metal at the points where the stippling was done. After the wax has been removed, the design is printed from the acid etched plate.

Mezzotints were first made in the early part of the seventeenth century. A copper plate is roughened by crisscrossing it with lines, using a sharp tool. This roughness is smoothed out and shaded in areas to create the picture in reverse. After being inked, these plates are used for printing, and several colors can be employed at one time. Shading to give better dimension to the work is possible with this technique. The English and French did excellent eighteenth century mezzotint work which is very collectible today.

Etching is done in much the same manner as line engravings in relief, in that acid is used to score unprotected areas on the plate's surface. It was refined so that an artist might repeat the acid baths in certain areas to effect shading. In dry-point etching, no acid is used, and a pointed tool is employed to do the entire job, requiring the hand of a master.

Aquatint was developed at the end of the eighteenth century. It is a refined form of etching in which masses are printed more easily. A finely powdered resin is spread over the plate and solidified by heat. After the design is traced through it, acid is applied and reapplied to create the design and shading.

Lithography

Lithography is a process in which a greasy crayon is used to trace a design on a very porous stone. The stone is then soaked in water, and it absorbs the moisture in its clear areas. Ink is rolled on the surface, and it clings to the crayon areas and is repelled by the wet stone. A sheet of paper is rolled on the stone, picking up the design from the remaining ink. Most colored lithographs were painted by artists after printing. There is a revival in this form of work today, and some fine artists are quickly being recognized for their work.

From a painting by William Aiken Walker   *Etching by Phillip Sage, New Orleans, Louisiana*

Plantation Workers

Philip Sage of New Orleans, a contemporary print maker, has turned out a series of copies of the oil paintings of William Aiken Walker. In limited editions, good work such as this represents present enjoyment and a fine investment for the future.

This work by contemporary artists is not to be confused with the reprints of old work being turned out on sophisticated presses today. The offset method of printing has made faithful reproduction of old work possible, and you must be careful to examine prints to determine their age and authenticity. Also, there are concerns turning out prints by contemporary artists, numbering them in a short series, and then selling the complete series in different areas of the country, deluding buyers into thinking they are getting limited edition originals. Most are dressed up in expensive frames which enhance their appearance.

Although the prints cost only a few cents to make, their frame dressings and a gullible public have resulted in quite a profitable business for the fakers.

Samplers

Another type of wall decoration is the sampler, created by hand-weaving threads into handwoven cloth. Most samplers were done on linen until the middle of the nineteenth century, when

New England christening blanket with crewel embroidery, worked on linen and cotton twill by Mary Fifield (born in Boston in 1694), about 1700–1713. (Museum of Fine Arts, Boston, gift of Miss Mary Avery White)

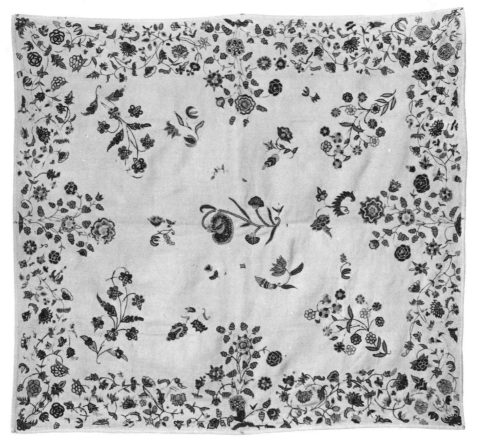

the less expensive cotton took over. Samplers tested a young girl's ability to sew an alphabet and figures, and to create an interesting and pleasing design. Those of the eighteenth century are the most desired, because of their age and primitive quality. They were not originally made to be framed, but in the early part of the nineteenth century it became fashionable to hang them as interesting works of art. They were more appreciated by the descendants of those who made them. In the second quarter of the nineteenth century, less attention was paid to the letters and figures, and more was given to scenic decoration, such as farm buildings, trees, flowers, and animals. These pictorial samplers are judged not only on workmanship but also on design. These were the work of the younger girls, with the older girls turning their attention to embroidered pictures.

The nineteenth century saw the arrival of "Berlin Work," named after a light wool which was used to make clothing and gloves. Designs would be woven to a base cloth in artistic fashion, and a three-dimensional effect could be achieved because the thread could be raised at the whim of the artist. Most designs were made on canvas, but some were done on the combed or worsted wools of the day. Patterns were copied from publications such as *Godey's Ladies Book,* and some were copied from the paisleys done in Scotland at the time.

Another product of the Victorian era is the Stevengraph, a silk picture framed as a wall hanging. The Jacquard loom was invented in France in 1801 and made weaving pictures into any fabric possible, and soon manufacturers everywhere were using it. The loom was computer-operated in that pierced cards were used to direct the pattern being woven. French silk was permitted free entry to England at the time of the Cobden Treaty in 1860, and this harmed the economy of the English mills. Coventry was a center of this work, and the enterprising Thomas Stevens of Coventry created bookmarks which caught the public fancy. He later turned to the production of pictures in silk, with the result that even those made by the other firms which followed are given the generic name Stevengraph. The first of these was made about 1879 and was introduced at an exhibition in York. Even postcards were made with woven silk panels, and these are collectors' items. Condition is most important in determining value today, and many will be found waterstained and/or faded. Some were unmounted, but those with aged frames are best.

Tapestries

Let me touch briefly on tapestries. It is not likely that you will be able to locate and purchase a tapestry wall hanging made before the seventeenth century. Tapestry weaving was a going art

Polychrome plate and block print on silk, English, about 1829–1830, taken from a series of caricatures by Paul Pry. It is called the Coaching Handkerchief because George IV and the "whups" of the political parties are represented expressing their views on the reform measure of 1829 designed to extend religious and civil liberties to non-Anglicans. (Colonial Williamsburg)

in the Netherlands then, and many artists were at work designing tapestries, while many others were engaged in making them. Even artists like Peter Paul Rubens were employed since most work was being done for the wealthy and for royalty. Tapestry work in wool and silk was later taken over by the Jacquard loom. At the end of the seventeenth century, a new type of tapestry called *Tenieres* was created featuring rustic scenes full of people and animals, and these are highly colored and quite lifelike. Commemorative scenes were in vogue later on, and even war events were immortalized in this manner. There is limited demand in America for even the large important hangings, since most end up in museums or in a few wealthy homes. The lesser tapestries which were ground out on looms by the thousands in the last century have little or no value, and should not be acquired as an investment. The handmade items are of more interest and value, if you can find them. Since there is no easy rule to follow in determining the manner of workmanship, you must seek competent advice before investing much money, or else study the field yourself in order to make your own appraisal.

Chapter 8

Clocks, Cloth,
Paper, and
Miscellaneous Collectibles

Timepieces

Increased interest in clock and watch collecting has brought with it the usual reproductions and outright fakes, which means buyers must be on their toes. The proliferation of American dealers purchasing antiques in Europe has brought about misrepresentation in timepieces, with the mistakes usually being discovered after the item arrives, when it is much too late to do anything about it. Americans are regarded as "hot clients" for just about anything, and the poorer peoples of the world are wont to help us part with our dollars in a hurried and unwise manner. There are no rules to this game—you have to sharpen up on your knowledge and get up real early in the morning to outwit your counterparts overseas. Everyone is fair game. Part of the problem in collecting pre-1800 clocks lies in making sure that the movements and case are original to each other. Many clockmakers engraved their names on the dials. The fakers have learned to grind off the names of lesser makers and replace them with famous names, like Thomas Tompion, Barraud, Perrigal, Dwerrihouse, and others. Some famous makers even bought inferior works and allowed their names to be engraved on them to keep up with the demand for their products. The old Stackfreed watches were imitated in at least three places in Germany, and recently in Belgium. Moving arm watches which were nineteenth century reproductions of much earlier pieces were imported from France, and these are old enough to defy detection as to whether they are original. Water clocks are thought to be very old, but they were listed in a catalog of English manufacture as late as 1914, and many of these fakes are revered today as centuries-old originals. Some are stamped with the year 1640. When you know of the fakery going on, it can make you quite nervous when it comes to appraising and buying old timepieces.

CLOCKS

If you are to collect clocks of the late eighteenth and nineteenth centuries, you will do well to concentrate on those of American make. Piece for piece, they will command more money than their foreign counterparts. The tall, or grandfather clock, is one of the most desired, and was made everywhere in the colonies. These are judged by determining if the works were made by the clockmaker, since many were assembled from parts which were bought elsewhere. Works and dials were imported from England, and many American makers merely made the weights and pendulums, had a cabinetmaker prepare the cases, and assembled the clocks for sale. Osborne's Manufactory in Birmingham, England, was a prolific concern, and many so-called American clocks house their works. However, as long as a clock is incorporated in an American case with native weights and pendulum, it is regarded as American. The desirability of these clocks is determined by whether the works came from England or were handmade in America, and the latter will command the most interest and value.

There were clock and watchmakers in America early in the eighteenth century, but it was not until after the Revolutionary War that their output was significant. Anyone who has a timepiece of any kind made in America before 1800 has an old and most often important item indeed. Connecticut became the breeding ground for some of the best and most prolific makers, and after the beginning of the nineteenth century their impact was felt around the world.

Even if a clock is signed with the name of a noted maker, you must do a little more research to document it. Witness the case of the famous Simon Willard, who worked in the Boston area during the Federal period. A master clockmaker, he was responsible for the training of many apprentices, and those who came from his

Connecticut peddler's clock by
Seth Thomas, around 1840.
The painted scene is quite
good. These are remarkably
accurate timepieces even to
this day.

Dutch peddler's clock
in cast iron which
stands about 16″ high
and weighs about 30
pounds. The clock in
front works and the
clock in the back is a
sample. Found at the
Amsterdam market-
place.

Early Dutch wag-on-
wall clock which rested
on a shelf to allow the
weight room to drop to
the floor and the pen-
dulum room to swing.
During the seventeenth
century someone had
the idea of encasing the
whole mechanism, and
the tall clock was born.

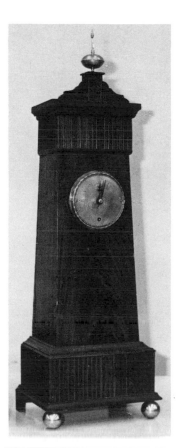

An unusual mantel clock with
works marked by Simon Willard, the noted Boston area
master clockmaker. I wonder if
Willard really made all of the
unusual timepieces which bear
his name.

shop are regarded as next to him in importance as craftsmen. Clocks by one such apprentice, Lemuel Curtis, often sell for more than the master's, but Willard is revered for his clocks and many fine ones grace homes and museums, not only in New England, but throughout the country.

Willard was known for creating masterpieces in unusual cases, such as his famous lighthouse clocks, one of which is in the White House. Shaped like a lighthouse, this clock features a face at the top, surrounded by a glass dome, with the pendulum and weight hidden by the tall body. Some scholars wonder if he was actually responsible for such oddities as this, or if they were the creation of apprentices with the works somehow appearing with Willard's name. In the absence of written proof, much of this was only conjecture until new evidence came to light.

Typical scene in a clockworker's shop featuring two pillar and scroll mantel clocks which were originally designed by Eli Terry in Connecticut (on the left). All clocks to the right of these two represent work done throughout the nineteenth century. Pillar and scroll clocks are being reproduced in many places today, so check the documentation carefully if you intend to buy one.

Wooden clockworks were made centuries ago and also enjoyed an American revival early in the nineteenth century. Men like Eli Terry and Silas Hoadley are known to have made many of these. They are not really practical as timepieces, although some do keep good time. The industrial age brought about the demise of wooden clockworks by making mechanical metal gear cutting possible.

An issue of the *Boston Evening Transcript* of Saturday, March 28, 1928, carries a revealing story about Simon Willard which should give rise to much conjecture and cause some uneasiness among owners of Willard clocks. It was written by a Charles Messer Stow, a highly regarded antiquarian of his time. He tells of visiting the showroom of Israel Sack, who was then in Boston, and he reprinted a bill of sale which was attached to the door of a tall clock. It read, "Clock Manufactory, Simon Willard, at his clock dial in Roxbury Street, manufactures every kind of clockwork, such as large clocks for steeples, made in the best manner and warranted; price with one dial, 500 dollars; with two dials, 600 dollars; with three dials, 700 dollars; with four dials, 900. Common eight-day clocks, with very elegant faces and mahogany cases, price from 50 to 60 dollars. Elegant eight-day timepieces, price 30 dollars. Timepieces which run 30 hours and warranted, price 10 dollars. Spring clocks of all kinds, price from 50 to 60 dollars. Clocks that will run one year, with once winding up, with very elegant cases, price 100 dollars. Timepieces for astronomical purposes, price 70 dollars. Timepieces for meeting houses, to place before the gallery, with neat enameled dials, price 55 dollars. Chime clocks that will play 6 tunes, price 120 dollars. Perambulators are also made at said place which can be affixed to any kind of carriage and will tell the miles and rods exact, price 15 dollars. Printed by I. Thomas, Jun. Worcester."

The advertisement tells us of many items made by Willard that have not yet turned up. Where is a clock that runs one year on one winding, where is the clock that plays six tunes, where is the perambulator device that tells the miles traveled with the baby, who ever knew that Willard made such devices? What will give comfort to Willard clock owners if the following statement, printed by Willard, and inserted inside the same case, is true? It reads, "I believe the public are not generally aware that my former patent right expired six years ago, which induces me to caution them against the frequent impositions practiced in vending spurious timepieces. It is true these have Patent printed on them and some with my name and their outward appearance resembles those formerly made by me. Thus they are palm'd on the public. Several of them have been brought to me for repairs, that would certainly put the greatest bungler to blush. Such is the country inundated with, and such I consider prejudicial to my reputation; I therefore disclaim being the manufacturer of such vile performances. S. Willard."

When Willard retired from business in 1839, he sold his tools and goodwill to an apprentice, Elnathan Taber. Taber was allowed to print Simon Willard on the face of the clocks he made, and these were sold by Simon Willard, Jr., at his store in Boston. All of this should be cause for reflection by owners of "Willard" clocks, as well as dealers and appraisers. In the light of the direct writing by Willard himself, you cannot be too careful in attribution to the master. You must apply some of this thinking to other makers as well.

Early in the nineteenth century, three noted clockmakers joined forces in one concern, though later they went out on their own.

Each was a true craftsman, and each left us a legacy in fine timepieces. Seth Thomas, Eli Terry, and Silas Hoadley made up this partnership and, along with other makers like Chauncey Jerome and Joseph Ives, brought the mechanization which made volume production possible to the industry. The Connecticut peddlers clock came into being—a shelf clock that sold for about ten dollars at a time when a tall one cost a hundred. These clocks were sold door-to-door, bringing a timepiece within the reach of almost everyone.

Until this time, clocks were powered by weights whose gravitational fall drove the hands and striking mechanisms. Until the mass production of spring-wound timepieces became practical, it was impossible to make a shelf clock which would run more than 30 hours with one winding due to the short distance a weight could fall. The tall clocks could run for eight days on one winding because of the long distance the weights could drop to the floor. Spring-wound mechanisms made the eight-day shelf clock a reality. Throughout the nineteenth century, various types of wall, shelf, mantel, and tall clocks were made, along with the clocks designed for commercial or industrial uses. Church and tower clocks were in demand, and many made way back in the last century are still keeping time for communities.

There are similarities between tall clocks made in Europe and in America. The Sheraton styled cases made in England are much the same as those made here, so it is advisable to check the works first to see if they are stamped with a maker's name. In upper New England, you will find that the makers used can type weights made from tin, which were soldered after being filled with metal, stone, or even beach sand. Most of the many Pennsylvania clockmakers utilized solid cast iron weights in the manner of the English clocks. However, most of the Pennsylvania clocks are quite tall, some standing as high as nine feet, and the English clocks are more the height of those made in New England. So if you find a tall clock of New England height (in the seven-and-a-half-foot range) with iron weights, you could be looking at one made in England. Can weights are generally a good sign of American make, but you must realize that clock weights are

Mid-nineteenth century Connecticut mantel clock in a Gothic revival mahogany case. The pendulum insert is porcelain, and you can see the alarm bell behind it.

A very fancy French clock from the mid-nineteenth century. It is gilded with ormolu mounts and has a porcelain face. The decorative molding of the case gives it interest and value.

Dies for stamping parts of clockworks, from the E. Howard Clock Company, Boston. (Owned by Elmer Stennis)

Mantel calendar clock which gives the month, day, and date, as well as the time, made by the Ithaca Calendar Clock Company, Ithaca, New York. It employs the H. B. Norton Patent, which was first recorded in 1863.

Wall clock from the Empire period, made by James Collins of Goffstown, New Hampshire. Mirror clocks seem to have originated in New Hampshire, where some of the best examples were made and are still found today.

interchangeable, so you must do some research to verify the place where the clock is reputed to have been made.

Mantel clocks took on different sizes and shapes. Most were made of wood, but marble, china, and iron cases are common. Some were made with scenes painted on the inside of the glass fronts, and this can heighten the value, especially if the work pictures some important place or person. Some had special movements or different means of powering the clock. One such device resembles a wagon spring—very few were made, and those appearing now command high prices. Some clocks were made with alarms, and these are of interest. The cases gradually evolved in style, keeping pace with furniture changes. Those made in the later nineteenth century in what is called "gingerbread" reflect the last true period change, that of Eastlake. They were made in these fancy styles as late as the 1920's, with the designs often pressed into the wood by machine.

School and regulator clocks have experienced a revival, and those with calendar devices are interesting, but are in short supply. China cased clocks are often a product of foreign manufacture, notably German. However, many have American works, which suggests that the cases might have been shipped here for the final assembly. There are some French marble and iron-cased mantel clocks with American works, and you have only to read the dial to confirm this.

Connecticut wall clock of the 1830–1840 period, when such timepieces were brought within the financial reach of most people. The painted fronts add to the interest and value of the clock, depending on the scene and workmanship, and this would rate as a very good specimen.

Reproductions of early banjo clocks are made today by Elmer Stennis of Weymouth, Massachusetts. Early ones utilized old works of the E. Howard Clock Company of Boston, while present-day ones contain handmade works which keep superb time. Buyers find that good reproductions like these are just as enjoyable as the old ones, and the price of the reproductions is within reach, as opposed to the inflated prices on the old ones.

Howard watches and clocks of the nineteenth century are highly regarded throughout the world. Made in Boston, this watch movement found its way to the Museum Technesches in Vienna, Austria, where it is on permanent exhibit as an example of American workmanship.

WATCHES

Watchmaking hit its stride in the nineteenth century, and watches were mass produced to meet the demand. The maker who had perhaps the greatest influence in the industry was Edward Howard, born in Boston in 1813. At age 16, he was apprenticed to the noted Aaron Willard, Junior, whose father was Simon Willard's brother and a great clockmaker in his own right. He worked there until 1842, when he left to form his own business with David P. Davis. During this period the clocks were labeled Howard and Davis. Howard was inventive and created a great deal of timesaving machinery during the growing age of industrialization. He joined forces with Aaron L. Dennison in 1848 to create the business which eventually became the Waltham Watch Company. It was known as Howard, Davis and Dennison in 1850; American Horologe Company, 1850; Warren Manufacturing Company, 1853; Boston Watch Company, 1853; Waltham Improvement Company, 1853–57; E. Howard and Company, 1857; Howard Clock and Watch Company, 1863; E. Howard Clock and Watch Company, 1881. He retired in 1882.

Howard is best known for his commercial and industrial clocks. Rare was the bank, factory, or railroad station which did not boast one of his timepieces. He made banjo clocks in both wood and marble cases, ranging in size from 30 inches to 60 inches. These came in five sizes, and collectors strive to get all five in each series. Many of his tower clocks are still used daily.

He made wall-hanging jewelers clocks—some with pendulum arms of different metals which would contract and expand with changing temperatures—in a manner to guarantee accurate timekeeping. His watches were the most elegant of his works, and it would be safe to say that an E. Howard watch in a gold case is the most desirable of the nineteenth century production watches to collect today. They are still as accurate as the finest timepiece available to us at this time. Many railroads ran their trains on them. I do not know of any Howard timepiece wearing out and so they are perhaps the ultimate in American manufacture of all time. Howard movements from outdated cases are now being put into reproductions of dwarf (grandmother) and tall clocks. Rest assured that the timepiece will outlive you if you buy one today, even if the movement is already over a hundred years old.

You would do well to study Brooks Palmer's *The Book of American Clocks* (listed in the bibliography) since it cites the known and recognized makers and is a good reference for research on timepieces.

Rugs

Early rugs are one of the most expressive forms of American folk art. When you consider that practically every young lady was taught to spin, weave, and sew, you would assume that there should be an abundance of floor coverings as millions must have been made since the Pilgrims landed. However, collectors do not find it easy to locate outstanding examples since, as with most art, few fit this description. There were thousands of artisans who plied every trade, yet only a few set themselves apart as true artists whose work is of great quality. Though most girls may have been proficient with tools such as looms, wheels, and winders, not all could be classed as true artists in their work—they made necessities for the home, perhaps with little or no talent for good design and decoration, nor in the execution of what they did.

Hooked rugs made of wool on a foundation of homespun linen between 1775 and 1840 are direct and original in design. Folk rugs were given an added brilliance with the introduction of turkey red dye in 1829. Chenille, the rarest method of hand manufacture, is done by threading a half-inch strip of cloth lengthwise, gathering and rolling it to appear like a furry caterpillar, and then stitching it on to a closely woven fabric.

Naturalistic floral medallions with scroll borders and corner spandrels appear frequently in rugs made in the latter part of the nineteenth century. These were first popularized by Edward Sands Frost of Biddeford, Maine, a tin peddler, whose stencilled burlap designs tolled the knell of the bold original patterns of the earlier period. While peddling tinware, Frost had noted many housewives at work at their rug frames, and vowed he could create better designs than the housewives had available. He traced and cut out tin stencils using his shears, reproduced them on burlap, and began peddling these along with his other products. His designs soon caught on and he created a full line, many of which are reproduced for visitors at Greenfield Village at the Henry Ford Museum in Dearborn, Michigan. Frost's pattern number two features the initials of a bride and groom worked into the border, about four feet apart. On the facing border is a place for the minister to stand, and all step into position for the wedding vows.

Large rugs were used as bed coverings at first, since they were considered too fine to suffer abuse on the floor. Their quality of warmth and the greater availability of materials soon resulted in

Quilts for sale at the annual auction sponsored by the Mennonites at Morgantown, Pennsylvania. All of the quilts are handmade, and they are sold to raise funds for charitable purposes.

their common use as floor coverings. Until that time, it had been popular to paint floors in colorful designs. Later on, canvas might be painted to spread as a covering, and this may have been the forerunner of the gaily printed linoleums. Braided rugs are in keeping with early homes, as are Orientals. Oriental rugs represent a complete study in themselves, as they are judged by pattern and workmanship. They were popular in wealthy homes, and many were carried here in the China-American trade. Rugs from the Near East gradually assumed greater importance to buyers in America, and the rugs from old Persia, now Iran, are among the best to collect. Rug weaving by hand is tiresome work, and a large rug will often consume up to five years in the making, with several people working at it. It is said that the art of making them may die out since young people are not eager to take on such a chore. I wonder at the abundance of these rugs coming into America at this time, and often sold in major cities at auction in order to dispose of them. Can it be possible that some machinery has been smuggled into the hills to help out in production? If this is a dying art, how can so many be offered at auction brand new? The People's Republic of China is responsible for some exceedingly fine rugs which are finding their way out to the open market via Hong Kong. The workmanship is superb, and prices for these rugs are on a par with the best from Iran, and in some cases exceed them. There has been a continual output of "Oriental" rugs from Belgium, and during the 1950's thousands must have been sold here at low prices. Dealers purchased the 9 x 12 size at three for a hundred dollars and pitched them out at auctions for fifty apiece. Although beautiful in design and color, they are quite thin, and wrinkle easily on the floor. Those from the Orient and Mid-East are much heavier and of better quality.

Quilts and Coverlets

Quilts and coverlets are common, as most old homes have a trunk or two full of them. The quality of each piece must be judged on the originality of the design, workmanship, color, and condition. If it is documented with the year and possibly the name of the maker or owner woven into it, a quilt will assume much more importance. Pennsylvania, Ohio, and New York take top marks for the production of quilts in the nineteenth century, as the designs are colorful, reflecting the German-Dutch heritage of many of their settlers. New England can be credited with much fine work, but there was less attention given to dating and naming these. There are many fine quilt makers at work today, and the outstanding place to see and buy their output is the annual Mennonite auction held in Morgantown, Pennsylvania. The ladies of this religious group spend the year making up to 300 quilts which are sold to raise money for relief purposes throughout the world. The quality is very good, and because of this the auction attracts about ten thousand people, which must make it the largest in the world.

Quilt designs have names, and patterns for quilts were circulated for all to use. Most were made from scrap material, and old discarded clothing was often cut up and utilized. Cooperative quilts were made by members of churches or organizations. Each member contributed a square of work, often signed, and these were later sewn together to make the finished product. Some quilts relate the history of a group or an event—witness the English regimental quilt which is at the Shelburne Museum in Shelburne, Vermont. This quilt depicts scenes from the many countries in which this particular regiment served, along with views of its permanent station in the British Isles. Others were made with materials from France, which might be separate squares with pictures of the Presidents or other famous people printed in the fabric. Some were made from cloth with designs already worked in it on Jacquard looms. Exotic fabrics like silk and embroidered cottons found their way here from India and were used to good advantage.

Pieced quilts are those which are made up of pieces of material sewn together. Appliqué quilts are often more bold in design, as pieces of cloth could be cut in fancy shapes and then stitched to another surface of cloth. Designs were printed in many of the ladies magazines of the day, but most quilts were the result of the material available and the individual taste of the maker. Some are quite geometric, others very floral, and some even approach pure abstract art. Making a quilt is a sort of painting with cloth, and it is in this light that each is judged today.

One of the most desired pieces is a Baltimore quilt, so named because of the city in which they were made. These were made by girls facing marriage, and most are really great works of art. Some have sold well into the four figures because of their superb quality and beauty. It would seem that the young ladies vied to outdo their friends and that such competition resulted in greatness.

In the later Victorian times and into this century, many odd quilts were made, such as those using parade ribbons, flags of all countries, advertising flags, and even neckties. These are judged in the same manner as the earlier ones, and should be preserved as interesting bits of Americana.

Most of the regular quilt patterns are named. I could begin citing those such as Double Irish Chain, Baby Blocks, Road to California, Grandma's Dream, Kaleidoscope, and on and on. *American Pieced Quilts* by Jonathan Holstein is an excellent book which carries a list of 87, along with pictures of each.

Our earliest collectible coverlet is called a linsey-woolsey. Those eighteenth century examples which have survived are treasured today. There is still a question as to whether they are all wool, or part linen, as implied by the name. Late research suggests they are named for the town of Linsey in England where they were reportedly first made. Identified by their wool-like quality, linsey-woolsies are really two layers of homespun stitched together, often in design. Each layer is a different color, with a lighter side for summer and a darker for winter. The cloth was dyed with readily available materials, such as onion skins, beets, bark, and ochres. They are subject to damage by moths, so most reveal a hole or two, but some were protected in cedar chests over the years and have found their way to some historic home or restoration. In later years, coverlets were decorated with embroidery, and some are works of art. The Shelburne Museum features a sample quilt on which the maker worked the alphabet and numerals in several different fashions, along with floral motifs and other decorations. A person ordering a coverlet from her would be able to choose the designs they liked best and the type of lettering and numbering they wished. Such sample quilts are rare.

Books and Manuscripts

Book and manuscript collecting is an area which requires considerable study if you want to keep aware of the value and desirability of each item. As with any antique, age alone is not enough. Desirability and the law of supply and demand set the prices for old books, and if you do not know these, you can get burned financially.

Two categories of books seem to command the most attention—the most important are the histories of towns and counties, and the atlases of states made in the nineteenth century. These are invaluable to researchers of American history, and are of special interest to residents of the areas which are covered in the books. Lawyers also make very good customers for the atlases and histories of the communities in which they practice, since genealogies, property lines, and past ownership of items are often revealed in these old books. Writers are continually preparing stories on the history of communities and the people in them, and owning books of this kind is much easier than going to the library and spending long hours reading and copying from the books there. This is a relatively safe area of collecting, and you can learn it quickly since the number of books written about any area is usually quite limited. Age helps value, because many copies of a particular printing probably did not survive. However, publishers today are issuing reprints of old books in order to fill the demand for them. This can hurt the value of the old books, as most buyers want them not for their historical value, but for the information in them instead, and could care less whether the printing is old or new. Keep in touch with your local friendly book dealer to find out what books are being reprinted and what is in demand.

Next in importance, but in many cases much higher in value, are first editions of works by noted authors. You will have to study to find out which books are most in demand. The demand changes from year to year, making it inadvisable to list any here. Publishers usually note the edition of the book by stating which printing it is. Some use the numeral system, printing those from 1 through 10. As each successive printing is done, a numeral is dropped to indicate which printing it is. In the past, some editions were not marked, and many others have been found marked with the first year the book was published, although they may have been issued years later from a new press run.

Perhaps the ultimate triumph is to acquire books that are first editions signed by the author. The signatures alone are good documentation, and may have value in themselves. When you buy books today, try to have the author sign them wherever possible, since this enhances their value.

Old books on art and antiques are in great demand. Buyers hunted for years for copies of Alice Morse Earle's *China Hunting in America,* first published in 1892. It was recently reissued by the Charles E. Tuttle Company in Vermont, making it available to all, and this must have reduced the value of the early editions. Ledlie Laughlin's *Pewter in America, Its Makers And Their Marks* was originally issued in two volumes, which were sold only a few years ago for as much as $250 when they could be found. Both were recently combined into one volume and made available at $27.50, which reinforces the fact that you must be aware of possible republication before investing too much money. However, many books would be too expensive to reprint today, although they are valuable research tools for antiquarians, writers, and collectors. So not hesitate to buy books on antiques and art, as long as you do not have to pay high prices. These books are rising in value every day. Old auction catalogs, with the prices written in, are also in demand. Museum exhibitions often result in catalogs being printed. These are valuable because they are a record of the public's taste at the time, and they also serve as valuable research tools because of the accuracy of the information gathered by the museum staff.

Old school books are plentiful, and there is little demand for them. Books about our native heros are quite valuable and those relating the deeds of Paul Revere, Kit Carson, Daniel Boone, and others bring the days in which they lived home to us. Diaries are good, as they can furnish a record of events, times, and places. One of the most collectible items today is the sailors' logs, as these are personal accounts of voyages and adventures. Those which include experiences with mutiny, pirates, storms, and

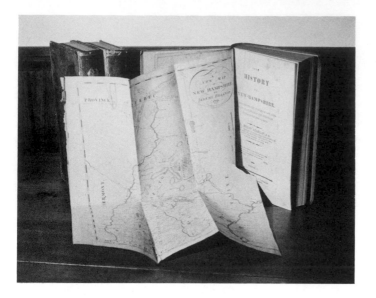

The earliest state history was probably Jeremy Belknap's *History of New Hampshire,* first published in 1794. In three volumes, it has its greatest value to New Hampshire residents. Belknap was responsible for the formation of the Massachusetts Historical Society, whose early start in collecting important documents has provided it with remarkable rarities in printed material.

Early notice relative to the granting of licenses for spiritous liquors in Boston, 1772. Such notices are historically important as well as interesting in themselves.

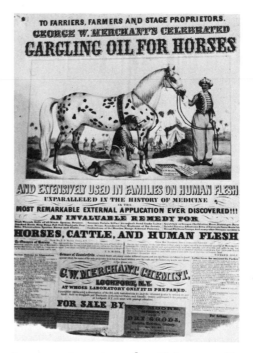

A way-out poster advertising gargling oil for horses hangs in the shed at the Calvin Coolidge Homestead in Plymouth, Vermont.

The famed *Ulster County Gazette,* which carried the account of the death of George Washington, dated January 4, 1800. Be cautioned that many reprints of this were made early in the nineteenth century; the many copies available cannot all be originals.

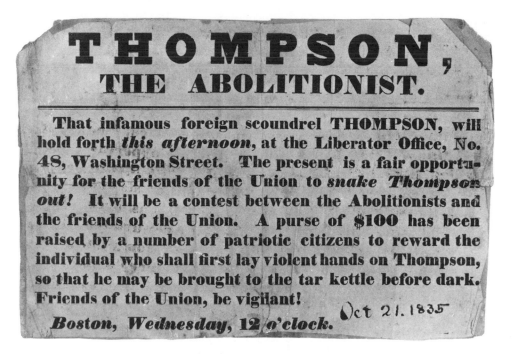

THOMPSON, THE ABOLITIONIST.

That infamous foreign scoundrel THOMPSON, will hold forth *this afternoon*, at the Liberator Office, No. 48, Washington Street. The present is a fair opportunity for the friends of the Union to *snake Thompson out!* It will be a contest between the Abolitionists and the friends of the Union. A purse of $100 has been raised by a number of patriotic citizens to reward the individual who shall first lay violent hands on Thompson, so that he may be brought to the tar kettle before dark. Friends of the Union, be vigilant!

Boston, Wednesday, 12 o'clock. Oct 21. 1835

Posters are a good collectible, but few can match this one owned and exhibited by the Bostonian Society at the Old State House in Boston.

other disasters are especially desirable. Captains' logs are always of interest, but there are few to be found. Most were turned in to the shipping companies, or were handed down in families which will not part with them.

BIBLES

The Bible is the most frequently printed book, and this keeps the price down on most. It is a book which survives since no one willingly destroys a copy, and the supply is large. However, some of the very early Bibles are valuable, and the following tips may help. The Bible has been published in more editions and in more countries than any other book. Many large sized old ones turn up in country homes, with the inner pages containing records of births, deaths, and marriages—many telling a rather poignant history of a family. As a basic rule, to be of collecting interest a Bible must go back to the eighteenth century when early presses and wooden type were still in use. Those with woodblock pictures are valuable, more for the pictures than for the Bible itself. If the pictures are hand colored, it will help raise the value.

Title page of the Genevan Bible, printed in 1608 by Robert Barker, "Printer to the King's Most Excellent Majesty." Bound in calf, this is a good early bible. Most bibles are not valuable because the supply exceeds the demand, but age is a helpful factor in this case.

The German Pietists at the Ephrata Cloister in Pennsylvania were the first to be able to take on the task of printing Bibles, and in the 1740's they turned out a massive copy, printed in German, for their neighbors the Mennonites. A Bible from the seventeenth century or earlier is preferable, and those printed in England turn up from time to time. Metal type was in use during this century, but some might still have been printed using wooden type. In the less expensive volumes there are few or no pictures, although some decorations may be found at the title page in the front and at the chapter headings. The best volumes had hand illumination done by painting and gilding, since this was painstaking work most often undertaken by monks. This hand work was a holdover from the Bibles which were completely handwritten by monks—very few of which have survived. When a buyer finds a Bible which has been hand written and hand illuminated, he has the best that he can collect. Single pages from such Bibles sell for enormous sums which is unfortunate because they must be torn apart for this purpose.

Other rare Bibles which you might look for are those which have errors in print. There is the Place Makers Bible, which stated, "Blessed are the place makers, for they shall be called the children of God." This extraordinary misprint occurred in the second edition of the Geneva Bible published in England in 1561–62. Then there is the Vinegar Bible, in which "The Parable of the Vinegar" instead of the "Parable of the Vineyard" appears in the chapter heading according to Luke XX in an Oxford edition of the authorized version, said to be the most sumptuous of all the Oxford Bibles. Then there is the Basket Bible, which had a "basketful of errors" according to critics. An edition printed by Robert Barker and Martin Lucas in England in 1631 is rare. It is called the Wicked Bible because the negative was left out of the seventh commandment. The printers were fined several thousand pounds by the king and most copies were destroyed, with only four known to exist today. While searching out copies of this Bible to destroy, the censors found a German edition repeating the error.

MAPS, DEEDS, AND WILLS

Old maps, deeds, wills, and other documents are academic in their value. Those relating to people who are historically important are of course the best, and the average ones found in boxes of papers during estate auctions are of little value. These can probably serve their best purpose as a gift to the local historical society which will preserve them for research. Old newspapers have research value only, and books like *Godey's Ladies Book* and magazines like *Petersons* and *Frank Harper's Weekly* serve as interesting references to the life and times in which they were printed, but have little material value. The *Godey's Ladies Books* are often stripped of their colored prints, which are then individually framed for resale.

Greeting and Trade Cards

Advertising and trade cards are fun collectibles, but few sell for much money. Some people collect cardboard fans which bear advertising messages on one side and colorful pictures on the other. These were given away at theaters on hot nights as promotional gimmicks.

Postcards are fun, as they are numerous and varied. Louis Prang of Boston is considered to be the father of American greeting cards. Born in Prussia in 1824, he later moved to New York where he was unable to find work in the lithography field for which he was trained. After moving to Boston, Prang set up his own business and in time in produced cards of all types. In 1874 his production of Christmas cards was very well accepted and his name became a household word. From this fine start, he went on to make cards for other holidays such as Easter and New Year's. Prang solicited the work of known artists and paid them well, and also developed a technique of printing as many as twenty colors to produce the finished product he wanted. Some of these cards were fringed with tassels and others were made partly of silk and other cloth. Prang's floral designs were among the best and he created exquisite Easter cards with the theme of Spring. Some sold for seventy-five cents a dozen and others cost as much as a dollar apiece, which was a lot of money at the time.

Santa Claus was a popular subject, and there were many makers, including foreign ones, who portrayed the jolly gent in different situations and likenesses. Cards with a standing Santa are worth more than those with a sitting Santa. Those showing him using different modes of travel such as the dirigible, airplane, automobile, and even balloon are very desirable.

Some collect cards by artists, and others by makers. Some want them merely for the old stamps, while others are looking for those with Christmas seals which have been cancelled by the postmark, as these bring good money. There are many collectors of specific scenes such as lighthouses, trains, seaside resorts, churches, etc., and all will pay according to their eagerness. Most cards are sold by the boxful to dealers who are much more canny about reselling them. The dealers allow buyers to examine the cards, hoping that they will show an interest which will help set a higher price. Get a price quoted on cards before you buy—this is one area where games can be played.

Dolls

Collectible dolls come from almost every country. Excellent examples have been found in pre-Columbian ruins in Mexico and South America as well as from early civilizations in Europe and Asia. Dolls have been made in a variety of materials including clay, wood, wax, rubber, parian porcelain, glazed porcelain, metals, bisque procelain, papier-mâché, celluloid, and other compositions too numerous to list. Wooden dolls were evident during the eighteenth century and into the early part of the nineteenth century, when the industrial revolution allowed mass

Dolls are quite popular, and they come in all sizes, types, and materials. Collecting them is a study in itself. Some nineteenth and twentieth century dolls made from various compositions (including papier mâché) are pictured.

production of dolls in other materials. The good early wooden dolls are rarities and are therefore high in price. The primitive ones were carved rigidly, while the better ones had pegged joints which allowed motion. These were gessoed or painted in a lifelike manner. Wooden dolls were made until the late nineteenth century, but these are inferior in quality to the earlier ones. Some were made with hinge joints which could rust over the years, so check this. During this time, the heads, hands, and feet might have been made of wood, and a stuffed body, arms, and legs attached. Some early dolls had plaster heads on wooden bodies, and these are quite rare. Springfield, Vermont was a doll making center in the late nineteenth century, and dolls made by Joel Ellis and Mason and Taylor are very desirable. Wooden dolls were also made as late as the 1920's by A. Schoenhut & Company of Philadelphia.

Porcelain dolls varied in their glazes, which included the shiny, bisque, and parian. In the dolls with a shiny glaze, you should look for those with brown hair as this is rarer than black. Brown eyes are also rarer. Facial coloring is important, and it should be as natural as possible. Dolls with set-in glass eyes are not common. Shoes with flat soles were used until about the time of the Civil War, when heels began to be added. As with most dolls, the style of clothing used can help to determine when they were made.

Parian is an unglazed porcelain, generally pure white. The hair of parian dolls is generally molded, they have glass or painted eyes, and some fancy ones even had pierced ears. Bisque doll heads are unglazed, and the coloring is generally more pronounced than on dolls in parian since the doll makers were not held rigidly to the white texture. The French and German makers are best known for bisque dolls—they made the busts (and often feet and arms to match) and the purchaser could add the body and clothing she wished. You can check the provenance of a doll by lowering its dress at the back of the neck, as this is where many manufacturers stamped their names and marks.

Papier-mâché is made of paper which has been torn to shreds and mixed with paste. This can be molded, will harden, and can then be gessoed or painted with ease. Papier-mâché dolls may have either painted or glass eyes. These were popular in the nineteenth century until dolls of this type and class gave way to other compositions which might have been made of similar materials. Ludwig Greiner of Philadelphia patented a method for making papier-mâché dolls in 1858, and some may be found with his mark on the upper back.

Charles Goodyear patented a process for making rubber, and this material was first used for dolls in the middle of the nineteenth century. Hard and soft rubber were both used. This has been modified by the use of foam and related materials in today's dolls. Not many of these dolls survived as they could go out of shape if they were stored with weight against them.

Wax was one of the earliest materials utilized in doll making. Some dolls were molded directly into shape, and others were made of wax poured over some other type of body material such as papier-mâché or cardboard. These are quite perishable as they are subject to heat, and therefore most are high in price due to the

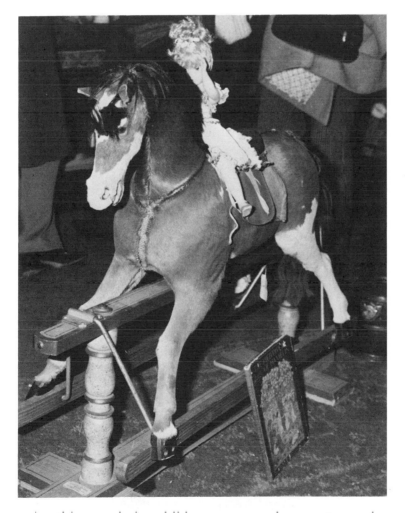

Anything made for children years ago has great appeal today. F.A.O. Schwartz advertised this horse 75 years ago, and its good condition attests to its quality.

small supply. These dolls were popular until the end of the last century.

Metal dolls are interesting, but do not command the high prices of most of those made with more exotic materials. They seem to have originated in Germany, and at one time were popular because of their durability. Most were made in this century, and metal heads, legs, and arms were often used as replacements for broken parts of other dolls.

Perhaps the most basic doll material is cloth, as it was readily available in every home and a mother could easily fashion her own gift to a child. Rag dolls fall into this category, as do those which were designed with a great deal more finesse. Companies were set up to print complete doll bodies in color, and these could then be stuffed and stitched up at home. These were offered as premiums for cereal box tops as recently as the Depression—not only in doll forms, but in animal forms as well. The Arnold Print Company of North Adams, Massachusetts is well known for this work.

Almost everyone has seen one of the celluloid Kewpie dolls which have been given away as prizes at fairs for years. Celluloid was first perfected just after the middle of the nineteenth century and was immediately put to use in making doll heads and bodies.

Dolls were made to walk and "talk" in the second quarter of the nineteenth century. They were used on pull toys, some were designed with mechanical features which permitted them to perform, others fell into the puppet category, and some were incorporated into music boxes where they danced to a tune. More recently, dolls have been made to cry, wet, and talk via a built-in tape recorder. The Barbie doll of today with all her attendant paraphernalia, which includes not only her clothing, but also sporting equipment, cars, boats, and campers will certainly be of interest to the collectors of the future. Many women who were girls during the Depression are seeing the type of dolls they played with on the flea market counters today. The Shirley Temple and Raggedy Anne dolls have their buyers, which indicates that you should preserve anything related to dolls of any period. Someday, someone will want them—and that day may not be far off in our quickly changing world.

Buttons

It is felt that button collecting first took hold in this country during the Depression. The National Button Society of America was organized to promote their collection and display, and new afficionados are being created almost daily as more information is published about buttons. The Just Buttons Museum is in Southington, Connecticut, and it features just that.

There are many classifications of this collectible, with a wide range of different types from which to choose. Eighteenth century buttons are rare since not many have survived. The most familiar are the military buttons, which were saved because of an attachment to the history of the American Revolution which prompted many people to save the uniforms of their ancestors. While the uniforms disappeared due to the ravages of moths or time, the buttons were most often saved as a final remembrance. Much of the clothing of the eighteenth century was held together by sashes, belts, and hooks.

In the early nineteenth century, fashionable women were dressed in the Greek Revival style, and buttons were used sparingly on their draped clothing. Their use was confined mostly to the men. It was not until the change of styles after the Civil War that buttons came into general use on clothing for all members of the family. Early buttons were made of copper, porcelain, precious metals such as gold and silver, glass, steel, bone, ivory, and even wood. Decoration was done by enameling, carving, molding, and gilding. Some buttons were silver plated after this technique was developed in the 1840's. Many housewives made buttons from the bones of farm animals by cutting, shaping, and polishing, and these were used frequently on undergarments. You can tell bone from ivory by examining the material with a magnifying glass—bone will have small black specks throughout, whereas ivory is clear. Many "gold" buttons are actually made of pinchbeck, which is a man-made product, so you must judge most of these in this light. The technique of decorating buttons by enameling them originated overseas many years ago, and was not practiced much in America, so most enameled buttons we find are probably European. Metal buttons were chased and engraved with decorations, and some are now called "steel cut," referring to the bright facets left by such work. Hunt clubs often had sporting buttons made up for their members with hunting scenes on them. Some buttons were enameled on metal, and others were done on porcelain. Some buttons were made in concave or convex fashion and joined together at the rims to form a hollow button. Exotic materials like shell, mother-of-pearl, and tortoise are found, but although these are not common, they do not command much interest. Housewives often made fabric buttons by sewing material over a shaped disc and then drilling holes to accommodate the thread. Some of the early steel buttons will rust, and they must be oiled or otherwise protected. Gems were used on royal buttons, but it is unlikely that you will find any of these in America.

Horn was used for button making to some extent; some was simply carved, and another technique involved molding the material by using heat. Most American "pearl-looking" buttons came from Birmingham, England, where they were made in abundance during the middle of the last century. This pearl look was later duplicated in plastic, which eventually dominated other materials in button manufacture. Compositions of plastic and other synthetic materials became the rule in button making and fine quality gradually disappeared except in buttons made for the carriage trade.

Other materials of exotic nature used in buttons were vegetables, ivory, nuts, and even seeds. Jet is best known for its use in jewelry, but it was also used for buttons. It is actually a natural material called lignite which has a coal black quality that was eventually reproduced in a black glass which can fool the uninitiated. Pressed glass buttons were turned out by major factories, but the quality of most is not great, and they are collected for their curiosity value alone. Paperweight buttons were made to look like the larger weights, and are interesting to collect. Then there are the charm string buttons—every string contains at least a thousand small buttons, each different from the others. A girl would collect these buttons with the final one supposed to be put on by the man she married. Some doubt that they ever existed, while others feel that the strings were long ago broken up as a practical matter when clothing needed mending.

The decorating motifs and shapes of buttons were influenced by the art forms prevalent in other decorative items, so a true collector can soon learn to classify his collection into different periods. You must keep abreast of the action in button buying and selling, but this can be difficult as there are few specialists in the field because of the low rewards. There are many buttons selling for just a few cents, and this brings a much lower return than antiques which sell for many dollars. You can learn a lot on your own by buying boxes of buttons at auctions and then sorting them out. Those of interesting and/or valuable materials, those with good design and decoration, and those which show some handwork in their making are ones that you can consider saving. You will assimilate much knowledge if you deal in buttons, and keep buying and selling until you learn what the collectors want, and this will guide you in what you should be collecting if profit is important to you. If buttons are represented as having come from the garments of famous people, be sure you have documentation before buying. The woods are full of good story tellers.

Fans

Not many people realize that men as well as women carried fans as far back as the seventeenth century. Their origin is lost in history, but it is known that fans were in use in the Orient many centuries ago. The Egyptians pictured huge fans which were used to cool the reigning Pharaohs, and smaller ones must have been in use even in their day. Those which are collectible today could have been made in either the Orient, Europe, or America, but the fanciest came from overseas. French fans were most popular in the eighteenth century, since this was an age of elegance there, and fans were a social necessity almost as important as good clothing if one wished to be properly dressed.

It is felt that the first hand fans did not fold, but were made in square, rectangular, round, or oval shapes. Materials were silk, parchment, leather, paper, bamboo, grass, linen, and even cane.

The folding fans utilize framing (called the "sticks") which is held together by the mount (the axis at which they open). In the sixteenth century a fan opened about 120 degrees, and they continued to progress in size until they could be spread beyond 180 degrees. The folding fan probably originated in the Orient and spread to Europe through the growing trade. Some fans were made totally of carved ivory, tortoiseshell, horn, or bone, and some featured these materials along with lacquered wood used as framing in the sticks and mount. Gold, silver, and jewels were imbedded in fans for the wealthy, and some fans even contained a small mirror which milady could use to look over her shoulder as she pretended to cool herself.

Painted decoration was popular, and was done on almost all the materials, particularly wood and cloth. Some fans had mounts covered with vellum (lamb skin) and others were decorated by cut or open work. Some of the painting was done by artists who signed their creations. Other fans with spangle and sequin decorations may be found.

The addition of a small scent pad or box near the mount was a helpful innovation for an area where the air was bad. A bride's fan could have been made of lace, and that of a portly matron may have had feathers attached as a decorative touch. You can look for the cords from which fans dangled from the wrist, since these can be quite fancy and made with good metals and decorations. Fan boxes were popular, and you will find them in a variety of materials. Papier-mâché must have been the most popular, perhaps because these boxes were inexpensive to make.

As with anything else, a fan must be judged according to the requirements of being an antique. Fans showing fine handwork, and good taste, design, and workmanship are the most desired. Carving, painting, and other decorations are important. Precious metals and gems, and exotic materials like ivory, bone, horn, and tortoiseshell contribute to desirability. Condition is important, so you must be careful not to invest in those which cannot be restored properly. Those with fine carvings and paintings are often framed as wall hangings and are quite effective. It is the workmanship, beautification, and art on the fans which generally give them the most value.

Paper and cardboard advertising fans were used during the late nineteenth century, and some of these were made to open a full 360 degrees. A color picture of a product, establishment, or pretty girl might appear on one side, with the reverse carrying the advertising message. These were issued at many public functions in an era when air conditioning was unknown. Most are on inexpensive wooden sticks. Although these fans are of interest, most do not command much money. Buy what appeals to you in fans of this type, with little thought of what you might get at resale someday. The number of collectors of these is quite limited, and you may have difficulty in getting your money back when you are ready to sell.

Guns

Gun collecting is interesting, as so many different types were made over such a long span of time that you have a wide field to choose from. Weapons which relate to American wars are very desirable; especially those from the Revolution, the War of 1812, and the Civil War. Insist on documentation if someone tells you that a gun was carried in certain battles, as family history is often not too reliable. A museum curator in Pennsylvania was approached by the descendants of a man who served in the Civil War. They claimed that he had served with distinction as a captain, and they wanted more information about a sword which had been handed down in the family as having been carried by him in some very famous battles. The curator recognized the "sword" as one of the long bayonets which were in use at that time, but rather than debate it with them, took down the man's name, regiment, and other pertinent information. His research revealed the man in question had deserted the Army two weeks after his induction, and was given a dishonorable discharge.

During the Revolution, most guns in use were of British origin. Others were made by local gunsmiths, or were French guns which had been taken as prizes in the French and Indian War of 1754–60. Locating weapons made in America before the Revolution is rather fruitless, since most people who own those

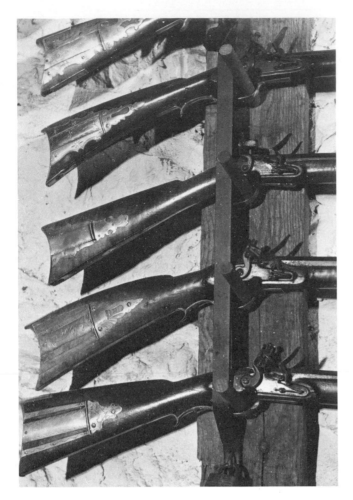

Collectors of militaria like old powder cans. Although this one was made in 1924 it is unlike anything made today, and it is therefore interesting even though it is not of great value.

Closeup of the stocks, locks, and patchboxes of the famed "Kentucky" rifles which were originally made in Pennsylvania. These are the products of noted Lancaster gunsmiths. (Pennsylvania Farm Museum)

guns will not sell them.

The first truly important American native rifle was the Kentucky rifle. About 2,000 Kentuckians fought with Andrew Jackson at New Orleans during the War of 1812, giving their name to the Kentucky rifle. However, the rifles probably did not come from Kentucky. It is known that these rifles originated in Pennsylvania, though others in this style were made in Ohio, Indiana, and even Tennessee. Very few, if any, had been made in Kentucky when they first saw service in the Revolutionary War. Legend grew around the rifles after the Battle of Saratoga. General Washington assigned southern sharpshooters equipped with these long rifles to every regiment because he had seen their effectiveness many times during the French and Indian War. At Saratoga, British General Fraser was at the head of his troops just before a decisive attack on the Americans. A sharpshooter in the Continental Army was called on to fire on him at a distance of more than 300 yards—a distance well out of range for most of the weapons then in use. He fired once, killing an aide next to the General. Another aide remarked, "It is evident you are marked out for particular aim; would it not be prudent for you to retire from this duty?" To which Fraser replied, "My duty forbids me to fly from danger." He was killed a moment later by the sharpshooter's next bullet, fired from a Kentucky rifle. This helped to disorganize the British, and they lost the day.

Rifle buffs are torn between calling them Kentucky rifles or Pennsylvania rifles—although most were made in Pennsylvania, they found their fame in the hands of Southerners. All of the experts agree that the weapon is uniquely American and represents the final stage in the development of the muzzle-loader. It evolved from two basic types—the graceful fowling pieces developed by the English and French, and the rifled "Jaeger" which was first developed in central Europe. Many of these rifles were made by blacksmiths in Pennsylvania, notably in the Lancaster area, between 1760 and 1860. They embellished their rifles with polished brass patchbox covers, butt plates, and decorative devices. This work spread into other regions and similar rifles were made as far north as New England and as far south as the Carolinas.

Kentucky rifles fall into three categories: those made before the Revolution, those made during the War, and those made in the nineteenth century before the percussion cap became common and replaced the earlier flintlock mechanism. Some rifles made in the early nineteenth century were decorated with silver, giving rise to the speculation that these were more important as presentation pieces than as actual hunting weapons. The most popular wood for the butt and stock was tiger maple, whose striping gave beautiful contrast to the iron, brass, or silver. It is said that some wood was striped by wrapping it with a waxed string, and then setting fire to the string and burning the pattern into the wood.

There are many stories about rifles and riflemakers, such as that of Melchior Fordney of Lancaster, Pennsylvania, who worked late in the period. Fordney lived with an unmarried woman, much to the consternation of his neighbors, and finally a religious fanatic killed him in 1846 because of his sinful life. J. P. Lindsay made superimposed-load rifles which featured a method of charging two loads at once, one atop the other. The loads were fired separately, using two hammers and two percussion caps. Since these rifles were muzzle-loaders, you can recognize the hazard of tamping one load atop another: Both charges usually went off, with disastrous results.

Various mechanisms were tried to give greater safety and rapidity of fire before Colt brought out his famous multi-shot guns. Double barrel rifles came into use, often with one barrel smooth for bird hunting and the other rifled for long range slugs. Though the over-and-under barrels were known in Germany at the time, few of these were made in America. The swivel breach weapon was not commonly made although it was popular on the frontier.

Gunsmiths in Pennsylvania and elsewhere are still making long rifles, so you must check your prospective purchases carefully to make sure you are not buying one of these. With the growing popularity of black powder shoots, some companies have begun reproducing all types of muzzle-loaders and these are available for sale everywhere. The originals will always be prized for their beauty, workmanship, and age, so be sure this is what you buy when you invest.

Other guns made during the nineteenth century have grown in value, especially those with the rapid-fire mechanisms that became popular during the Civil War. The North entered the war with an arsenal of about 9,000 rifles, 7,000 of which were the old flintlocks which had long been out of favor due to the advent of the percussion cap. By the time the war ended the men had been equipped with all sorts of rifles and handguns, and the first brass cartridges had completely outdated all of the previous firing mechanisms. Samuel Colt of Connecticut perfected the five shot pistol as early as 1834, but the Government did not give him the expected orders for these, and their production was low. Colt's principal customers were the wealthy since his guns were expensive. The war changed this, and the many Colt models made at that time are very desirable today. Colt is best known for his handguns, but he also made rifles. The multi-shot Henrys and Spencers, along with the Remington handguns, are very good items to locate. Winchesters were not made until 1866, when Oliver Winchester, who until this time had been a textile manufacturer, bought the patents and rights to both the Henry and Spencer rifles, the latter just to remove them as competition. The model 1873 Winchester was the first rifle to use a center-fire cartridge, and also had a chamber for twelve .44-caliber bullets. This is the weapon which is credited with helping to win the West. The first rifle designed to shoot the new smokeless powder was the model 1894 Winchester in a 30-30 caliber. This is still one of the most popular hunting weapons and it is available at sporting goods stores with only minor modifications of the original patent.

Most guns with any age are of interest, but you must acquaint yourself with the going market price before you invest. The popular Model 62, 22-caliber Winchester pump gun sold in the late 1930's for about eighteen dollars, and is now selling at auctions for well over a hundred because the model has been discontinued. This is the type of gun still used in shooting galleries. It is next to impossible to wear them out and they are fantastically accurate and reliable. This proves that age is not the only factor in determining value.

Most gun parts are marked with the same serial number, which makes it possible to check the originality of the pieces and to look for replacements. It is important that all parts be original to the gun. If you are collecting weapons from the first half of the nineteenth century you should check to make sure that they are not conversions. The early ones used a flintlock firing mechanism, and many were later converted to the more reliable percussion cap. This alteration must be taken into consideration. Some gunsmiths are clever at returning these pieces to their original flintlock condition, and this may be done with another lock not original to the piece.

There are many foreign guns in America, and perhaps the most collectable are those which are rarities in their countries of origin. About 2,500 percussion-operated and reliable Tower rifles were sent to the Confederate forces during the Civil War. These turn up from time to time, but their quantity is limited. The famed Luger, Mannlicher, and Mauser sporting and military arms are very fine collectibles of the twentieth century.

Jewelry

Jewelry is made up of minerals and metals, and the more valuable these are, the higher the cost of the jewelry. Gold is rated in carats (1 carat = 200 milligrams) by weight. Pure gold is rated at 24 carats (24K). A 14K gold piece or plating is made of 14 parts of gold and 10 parts of alloy; the carat represents the recipe of the mixture and depends on the amount of alloy. Most good gold jewelry is made with gold of at least 14K. In the better grade 18K is used, but pure 24K gold is rarely used because it is too soft. The carat weight is required to be stamped on all gold items of 10K and above. The terms gold-filled or gold-plated are used to designate a base metal which is covered with a layer of gold of the grade indicated by its carat weight stamp. There is some electroplating in gold, but the thickness is minute and can even be measured in millionths of an inch. Gold wash, which is a method of dipping of another metal to brighten it with a gold finish, may be even thinner.

Silver plate has a greater thickness than gold plate. Silver plate made before World War II is marked accordingly with the plating designations. Other important metals used in jewelry are platinum, palladium, iridium, ruthenium, and rhodium. Although it is a member of this family, osmium is not used in jewelry. These metals are alloyed with others to make expensive pieces, and they are often used in plating to give an expensive finish to lesser metals.

The diamond is the hardest and brightest of any of the gems. Diamonds are graded, flawless, or perfect; very, very slightly imperfect—VVS; very slightly imperfect—VS; slightly imperfect—SI; and imperfect—I. Diamonds come in tints of yellow or blue. A clear stone is most desired, although some of bluish tint are quite rare and good. Diamond weights are measured in carats and points. A carat contains 100 points.

Jewelry of the Victorian period is quite fancy. This magnificent parure and earring set is delicately enameled.

Emeralds and rubies are next in line in importance as gems. Following behind these are the semiprecious stones such as aquamarine, jade, garnet, lapis lazuli, opal, pearl, sapphire, topaz, zircon, and turquoise. Good imitations of all of these are made, so you must do business with reliable people, or else learn the game. This field is full of imitations, so be careful.

Back in the eighteenth century, a man by the name of Christopher Pinchbeck invented a metal which bears his name, and this metal bears a close resemblance to gold. It is so good that even royalty had pieces made of it, and some of the crown jewels we see today may possibly be imbedded in this phony material. Age has given it a great patina.

A paste known as strass was also invented in the eighteenth century. It can be turned into gems that rival the finest diamonds in brilliance. Much phony jewelry has been turned out in strass, and you have to be an expert to detect it today.

Early diamonds were cut in as few as 24 facets, which accounts for their lack of brilliance when they are compared with modern diamonds cut in 58 facets. Some people buy old diamonds, have them recut to today's standards, and feel that they have improved them. The present-day, man-made diamond was created for industry alone, but these are now being improved for jewelry use.

Jewelry designs were influenced by the prevailing styles in the decorative arts. The Georgian designs of the eighteenth century were classic, and those of the Victorian period of the nineteenth century were rococo with floral inspiration. The designs of the Edwardian era which followed were bold and austere. The Art Nouveau period was reflected in light and airy creations, and those of Art Deco are garish in comparison.

If you are to collect jewelry, you must first learn to identify the metals and gems. This is not as difficult as it sounds, as there are really very few with which you must become familiar. Beyond that, you must appraise a piece in light of its design and condition. Age enhances a piece, but it must be of quality to begin with. Most of the better nineteenth-century jewelry you might find today came from overseas, while quality costume jewelry was made in great quantities in America, particularly in the Attleboro and Fall River areas in Massachusetts. Good costume jewelry is in great demand and relatively inexpensive. The design of costume jewelry is more important than its material content. Earrings, brooches, lockets, and chains are always good sellers. Bar pins and bracelets are plentiful and less in demand, so prices are lower.

Amber has been and is popular, but you must be sure that you are buying the real thing. Amber is petrified pitch which has lain for millions of years at the bottom of the sea, notably the Finnish gulf, and it often contains bits of insects, bark, and other impurities. Most buyers feel that this enhances its value and they look for deeper-toned pieces filled with the relics of a long gone age. Amber comes in shades all the way from white to black, but the most popular color is a rich amber brown; followed by the opaque amber; then the cloudy buttercup yellow; and finally the golden transparent yellow. Amber shares the distinction of being a gem of vegetable origin with the diamond alone. It was used in the earliest known jewelry, and the ancients thought that it had curative powers due to the fact that you can generate electricity on its surface by rubbing it rapidly. Some of the world's best rosaries are made of amber, and collectors vie to locate these, some of which date all the way back to the fifteenth century.

Fine amber jewelry is obtainable today in the Iron Curtain countries at a fraction of its free world cost, and most tourists avail themselves of some of it. The Beriovska stores, which are maintained for the sale of such items to tourists in exchange for foreign currency, are the best places in which to buy. Amber has been copied in glass, but you can tell the imitations quite quickly, as the true amber is warm to the touch. If you are still in doubt, do what the dealers do—heat the end of a needle or pin, and apply it to a relatively hidden surface, such as the inside of a hole where a bead is strung. If the piece is amber, smoke and the odor of pine will rise from it.

Enamel

The art of enameling reached its peak many centuries ago in Byzantium and Georgia, which are now part of the USSR. There are three ways in which it was done, and the first is probably a lost art today. This technique is called champlevé. Cavities are punched, ground, or chiseled into the surface of a material, often gold, and then filled with colored smalt. Smalt is made of powdered glass which is colored and then mixed with an adhesive which binds it to the surface. Colors are put into the cavities to form a picture or design, and then the entire work is polished to remove the excess material, leaving behind a true work of art. When you consider that much of this work was done on gold, often on tiny items as beads and hanging pendants, it is little wonder that artisans today marvel at it.

The next technique was that of raising a wall of material on a surface, and the early work was done by soldering fine gold wire to a gold surface in the desired design. This was done by the cold solder method, using mercury as a flux since mercury is a solvent of gold. The outlined areas would be filled with smalt and then

Most of the cloissoné we collect today comes from China or France. These pieces date back to about 1900. Most cloissoné is rising in price because this delicate handwork is rarely done today.

polished. This technique is called cloisonné, and was used extensively not only in the Georgian area, but also in the Orient and in France. It is mostly the production of China and France that we collect today, since their output during the last century must have been tremendous. This work was done in a less expensive manner, using brass or bronze as the metals. Cloissone work is quite desirable as it is demanding on the artist. The production coming out of the People's Republic of China today is very good, and a simple new eight-to-ten-inch vase will command over a hundred dollars.

The third technique is simply called enameling. Materials such as those used to beautify porcelain and glass are merely painted on the surface, with lines of gilding detailing the design between the colors. This line can be mistaken for the raised brass wall in cloisonné, so you must examine it carefully to determine what you are buying. The value of enameled metal pieces is not as high as that of those made with the raised walls and smalt. A large amount of this imitation cloisonné was made, and is still being made today, so be careful when you buy.

Musical Instruments

There is some interest in old musical instruments, but collectors are really few and far between. Prices are not high, so you must regard these more as curiosity pieces than as antiques. The large rectangular spinet pianos are still a drug on the market, so do not invest much money in them. Many are being sold so that they may be dismantled for the fine wood used in them, since most of this may consist of huge, aged mahogany boards. Brass instruments have little value, and the woodwinds are mere curiosity items. Zithers and other stringed instruments have had a brief revival due to the current trends in music, but most are still low in value.

Old violins keep turning up at auctions and buyers often get excited: through the cutouts on top, they see a label which reads, "A. Stradivarius, Anno 1730," with perhaps a variation on the date. They visualize a trip around the world after reselling the violin, until the truth comes home after appraisal. These violins are no more than reproductions made in the Black Forest in Germany or even in Switzerland late in the nineteenth century or early in the twentieth. Violins were quite popular then and the fine woodworkers in those countries took advantage of this, modeling their products after those of famous makers. You can find the names of Stradivarius, Nicolo Amati, or Guiseppe Antonio Guarnerius as they were often copied.

Antonio Stradivarius was born in 1644, and by the time of his death in 1737 is known to have made about 1100 violins. Violin purchasers hope to gain ownership of one of the 500 or so which have never turned up or been accounted for. It is unlikely that such fine instruments would have been destroyed wilfully, so there is always the chance that an original will turn up. Most Strads sell well into the five figure price range, so you can understand the excitement someone feels when he thinks he has discovered one. The ones with paper labels are reproductions, so curb your enthusiasm.

If your violin happens to be in a wooden case which resembles a coffin, it was probably made by a coffin maker near Charleston, New Hampshire, who must have gotten rich on this product. The

Violins made in the style of (left to right) Nicolo Amati, Giuseppe Antonin Guarnerius, and Antonio Stradivarius, late seventeenth and early eighteenth century Italian craftsmen. Most violins of this type contain a paper label inside which identifies the maker's design—these are reproductions made in the late nineteenth or early twentieth centuries.

Before you buy an organ such as this be sure that you know someone who can service it if it needs it; they are worthless if they do not play. This fine example was made in the nineteenth century by J. Estey and Company, Brattleboro, Vermont. You can electrify an old organ by using the air blown from a vacuum cleaner.

cases are just about indestructible and saved many a violin from unfortunate death.

Guarnerius was born in Italy in 1683 and died in 1745. His violins rank with the Strads. The only other maker whose work approaches theirs is Amati, who was a teacher to Stradivarius. You should also look for cellos made by Carlo Berkonzi of Italy, who worked early in the eighteenth century. Many of his instruments are missing.

The average instrument turning up at auctions is worth little, and a hundred dollars is a lot to pay. Most sell in the five-to-twenty-dollar price range, which is enough. Actually, many people feel that these old violins are much better than the new ones, so if your child is going to learn this instrument, one of the Black Forest models might be the best investment. At least it will be cheaper than a new one.

Lamps

A great deal of the world is still lighted by oil and candles, which means that many of the lighting devices we consider antique are still in use in various lands. Fats and oils of all kinds were common fuel for early American lamps, and many homes were lighted with them well into the nineteenth century. Lard was a popular fuel at the end of the eighteenth century, but this gave way to whale oil early in the nineteenth century. Whale oil was made by rendering the blubber from a sperm whale. In the mid-1830's a new fuel, camphene, was introduced and widely accepted because it was cleaner burning and gave off less odor and smoke than the whale oil. Camphene was made of about one part turpentine to seven parts alcohol. Lemon, balsam, and juniper were among the other ingredients introduced to camphene fluid to give it a better scent and burning quality. Unfortunately, camphene was quite volatile and many fires were started by careless people who put it into lamps other than those designed for it. Camphene lamps look almost identical to whale oil lamps, but you can tell them apart by the length of their wick spouts. Camphene lamp spouts are longer in order to keep the

The candle shop in all its eighteenth century glory at the Museum Village, Smith's Clove, Monroe, New York.

Solid brass chandelier which has been electrified. Probably made in France, it is quite rococo in design, in keeping with its eighteenth century origin. (The Hermitage, Leningrad)

Nineteenth century hanging oil lamp with painted glass shade and font, hung on a mechanism that allows the lamp to be raised or lowered. The prisms are cut glass. This lamp reflects the gingerbread decoration of the time.

Wisteria lamp with a bronze base made by Louis Comfort Tiffany. At one time such lamps were too gaudy for American tastes, but they have gradually come back into favor as works of art. (Sotheby-Parke Bernet, New York)

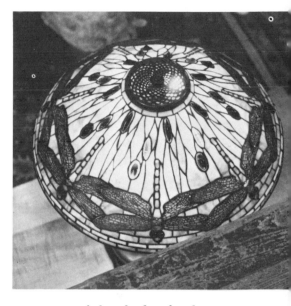

Top view of the shade of a dragonfly lamp made by Louis Comfort Tiffany, a pioneer in the American art nouveau movement. It reveals the intricate workmanship which elevates it from other lamps of this type.

Railroad lanterns. A switch signal lantern is shown at the center top. Each colored lens in this lantern signaled a particular instruction. (Canal Museum, Syracuse, New York)

flame farther away from the fuel supply.

The Argand lamp was invented in Switzerland in 1783, and was the first radical change in lighting since the beginning of time. Until then, fats and oils were burned in the open, either in cruzie or Betty lamps or hardened into candle form. The new principle allowed fats to be burned through a wick, using a draft of air introduced beneath the wick and a glass chimney to draw the air upward. All oil lamps operate on this principle to this day. However, it was not until the first oil well was drilled at Titusville, Pennsylvania, by Colonel Edwin Drake, beginning the petroleum industry, that petroleum oil lamps began to dominate lighting. Coal oil (a residue which came from diggings at mines) had been used before that time, but it did not have much impact as production was limited.

The birth of kerosene as a fuel during the growing industrial age brought with it a tremendous surge towards making lighting devices, notably the glass oil lamp. These lamps could be pressed out cheaply and soon practically every home had one or more. The multitude of such lamps made in glass as well as in metal provide enough information to make another book. However, here are some tips that can be useful. Color in the glass is important, as well as the type of decoration, especially that of hand-painted shades. Some people collect lamps by pattern, so this should be checked. The popular "Gone With The Wind Lamp" which made its appearance in that movie was actually not around at the time of the Civil War. This is the double globed type, usually with painted decoration on the upper and lower sections. The upper globe has quite often been broken and replaced with a reproduction. If this is well done it is acceptable, but if the replacement is obvious, it harms the value. Many lamps were made with bases of metals of all kinds and even of marble and alabaster, either in simple turned style or else fancied up with figurines. These must be judged on their quality and appeal.

The astral lamp was designed to carry fuel from a font to the burner via a tube, which made an overhanging light possible. A special fuel, called astral oil, was created for this lamp. Many of the old astral lamps are high on the desirable list since they were made with cut glass shades and prisms for elegant homes.

The advent of gas and electricity for lighting at the end of the nineteenth century caused the slow demise of oil lamps as lighting devices in America, but it was not until after the implementation of the rural electrification program in the 1920's and 1930's that they made a rapid disappearance. Most country people keep a supply of oil lamps in case of power line failures, and they keep turning up at auctions when old estates are liquidated.

The hand lantern was a necessary device, whether it burned oil or used a candle. The early pierced tin lanterns date back to before the Revolution. At the turn of the century these gave way to lanterns faced with glass as the glass industry grew to meet the demand. The Dietz Company is still very much in the lantern business, and advertises that it has a plant in Hong Kong which turns out over a million units a year—mostly for the under-developed nations. More lanterns are being made today than at any other time in history, so you must never regard the oil lantern as a disappearing item. However, some of the old ones make good collectibles, especially those made for the railroads. Some utilize brass, and these are the best. You can see a great collection of lanterns of all generations at the Canal Museum in Syracuse, New York.

Old coach lanterns and automobile lights are rising in value. The early ones burned the carbide gas which is given off when calcium carbide is moistened with water. Kerosene was used in some as late as World War I, and many have turned up from Government warehouses still dressed in their khaki color. These must be judged on interest and condition. As is the case with many types of collectibles, pairs of lanterns are more desired than singles.

The most desirable of the electric lights are those which are popularly called "Tiffany type" lamps. These feature shades of iridescent or colored glass set in either leaded or bronze framing. Those made by Tiffany are commanding huge prices, but the workmanship in the coloring, design, and iridescence of his lamps is unmatched. Some of the lesser types are referred to as oyster shell shaded lamps and are quite Gothic in their look. The coloring and design in the glass is most important in judging their values.

The field of memoribilia collecting is limitless. Let your eye be your guide as to quality, and your experiences at auctions, shows, and flea markets your guide to values. One must be immersed in this business to buy and sell wisely—a part time, on-again, off-again collector will not keep himself advised sufficiently to do well at it. Talk with dealers and collectors in the field in which you are interested. Go to museums and see the objects on display and study their characteristics. Above all, read good books on the subject—you will find there is a wealth of material that will help you, if you will but seek it out.

A great reminder of America's past—a windowful of lighting devices. (Museum Village, Smith's Clove, Monroe, New York)

Bibliography

Ceramics

Barber, Edwin Atlee. *Marks of American Potters.* Cracker Barrel Press, Southampton, New York.

Barret, Richard Carter. *How to Identify Bennington Pottery.* Stephen Greene Press, Brattleboro, Vermont.

Chaffers, William. *Marks and Monograms on Pottery and Porcelain.* William Reeves, London.

Cox, Warren. *The Book on Pottery and Porcelain.* Crown Publishers, New York.

Klamkin, Marian. *American Patriotic and Political China.* Charles Scribner's Sons, New York.

Penkala, Maria. *European Porcelains.* Charles E. Tuttle Co., Rutland, Vermont.

Quimby, M. G. *Ceramics in America—Winterthur Conference Report 1972.* University Press, Charlottesville, Virginia.

Schwartz, Marvin. *Collector's Guide to Antique American Ceramics.* Doubleday & Co., Garden City, New York.

Folk Art

American Folk Art, The Art of the Common Man in America, 1750–1900. Museum of Modern Art, New York.

Drepperd, Carl W. *American Pioneer Art and Artists.* Pond-Ekberg Publishing Co., Springfield, Massachusetts.

Fales, Dean A. *American Painted Furniture.* E. P. Dutton Publishing Co., New York.

Kauffman, Henry J. *Pennsylvania Dutch American Folk Art.* American Studio Books, New York.

Lewis Miller, Sketches and Chronicles. Historical Society of York County, York, Pennsylvania.

Lipman, Jean. *American Folk Art in Wood, Metal and Stone.* Panthon Press, New York.

Little, Nina Fletcher. *The Abby Aldrich Rockefeller Folk Art Collection.* Little Brown and Company, Boston, for Colonial Williamsburg.

Furniture

Bjerkoe, Ethel Hall. *The Cabinetmakers of America.* Bonanza Books, New York.

Burroughs, Paul. *Southern Antiques.* Bonanza Books, New York.

Comstock, Helen, and Ramsey, L.G.G. *Antique Furniture.* Hawthorn Books, Inc., New York.

Country Cabinetwork and Simple City Furniture. Morse, John D., ed. University Press of Virginia, Charlottesville, for Henry Francis du Pont Winterthur Museum.

Cousins, Frank, and Riley, Phil. M. *The Woodcarver of Salem.* Little Brown and Co., Boston.

Fastnedge, Ralph. *English Furniture Styles.* A. S. Barnes & Co., New York.

Montgomery, Charles. *American Furniture of the Federal Period.* Viking Press, New York.

Nutting, Wallace. *Furniture Treasury.* MacMillan Co., New York.

Parsons, Charles. *The Dunlaps and Their Furniture.* Currier Gallery of Art, Manchester, New Hampshire.

Sack, Albert. *Fine Points of Furniture.* Crown Publishers, New York.

Glass

Avila, George C. *The Pairpoint Glass Story.* Mattapoisett, Massachusetts.

Barret, Richard Carter. *Popular American Ruby Stained Glass.* Forward's Color Productions, Inc., Manchester, Vermont.

Barret, Richard Carter. *Blown and Pressed American Glass.* Forward's Color Productions, Inc., Manchester, Vermont.

Cloak, Evelyn Campbell. *Glass Paperweights of the Bergstrom Art Center.* Bonanza Books, New York.

Davis, Frank. *Continental Glass.* Praeger Publishers, New York.

Lee, Ruth Webb. *Nineteenth Century Art Glass.* M. Barrows & Co., Inc., New York.

Lindsey, Bessie M. *American Historical Glass.* Charles E. Tuttle Co., Rutland, Vermont.

McKearin, Helen and George. *American Glass.* Crown Publishers, New York.

McKearin, Helen and George. *Two Hundred Years of American Blown Glass.* Crown Publishers, New York.

Munsey, Cecil. *The Illustrated Guide to Collecting Bottles.* Hawthorn Books, Inc., New York.

Pepper, Adeline. *The Glass Gaffers of New Jersey.* Charles Scribner's Sons, New York.

Weatherman, Hazel Marie. *Colored Glass of the Depression Era.* Springfield, Missouri.

Wilson, Kenneth M. *New England Glass & Glassmaking.* Thomas Y. Crowell Co., New York.

Metals

Bigelow, Francis Hill. *Historic Silver of the Colonies and its Makers.* MacMillan & Co., New York.

Buhler, Kathryn C. *American Silver, 1655–1825, in the Museum of Fine Arts, Boston.* Museum of Fine Arts, Boston.

Cotterell, Howard H. *Old Pewter, its Makers and Marks.* Charles Scribner's Sons, New York.

Currier, Ernest M. *Marks of Early American Silversmiths.* Southworth Athoensen Press, Portland, Maine.

Gould, Mary Earle. *Antique Tole and Tinware.* Charles E. Tuttle Co., Rutland, Vermont.

Hammerslough, Philip. *American Silver, Vols. I, II, III, and IV.* Published by the author in limited edition.

Jacobs, Carl. *Guide to American Pewter.* The McBride Company, New York.

Kauffman, Henry J. *American Copper and Brass.* Thomas Nelson, Camden, New Jersey.

Kauffman, Henry J. *Early American Ironware.* Thomas Nelson, Camden, New Jersey.

Kerfoot, J. B. *American Pewter.* Houghton Mifflin Co., Boston.

Laughlin, Ledlie I. *Pewter in America.* Barre Publishers, Barre, Massachusetts.

Lindsay, Seymour. *Iron and Brass Implements of the American Home.* Medici Society, Boston.

McClinton, Katharine M. *Collecting American 19th Century Silver.* Charles Scribner's Sons, New York.

Wyler, Seymour B. *Old Silver.* Crown Publishers, New York.

Miscellaneous Collectibles

Baines, Anthony. *Musical Instruments Through the Ages.* Cox & Wyman Ltd., London.

Butler, Joseph T. *Candleholders in America, 1650–1900.* Crown Publishers, Inc., New York.

Farga, Franz. *Violins and Violinists.* Macmillan Company, London.

Finley, Ruth. *Old Patchwork Quilts and the Women Who Made Them.* Charles T. Brantford, Newton Center, Massachusetts.

Hebard, Helen B. *Early Lighting in New England, 1620–1861.* Charles E. Tuttle Co., Rutland, Vermont.

Holstein, Jonathan. *American Pieced Quilts.* Smithsonian Institution, Washington, D. C.

Lantz, Louise K. *Old American Kitchenware.* Thomas Nelson, Inc., Camden, New Jersey.

Peto, Florence. *American Quilts and Coverlets.* Chanticleer Press, New York.
Webster, Marie. *Quilts, Their History and How to Make Them.* Gale Research Company, Detroit.

Paintings and Prints

Ashton, Dore. *The New York School.* Viking Press, New York.
Burgess, Fred W. *Old Prints and Engravings.* Tudor Publishing Co., New York.
Drepperd, Carl W. *Early American Prints.* The Century Co., New York.
Elliott, George. *Sculpture Inuit.* University of Toronto Press for the Canadian Eskimo Arts Council.
Fielding, Mantle. *Dictionary of American Painters, Sculptors and Engravers.* James F. Carr, New York.
Groce, George C., and Wallace, David H. *Dictionary of Artists in America.* Yale University Press for the New York Historical Society, New York.
Howat, John K. *The Hudson River and its Painters.* Viking Press, New York, for Scenic Hudson Preservation Conference.
Peters, Harry T. *Currier and Ives, Printmakers to the American People.* Doubleday, Doran & Co., Inc., Garden City, New York.
Prints in and of America to 1850. Morse, John D., ed. University Press of Virginia for the Henry Francis du Pont Winterthur Museum.
19th Century America, Paintings and Sculpture. Metropolitan Museum of Art, New York.

Index